Introducing WebTV

Jill T. and Wayne S. Freeze

Microsoft Press

Introducing WebTV

Published by **Microsoft Press**
A Division of Microsoft Corporation
One Microsoft Way
Redmond, Washington 98052-6399

Copyright © 1998 by Jill T. Freeze and Wayne S. Freeze

All rights reserved. No part of the contents of this book may be reproduced or transmitted in any form or by any means without the written permission of the publisher.

Library of Congress Cataloging-in-Publication Data
Freeze, Wayne S.
    Introducing WebTV / Jill T. and Wayne S. Freeze.
       p.   cm.
    Includes index.
    ISBN 1-57231-715-9
    1. WebTV (Trademark)   I. Freeze, Jill T.   II. Title.
TK5105.883.W43F74   1997
004.67'8--dc21   97-31954
                                                                                                              CIP
Printed and bound in the United States of America.

1 2 3 4 5 6 7 8 9   QMQM   3 2 1 0 9 8

Distributed to the book trade in Canada by Macmillan of Canada, a division of Canada Publishing Corporation.

A CIP catalogue record for this book is available from the British Library.

Microsoft Press books are available through booksellers and distributors worldwide. For further information about international editions, contact your local Microsoft Corporation office. Or contact Microsoft Press International directly at fax (425) 936-7329. Visit our Web site at mspress.microsoft.com.

Barney is a trademark of Lyons Partnership, L.P. Microsoft and Microsoft Press are registered trademarks of Microsoft Corporation. Star Trek and related marks are trademarks of Paramount Pictures Corporation. Nickelodeon and the Nickelodeon logo are registered trademarks of Viacom New Media. WebTV is a registered trademark and the WebTV logo and the WebTV Network are trademarks of WebTV Networks, Inc. Other product and company names mentioned herein may be the trademarks of their respective owners.

Companies, names, and/or data used in screens and sample output are fictitious unless otherwise noted.

Acquisitions Editor: **Kim Fryer**
Project Editor: **Wendy Zucker**
Technical Editor: **Jon Forrest**

To Dad and Goose...enjoy your new life as Web surfers!

—Jill

CONTENTS *at a Glance*

Introduction — xiii

PART 1 — Getting Started

Chapter 1	A Brief History of the Internet and How the WebTV Network Evolved	3
Chapter 2	The WebTV Internet Terminal Versus the PC—What's the Difference?	11
Chapter 3	Before You Buy a WebTV Internet Terminal	21
Chapter 4	Anatomy of a WebTV Internet Terminal	29
Chapter 5	Subscribing to the WebTV Network	37
Chapter 6	Get with the Program	55
Chapter 7	It's a Setup	65

PART 2 — WebTV Basics

Chapter 8	E-Mail 101	81
Chapter 9	Reading, Writing, and E-Mail Management	91
Chapter 10	Everything You Always Wanted to Know About the Web	101
Chapter 11	A Nose for News (or Gossip?)	117
Chapter 12	Virtual Chatrooms and Cybercommunities	125
Chapter 13	Traffic Jams and Other Roadblocks	139
Chapter 14	Push Your WebTV Internet Terminal to the Limit	149

PART 3 Internet Culture

Chapter 15	Netiquette, the Rules of the Road	169
Chapter 16	BTW, About Those Abbreviations and Emoticons :-)	185
Chapter 17	Safety in Numbers (and in User Names)	193
Chapter 18	All That Glitters Is Not Gold	203

PART 4 The Fun Part

Chapter 19	Over a Dozen Creative Uses for Your WebTV Internet Terminal	215
Chapter 20	Over a Dozen Ways to Save Time and Money Surfing the Net	227
Chapter 21	Become a Virtual Bloodhound	239
Chapter 22	Web Sites of Interest to Young and Old	251
	Appendix	259
	Glossary	263
	Index	269

Table of Contents

Introduction	xiii
Read Me First	xiii
Who Should Read This Book?	xiii
How This Book Is Organized	xiv
What Do You Mean I've Got an Identity Crisis?	xiv
Conventions Used Within the Book	xv
Do You See What I See?	xv

PART 1 Getting Started

Chapter 1 A Brief History of the Internet and How the WebTV Network Evolved — 3

The Internet	4
How the WebTV Network Fits In	8
Enter: Microsoft	9

Chapter 2 The WebTV Internet Terminal Versus the PC—What's the Difference? — 11

The Eye of the Beholder	11
Real People Use the WebTV Network	17
WebTV Classic Versus WebTV Plus—Which Is Best for You?	18

Chapter 3 Before You Buy a WebTV Internet Terminal — 21

Local Access Charges?	21
Check Out Your TV	22
Put It in Writing	25
Make a List and Check It Twice…	26

Chapter 4 Anatomy of a WebTV Internet Terminal — 29

It's What's Up Front That Counts	29
On the Side	31
The Flip Side	31
Other Cool Bits and Pieces	34

Chapter 5	**Subscribing to the WebTV Network**	**37**
	The Lowdown on ISPs	38
	OpenISP: The Whole Truth and Nothing But the Truth	38
	The Search for an ISP	40
	Ask All the Right Questions	41
	OpenISP: Get the Best for Less	42
	Sign Me Up!	43
Chapter 6	**Get with the Program**	**55**
	Thumb-Surfing Basics	55
	One-Finger Typing	58
	Get Attached	59
	Look, Ma, No Cords	61
Chapter 7	**It's a Setup**	**65**
	Customize Your Web Surfing Environment	65
	Master Controls	71
	Anatomy of Your Home Base	76

PART 2 WebTV Basics

Chapter 8	**E-Mail 101**	**81**
	What Happens to My E-Mail When I'm Offline?	83
	Set the E-Mail Stage	84
	Fill Up Your Address Book	88
Chapter 9	**Reading, Writing, and E-Mail Management**	**91**
	Read Your Messages	91
	Revisit Saved Messages	93
	Write to Others for Free	95
	Unfinished Business	97
	Clean Up, Clean Up…	98
	Retrieve Your E-Mail Daily	99

Table of Contents

Chapter 10	**Everything You Always Wanted to Know About the Web**	**101**
	What Is the Web and How Does It Work?	101
	Form Opinions on the Web	103
	Play Favorites	105
	Web Surfing Tricks	113
Chapter 11	**A Nose for News (or Gossip?)**	**117**
	So How Do the Groups Work?	118
	Get to the Goodies	119
	Get Involved in the Discussion Groups	121
Chapter 12	**Virtual Chatrooms and Cybercommunities**	**125**
	Let's Chat a Moment	125
	IRC on the WebTV Network	128
	Tales of Friendship and Camaraderie on the Internet	136
	So What Is a Cybercommunity, Anyway?	137
Chapter 13	**Traffic Jams and Other Roadblocks**	**139**
	Red Alert!	141
	Virtual Gridlock During Rush Hour	146
	The WebTV Network, Unplugged	147
	Don't Try This at Home	147
Chapter 14	**Push Your WebTV Internet Terminal to the Limit**	**149**
	A Printout's Worth a Thousand Words	149
	WebTV Plus—The Ultimate TV Experience	154
PART 3	**Internet Culture**	
Chapter 15	**Netiquette, the Rules of the Road**	**169**
	What Is Netiquette, Anyway?	170
	Top 10 E-Mail Rules of the Road	171
	Top 10 Discussion Group Rules of the Road	178

Table of Contents

Chapter 16	**BTW, About Those Abbreviations and Emoticons :-)**	**185**
	Alphabet Soup	186
	I Second That Emotion!	189
	Express Yourself	191
Chapter 17	**Safety in Numbers (and in User Names)**	**193**
	Protect Your Privacy	193
	The Nuisance of Virtual Junk Mail	195
	Shop on the Information Superhighway	198
	Smart Shopping	201
	Shop till Your Modem Drops!	201
Chapter 18	**All That Glitters Is Not Gold**	**203**
	The Importance of Evaluating Online Information	205
	Question Your Sources	211

PART 4 The Fun Part

Chapter 19	**Over a Dozen Creative Uses for Your WebTV Internet Terminal**	**215**
	Make a New Friend	215
	Pick the Best College	216
	Put Those Leftovers to Good Use	217
	Pick the Perfect Pooch	217
	Chart a Path	218
	Become a Virtual Volunteer	219
	Expand Your Collection, or Learn More About It	219
	Plan Your Dream House	221
	Choose Your Junk Mail	222
	Learn More About a Medical Condition	222
	Have a Good Laugh	224
	Plan Your Vacation	224
	Extend Your TV Viewing Experience	225

Table of Contents

Chapter 20	**Over a Dozen Ways to Save Time and Money Surfing the Net**	**227**
	Hang Up the Phone and Grab the Remote	227
	SOS (Save Our Stamps)	228
	Magazine Mania	229
	No News Is Good News (or Is It?)	230
	Avoid Club Confusion	231
	Finance Your Dream Home	231
	Get Carded	232
	Listen Up!	233
	Get There Inexpensively	234
	Taxing Times	235
	Read 'Em and Weep (or Buy 'Em)	236
	Comparison Shop Without Wearing Out Your Shoes	236
	Lose Your Package?	237
	Be Your Own Operator	237
Chapter 21	**Become a Virtual Bloodhound**	**239**
	Systematic Surfing: When You Kinda Know What You Want	241
	Search for Answers	243
	Check Up on Old Friends (and Enemies)	249
Chapter 22	**Web Sites of Interest to Young and Old**	**251**
	Kiddie Links	251
	Golden Web Sites	255
	So Many Sites, So Little Time	258
	Appendix	
	The WebTV Internet Terminal and WebTV Network Troubleshooting Guide	259
	Glossary	**263**
	Index	**269**

Acknowledgments

The seeds of this project were planted over a year ago when I ran the idea of a WebTV book past our agents, Bill Adler, Jr., and Laura Belt. Bill and Laura pounded the pavement faithfully in search of a home for the project.

At about the same time, I began speaking with John Lee, Colleen Bertiglia, and Jamie Biggs of WebTV Networks to get their support for an official WebTV book. Each spent countless hours on the phone with me discussing WebTV's history and future. Later, Aaron Mata, Robert Laws, Carol Sacks, and other WebTV Networks personnel helped to pull the book together as well.

Thanks to the efforts of Kim Fryer, an acquisitions editor for Microsoft Press, I was linked up with a team of top-notch professionals. Project editor Wendy Zucker, with a sense of humor almost as bizarre as mine, did a stellar job of keeping things on track. Her constant communication was integral to the success of this project. You're the best, Wendy! Bill Teel deserves a big thanks for working magic with the screen shots you'll see on the pages that follow. Thanks to Travis Beaven, the book's electronic artist, who added the funky graphics throughout the earlier chapters. I love the way the WebTV logo's shape was incorporated into the illustrations.

I want to thank technical editor Jon Forrest for his work on this project. Performing technical edits on software that's still in the testing stages can be like shooting at a moving target. Thanks also to Kurt Meyer for providing another technical review in the book's later stage.

Acknowledgments

Countless behind-the-scenes people added their talents to the project, most of whom I haven't had the pleasure of meeting. Your work has not gone unappreciated. You've done a spectacular job of making those marked-up manuscript pages look like a real book. Thanks a million!

Thanks to Wayne, Christopher, and Samantha, who kept me constantly supplied with Diet Coke and Pop-Tarts (but most of all love, hugs, support, and tons of patience)—you three mean the world to me! Wayne, you're my best friend in the whole wide world. How many people get to share every part of their life with their best friend? Chris, Mommy cherishes those "Need for Speed" races of ours. I still can't believe you can run your own computer at age four. Sammy, you are a beautiful girl both inside and out. Thanks for letting me sleep with Boo Bear when I had the flu—it really helped!

While this is actually my second book to hit the stores, I still consider it my first book in many ways. I poured a lot of myself into this project for over a year, so I'd like to take this opportunity to thank the many people who believed in me and my writing throughout the years. Mom (a.k.a. Goose) and Dad, at least this book will be fun to read! Donna Lynch, few people have believed in me as strongly as you have. I wish I had the confidence in myself that you've always had in me! Sister Joyce Leibly, remember in fourth grade I promised to mention you in my first book? Well, here you go! Julie Smith, thanks for helping me stay in touch with the performing arts, even if it did mean I played hooky in the middle of this book to go see Jean-Pierre Rampal. Veronica Dau, I treasure our growing friendship. Now that this book is done, it's Dave and Buster's time, girl! Tracy Tonner and Becky Dinkins, I haven't had time to e-mail you guys during the past few months, but you've been in my thoughts. I can't wait to start writing e-mail for fun again (no offense, Wendy). Aunt Betsy, Uncle Troy, get out that WebTV remote control and start surfing again. And when you do, drop me a note at *netwriter@webtv.net*.

Jill T. Freeze
Beltsville, Maryland
November 1997

Introduction

Read Me First

In the beginning, the Internet was without form and void, so Vint Cerf (the father of the Internet) hooked four computers together and thus the Internet was born. As time progressed, those four computers became eight, and those eight became sixteen, and so forth until the Internet consisted of millions of computers. Each computer was complex and needed to be managed by a specialist. Then came personal computers. While they were much easier to use, they still required a great deal of knowledge and money. Steve Perlman saw this and said the Internet should be available for everyone, thus the WebTV Internet terminal was created.

It's not every day something is created that has the potential to have profound effects on people of all ages, educational levels, and economic backgrounds. The WebTV Internet terminal is such a device, and you're right at the forefront of this revolutionary breakthrough. This book will arm you with all the information you'll need to make the most of this emerging technology, so sit back and enjoy the ride.

Who Should Read This Book?

Introducing WebTV was written with a variety of people in mind. If you're new to the Internet, this book will not only show you how to get the most out of your WebTV Internet terminal, but it will also introduce you to the

Introduction

subtleties of life online. You'll learn all about Internet culture, "netiquette," "emoticons," and everything you'll need to have a fun and positive Internet experience.

If you're contemplating the purchase of a WebTV Internet terminal, you might want to pick up this book before you do so to see what exactly you'll need to have on hand so that you can begin enjoying your investment the moment you get home. *Introducing WebTV* is also useful in helping you decide between WebTV Classic and WebTV Plus.

How This Book Is Organized

For your convenience, I've organized this book into four sections. The first section is dedicated to getting you all set up to surf the Internet. The second section gives you the ins and outs of e-mailing, browsing discussion groups, chatting, and surfing the Web with your Internet terminal. With the third section, I try to acclimate you to all the cultural subtleties of life online, whether it's defining all those funny acronyms you stumble onto or priming you on basic Internet etiquette (netiquette). I also delve into topics not always addressed in other Internet books, such as how to evaluate the integrity of the information you find online. The final section teaches you how to find anything you want on the Net. This section also introduces you to some creative ways to save time and money with your Internet terminal. And, of course, I couldn't resist adding some blurbs about a few Web sites I think you might enjoy.

The chapters within each section are designed to be relatively self-contained so that you can read them in the order you need them, not in the order some author thinks you'll need—or want—them. And best of all, they're written to be fun to read. A point can be made just as effectively through humor. But make no mistake about it, I've crammed a lot of information into these pages.

What Do You Mean I've Got an Identity Crisis?

If you're really observant, you're probably wondering why this book is written in first person singular when there are two authors listed on the cover. Here's the scoop—I (Jill) wrote the book, while Wayne acted as the official screen shot–tweaker and technical consultant to the project. In a way, he could be considered "collateral" for ensuring that the book got done in a timely, professional manner. So while his name does appear on the book, I must point out that the editorial remarks contained within are mine and mine alone (except for the first paragraph in this introduction, of which he was the mastermind).

Conventions Used Within the Book

I'd like to point out a few book elements that I've used for clarification. I've used special Note boxes to elaborate on points made in text. While this expanded discussion is not critical to your understanding of the topic, it might touch on issues you'll find interesting.

Tip boxes are used to provide shortcuts or alternative ways of doing things. For example, you might see step-by-step instructions in the text for reloading a Web page, but the Tip box might contain a keyboard shortcut. Those using the optional wireless keyboard will often find these tips an invaluable resource.

One type of box that you should always read is the Caution box. These elements contain vital information for helping you to avoid getting into trouble.

Finally, for this book alone, Microsoft Press was gracious enough to let me create my own book element: the Technobabble box. These boxes define a term or technology in such a way that you, too, can speak technobabble at the company party. And yes, pronunciations are included where necessary.

Do You See What I See?

Does your screen differ from one pictured or described in this book? While every effort was made to deliver the most accurate, up-to-date information possible, *Introducing WebTV* was written while WebTV Plus was in the testing stages, so it's possible that some screens or steps might have changed slightly. We've been assured by the fine folks at WebTV Networks that there won't be any dramatic changes (at least in the immediate future), but I wanted you to be prepared just the same. Also remember that since WebTV Networks is committed to giving its customers the best service possible, a newly available update might cause the screen's appearance to vary as well.

Introduction

I should also prepare you for the possibility that a Web address might have changed or disappeared between the time this book was printed and the time you visit one of the sites listed in this book. If that should happen, the old Web page will often provide a link to the new address. If you aren't led to the new address and you're certain the site still exists, simply perform a search on the title of the desired Web site as demonstrated in Chapter 21, "Become a Virtual Bloodhound."

Another thing to keep in mind when executing the steps presented in this book is that the Go button or Return key must always be pressed after each selection. Go is the round button found in the center of the arrows on your remote control. Some Internet terminal manufacturers label it while others do not. Alternatively, you can press the Return or Enter key on your keyboard, whether it's the optional infrared wireless keyboard or an attached computer keyboard.

Most important, have fun with this book. Getting on the Internet can be a blast if you just relax. I'd love to hear stories of how you use your WebTV Internet terminal, or whether using it has changed your life. Use any of the tricks you'll learn in the e-mail chapters and send a note to *netwriter@webtv.net*. I promise to answer each note personally as soon as I can. And if you're looking for more places to surf, check out our Web site at *www.justpc.com*. While visiting, you can sign our guestbook or look at other reader's reactions to this book and to the WebTV Network in general.

To stay on top of all the latest breaking WebTV Network news, visit *www.news.com* and search on "WebTV." You can also go directly to the official Web site of WebTV Networks at *www.webtv.net*. And don't forget to read the Club WebTV News, the WebTV Network's monthly online newsletter. The next few months are bound to get exciting as Microsoft takes a more active role in the WebTV Network's direction, but we, the users, are the ones who stand to gain the most.

Hang on to your remotes, folks, and buckle up for your guided tour of the information superhighway!

Getting Started

Chapter

1 A Brief History of the Internet and How the WebTV Network Evolved — 3

2 The WebTV Network Versus the PC—What's the Difference? — 11

3 Before You Buy a WebTV Internet Terminal — 21

4 Anatomy of a WebTV Internet Terminal — 29

5 Subscribing to the WebTV Network — 37

6 Get with the Program — 55

7 It's a Setup — 65

Chapter 1

A Brief History of the Internet and How the WebTV Network Evolved

The Internet is big, and I mean really big. Try this little game some night while watching television. Watch each of the commercials carefully, and keep a mental tally of how many companies have World Wide Web sites listed in addition to, or even in place of, a toll-free number. You'll be surprised at just how many companies have made their presence known in cyberspace. What's more, "Internet," "information superhighway," and "e-mail" have become household words, and some sources estimate that as many as 35 million people in the U.S. alone surf the Net.

In this chapter, I'll take you on a brief tour of the Internet's 30-year history. (Yes, it really is that old!) I'll also explore how the WebTV Network came onto the scene and where Microsoft plans to take this emerging technology.

The Internet

When people think of the Internet, the World Wide Web (or just "the Web") and e-mail often come to mind. In actuality, the Internet is not these things at all. The Internet is really a group of computers that are hooked together and capable of speaking to one another in a common language. Figure 1-1 illustrates how the Internet is formed. The Web and e-mail are simply modes of communication. Just as humans rely on letters and telephones to communicate, computers rely on things like Usenet, the Web, and e-mail. (You'll learn much more about each of these in Part II, "WebTV Basics.")

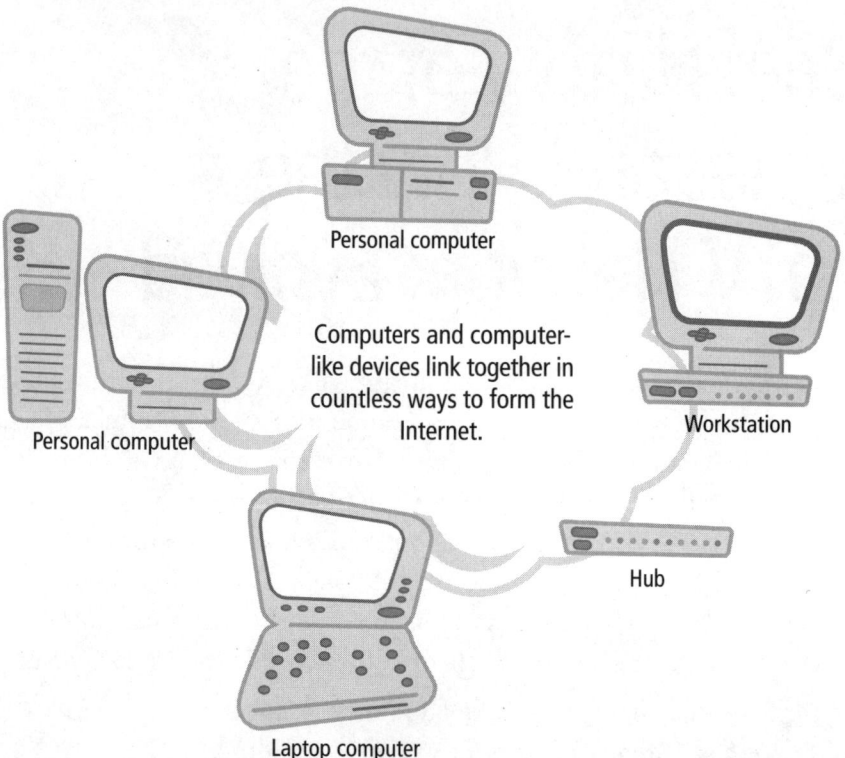

Figure 1-1. *The Internet is made up of computers that are connected together. These machines may be anything from small desktop computers to large mainframes at major universities to set-top boxes like the WebTV box.*

To say the Internet has experienced explosive growth over the past decade could be considered a gross understatement. Take a look at Table 1-1 on the facing page:

Table 1-1. **Growth of the Internet**

Year	Number of Computers	Year	Number of Computers
1969	4	1990	313,000
1971	23	1991	617,000
1981	213	1992	1,136,000
1984	1,024	1993	2,056,000
1986	5,089	1994	3,864,000
1987	28,174	1995	6,642,000
1988	56,000	1996	12,881,000
1989	159,000		

From Winding Dirt Road…

This staggering growth is no accident—many key events and technological breakthroughs led to the Internet becoming what it is today.

Back in 1969, when Neil Armstrong first walked on the moon and people were bopping along to "Sugar, Sugar" by the Archies, the Department of Defense (DOD) commissioned the Advanced Research Projects Agency (ARPA) to research computer networking. What better way for researchers to share their knowledge than to exchange data via computer? The result was a network of four computers that became known as the ARPANET.

A mere two years later, e-mail was invented and the ARPANET nearly quadrupled in size. Just to give you an idea of how long ago that was, sending a letter first class in the United States cost only eight cents back then. (Luckily for us, postal rates didn't increase as quickly as the size of the ARPANET; it only seems like it.)

Over the following decade, the ARPANET grew at a steady clip, adding its first international connection in 1973. Colleges and universities were tapped into the network as well. Researchers at two universities, Duke and the University of North Carolina, established Usenet in 1979. Usenet gave researchers and scholars a forum to discuss information on very specific topics. Instead of e-mailing all interested parties about a finding or idea, researchers could post their thoughts for all to see and discuss.

> **NOTE** Usenet goes by the name "Discussions" for the WebTV Network subscribers. These groups can be found by selecting the Community button on the WebTV Network's default home page and then selecting Discussions. For quick reference, you might want to save the All Groups page to your Favorites list. You'll find more on selecting Favorites in Chapter 10, "Everything You Always Wanted to Know About the Web."

But something was still missing. Not every computer could speak the "language" of the ARPANET. It was like having a bunch of brilliant scientists gathered from around the world all speaking in different languages. For this reason, ARPA declared the Transmission Control Protocol/Internet Protocol (TCP/IP) as the protocol (language) for the ARPANET in 1982.

Now before all these acronyms cause you to put down this book in frustration, let me explain why this development is so important. TCP/IP gave computers of all kinds a common way to exchange information. In other words, those brilliant scientists from around the world finally found a way to speak the same language. This development planted the seeds for the growth of the Internet as we know it in the late 1990s.

...To Paved Two-Lane Highway...

As the number of computers linked to the Internet passed the 10,000 mark in 1987, there was no question that the Internet had reached adolescence. It grew seven times its size between 1987 and 1989, but it was still considered far from mainstream technology. You had to know the right people in the right places to use the Internet, since access was still mostly limited to researchers and scientists.

And let's be honest here—the Internet wasn't terribly exciting back then anyway. Not only was information next to impossible to find, but what you did find was in bland fixed-font text or, worse yet, a bunch of jumbled characters that you needed to decode in order to read. But remember that the Internet existed initially for the exchange of information, not for drooling over pictures of (insert your favorite object of browsing here)—that came later!

...To Information Superhighway!

By the time 1991 rolled around, a whopping one-half million computers were linked to the Internet. But that was just the beginning—1991 can easily be considered the birth of the information superhighway. The University of Minnesota gave us Gopher, a program that allowed users to move through menus of information made available to all Internet users. Figure 1-2 shows a sample Gopher screen. Finally, people could surf for the good stuff without necessarily knowing what was where. Gopher might seem a little old-fashioned and unproductive when you compare it to the Web pages and search engines we know today, but it was a major breakthrough for its time.

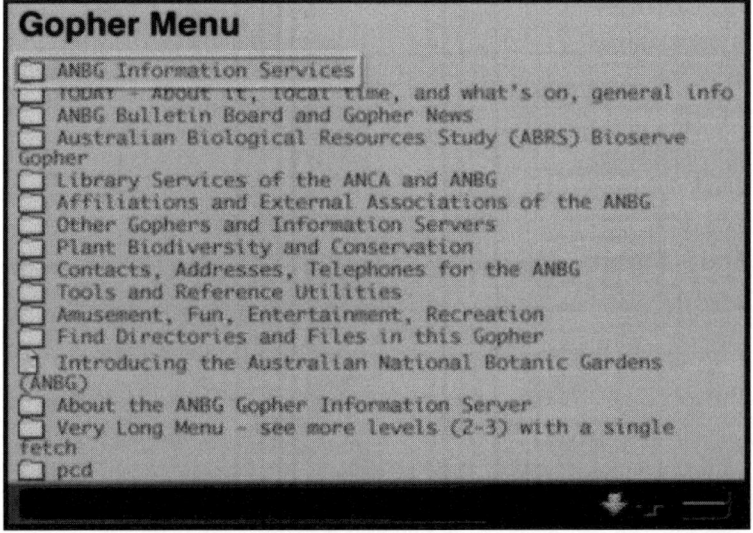

Figure 1-2. *Gopher was a surfer's dream come true. Without knowing where to find information, you could move your way through a series of menus until you stumbled across an item of interest.*

While the World Wide Web also made its debut in 1991, it wasn't until 1993—the year Mosaic (the first graphical Web browser) took the Internet by storm—that the Web stepped into the limelight. Not only had the number of computers on the Internet passed two million, but the White House was online with a Web page and e-mail addresses for the First Couple. The Internet was indeed starting to make its presence known.

The plot thickened in 1994 as electronic shopping malls appeared and Pizza Hut began accepting orders online. Some ingenious college students even found a way to program Coke machines to respond to commands given over the Internet. More and more people were taking an interest in the Internet and tailoring it to their needs each day.

In mid-1996, nearly 13 million computers made up the Internet, and some sources estimate that the Net doubles in size each week. Even though Internet access has become easy to obtain, some limitations still exist. Computers capable of accessing the Internet can be expensive, and you really need to know what you're doing to get online successfully. Busy telephone lines mean a long wait to get online. Then there's the confusing hunt for an Internet Service Provider (ISP), an experience in exasperation, at best. However, WebTV Networks is offering a new option called OpenISP, which lessens the pain of finding your own local ISP. I'll go through all the details of finding and registering with an ISP in Chapter 5, "Subscribing to the WebTV Network." I'll even help you decide whether OpenISP is the right option for you.

How the WebTV Network Fits In

No one will ever be able to tell the story as well as the WebTV Network founder and creator Steve Perlman, but here's the quick version. While the Internet was growing by leaps and bounds, the concept for the WebTV Network was gaining momentum. Steve Perlman had worked in the computer industry for many years, and one of his dreams was to bring easy e-mail access to consumers at large, without the expense of purchasing a computer. Upon witnessing the rapid growth of the Internet, his focus widened to include the World Wide Web as well.

Having figured out how to reduce TV screen flicker, Perlman was determined to test his idea. He ran to an electronics store and bought several thousands of dollars in parts. Three sleepless nights (and I'm betting a fair amount of caffeine consumption) later, he was ready to share the idea with a friend. Bruce Leak, now WebTV Network's Chief Operating Officer and Executive Vice President of Engineering, was that friend. Almost instantly, Perlman and Leak decided to form a business to produce a product and online service centered around the concept. A third colleague, Phil Goldman, was brought in to complete the management team.

For many months, the team worked in total secrecy (under the name of Artemis Research) out of a converted BMW garage in Palo Alto, California. Security was so tight that the WebTV Network's unveiling in July 1996 took PC makers and other members of the electronics industry by storm with its revolutionary technology and compelling business strategy. A mere two months later, WebTV Network's partners, Sony and Philips Magnavox, had the WebTV Internet terminals in stores nationwide. The marketing for the WebTV Network was so aggressive that everyone knew it existed before the holidays. The technology held much promise for the eventual merger of television and the Internet.

Enter: Microsoft

The clues about where this emerging technology is headed are everywhere—in the media, in the documentation that came with your Internet terminal, even in the construction of the Internet terminal itself. While no one of authority will come right out and say, "This is where the WebTV Network is headed," we can assume a few things:

- You will be able to hook up your camcorder to the Internet terminal to create full-motion videos that can be sent to others via the Internet.

- You will be able to use a microphone in much the same way as the camcorder to send sound files to friends and family.

- Smart-card technology will continue to evolve as a safer way to make purchases online and to engage in online banking.

- The possible incorporation of Windows CE into the Internet terminal would make the units even more functional for a wider range of audiences. My big prediction? Microsoft Word for WebTV, a lightweight word processing application, is only a few upgrades away! (This does not come from any inside information; it's been a running joke of mine since the Microsoft acquisition of WebTV Networks.)

Getting Started

- Television and the Internet will become even more seamlessly integrated. WebTV Plus is a great start. (Those who are currently using what has become known as WebTV Classic might want to check out Chapter 14, "Push Your WebTV Internet Terminal to the Limit," to see just how WebTV Plus works with your TV.)

When you consider how much the WebTV Network changed in its first year alone, none of these possibilities seems out of line. In fact, don't be surprised if you see changes and enhancements even more exciting than those presented above.

Will there be yet another Internet terminal with Windows CE incorporated? Will the original models remain for the cost conscious and computerphobic among us? Tune into "Club WebTV News" (select Using WebTV from the WebTV home page, and then select Club WebTV News) each month to learn all the answers as they unfold.

Chapter 2

The WebTV Internet Terminal Versus the PC—What's the Difference?

Whether you're contemplating buying a WebTV Internet terminal or are merely trying to understand the differences between it and a PC, this chapter gives you everything you need to know in plain English. Other useful tidbits are sprinkled throughout the book.

It might sound like I'm pro–WebTV Internet terminal and anti-PC, but that's really not the case at all. My husband and I make our living writing computer books, so I'd be crazy to knock PCs. Likewise, I've been given the opportunity to write this book about the WebTV Network, so naturally I want to see the product do well. I want to give you everything you need to feel confident about your decision and to help you get the most out of your WebTV Internet terminal. Who says we can't have some fun along the way?

The Eye of the Beholder

If you've read any of the reviews about WebTV Internet terminals, you might have heard some complaints about blurry text and poor image quality. While the display quality admittedly can leave something to be desired, there are some important points to keep in mind:

- In most of the articles I've read, the reviewers tended to be people spoiled by years of experience with a PC. Interestingly, the most complimentary articles were written by those experiencing the Internet for the first time on a WebTV Internet terminal.

- TV screens simply aren't capable of displaying images at a quality comparable to that of a computer monitor. Pictures on TV screens and monitors are both made up of dots (*pixels* in technobabble). Monitors are capable of cramming more dots on the viewing surface than are TV screens. What's more, these dots are smaller, which means that a monitor's image quality is superior in many cases.

- Those of you who have explored the Web using WebTV Internet terminals already know that pages designed by WebTV Networks look very nice. Why? Because the talented folks at WebTV Networks have spent countless months finessing Web page design and fine-tuning the unit's technology.

- As the WebTV Network subscriber base continues to grow, Web-masters will optimize their pages for viewing on a TV set. Because one communications research group optimistically estimates that over five million people will be surfing the Net on their TVs by the year 2000, some sites have already started work in this direction.

- Now that Microsoft is involved, the expertise of both corporations will come together to bring you a product that is second to none.

Everyone knows there is no such thing as a perfect invention—improvements can nearly always be made. And, as always, there are trade-offs. For a visually impaired person like me, surfing the Net on a 32-inch TV screen is incredible! Then there are the families unable to afford a $2,000 investment in a PC. A WebTV Internet terminal is a far more attainable goal, coming at $99 with a rebate from WebTV Networks (the sticker price is $199) for WebTV Classic and under $300 for WebTV Plus. Finally, we all know people who are terrified of computers. Heck, I was incredibly computerphobic myself ten years ago. But how many of us know people who are afraid of their TV? Their VCR, maybe, but their TV? Never!

2: The WebTV Internet Terminal Versus the PC—What's the Difference?

For the time being, WebTV Internet terminals might have a bit of a disadvantage when it comes to display quality, but it won't stay that way for long. It's still the best, most economical Internet surfing tool for many of us.

Easy Does It

One of the things I like most about a WebTV Internet terminal is how easily it can be updated. PC users must often upgrade their software to get the latest and greatest tools. These upgrades are not only time-consuming, but they can be expensive as well. With WebTV Internet terminals, it's different. One day while you're connecting to the WebTV Network, you'll see a little box pop up on the screen that says there's a new WebTV Network software update available. (See Figure 2-1 and Figure 2-2.) The message box will tell you approximately how much time you'll need to download the update, and then ask if you'd like to install it now or later. Within a few short minutes, you'll be able to take advantage of all the WebTV Network's newest features without further cost. No messing with disks or rearranging files; it's a dream come true.

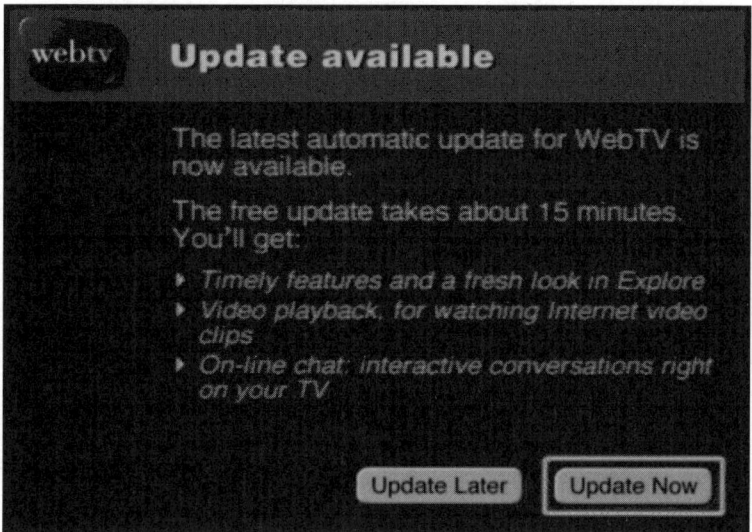

Figure 2-1.   *The Update Available screen makes it possible for users to have the latest and greatest version of the WebTV Network software promptly, easily, and—best of all—free!*

Getting Started

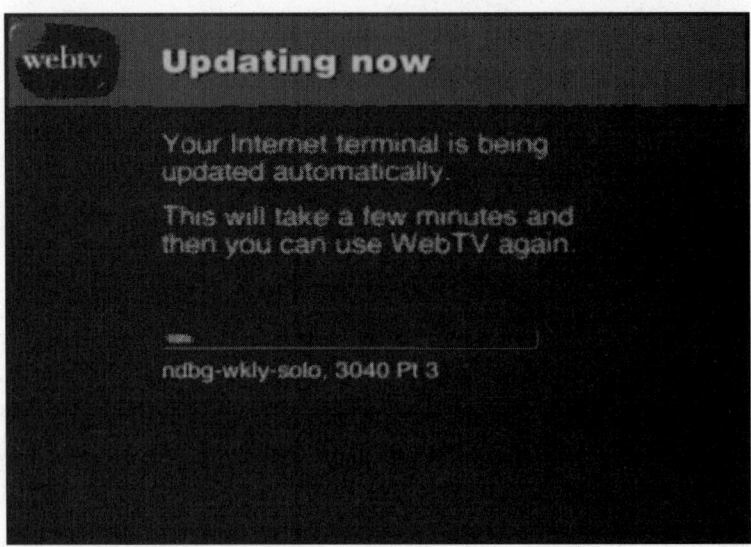

Figure 2-2. *The Updating Now screen lets you know everything's going smoothly.*

With a PC you could spend years (not to mention hundreds of dollars) trying to find, for example, a good e-mail program. Many such programs exist, but you don't necessarily know if you like them until you use them for a while. Repeat that process with a newsreader and a Web browser and it really gets messy. At least with the WebTV Network you don't have numerous expensive decisions to make. You get the software they give you, it gets updated regularly without cost, and you don't even have to engage in the great Internet Service Provider search, because it's already done for you.

Another thing that makes a WebTV Internet terminal easier to deal with than a PC is the ability to use a remote control instead of a mouse. Anyone who's ever attempted to use a mouse knows that it requires a bit of practice and coordination to get the hang of it. With the remote, the next Web page is a quick select-and-push away. This feature also makes the WebTV Internet terminal a good choice for younger children, people with a touch of arthritis, or people suffering from carpal tunnel syndrome. I know my hand gets less fatigued with the remote than with the mouse.

I promise to be totally honest with you throughout this book, so I need to say something about surfing the Internet solely by remote control. Technically it can be done, but it's probably not something you want to try for an extended period of time unless you have the patience of Job and endless amounts of free time. In the next chapter, I'll discuss your options in greater detail, but suffice it to say that I think a keyboard should come standard with the unit, not as an option. Granted, typing à la remote was a lot better than I expected, but a keyboard makes it so much easier. You'll actually look forward to typing that lengthy e-mail note to a long lost classmate, instead of cringing at the thought of it.

Dollars and Sense

If you've contemplated getting online for any amount of time, chances are you've been overwhelmed by your choices. Do you spring for a $5,000 PC Theater or a $2,000 computer? If your kids have a Sega Saturn, you could buy NetLink for $200. Then there's the WebTV Network—the options are staggering. In fact, it's almost as overwhelming as selecting a long distance phone carrier. But help is on the way. I've come up with a list of questions and answers that not only will help with the big decision but also will highlight the differences between WebTV Internet terminals and PCs.

1. **How much is too much?** The first question you should ask yourself is how much can you afford to spend on this device, whatever it might be. I've already illustrated the wide range in prices—only you can decide how much is too much to spend on this investment. Even if you can afford the most expensive option, it still might not be the most practical one. Keep in mind that PC ownership includes a host of indirect costs. While software bundles frequently are included with a machine, odds are you'll want something different. You might also find yourself upgrading your PC's hardware to keep up with the software's demands. This should all factor into your final cost analysis.

2. **Who will use it?** Will the primary user be a computerphobic grandmother hoping to stay in contact with her grandchildren? A WebTV Internet terminal might be all she needs or wants. Will this device be used to free up the family's PC so dad can pay the bills and mom can write her dissertation while the kids surf elsewhere? If so, you might not want to plunk down several thousand dollars for a second PC even if you have money to spare. However, if the kids will be

researching school papers on the Internet and then writing them on the PC, another computer could in fact be needed. Keep in mind that PCs generally have a life span of about two or three years before they become obsolete. Software changes so frequently that faster processors and bigger hard drives are often needed after that period of time.

3. **Where do you spend most of your time?** If you're going to spend your hard-earned money on an Internet-surfing device, you might as well choose something that fits in with your lifestyle. If you live in an efficiency apartment, you might not have the space for a computer. If you invest in a computer that needs to be kept in a room far away from all the action, you might not use it as much as you'd like. If you find yourself on the road a lot, a laptop or palmtop computer could be your surfboard of choice.

4. **What do you need the equipment to accomplish?** As you will see in Chapter 13, "Traffic Jams and Other Roadblocks," there are things WebTV Internet terminals can't do. They don't claim to be full-scale PCs capable of running word processors and spreadsheets, but they are able to read and print a majority of the file types encountered on the Internet. If you plan to play games (except for a few online games), download shareware, or establish a home office, a PC is your obvious choice. If you simply want to enjoy the Internet, use it for research, and want an increased image size, a WebTV Internet terminal is your device of choice.

5. **Do you or the device's primary user find computers intimidating?** I touched upon this before, but it's a point worth repeating. If the person planning to use the Internet the most is petrified of computers, there's no point in getting one. It'll just become an expensive dust collector. A WebTV Internet terminal, on the other hand, might be just the ticket for someone afraid of computers—it's nonthreatening and is bound to get even the biggest skeptics addicted to the Internet.

6. **Do you want your surfing device to be tightly integrated with your TV?** If watching a TV show and being able to jump to related Web sites is appealing to you, you'll love WebTV Plus. Likewise, if you'd

2: The WebTV Internet Terminal Versus the PC—What's the Difference?

like to be able to surf while you watch TV, you'll love the WebTV Plus picture-in-picture capability. For more on the differences between WebTV Classic and WebTV Plus, see the final section in this chapter.

Having read these questions and reflected on your answers to them, you should have even more confidence in your decision. No solution is right or wrong, since everyone has his or her own unique set of circumstances. For those who already own a WebTV Internet terminal, these questions and answers should give you a hair more insight into the differences between a PC and a WebTV Internet terminal.

Real People Use the WebTV Network

A few days after I purchased my WebTV Internet terminal, several of my husband's friends came over for a party. They were a group of electrical engineers, physicists, and computer professionals. One of them walked past the box, looked down at it, scrunched up his face, and said, "A WebTV? You actually bought one of those things?" It was as if I had dog dung on my shoe, the way he carried on. Another friend of my husband's wanted to get his mother a laptop for Mother's Day because she wanted to get on the Internet. I couldn't understand why someone who only wanted to surf the Net would pay $2,000 or more for an Internet-ready laptop when a WebTV Internet terminal would do the job commendably. To each his own, I guess.

While I'd like to say that everyone will enthusiastically embrace your decision to get a WebTV Internet terminal, this is the real world; you're bound to get some ribbing from a few of your friends and associates. They might tease you for not having a "real" computer. So what? For what they most likely paid for their computer, you could have a WebTV Internet terminal and a first class trip to Walt Disney World. And when they see how quickly you learn to navigate your way around the Web, they'll surely be impressed. So hold your head up high—you should be proud of your decision.

While out surfing around the WebTV Network discussion groups, I found these tidbits, which provide a little insight into the typical WebTV Network user. One of my favorites was a 75-year-old lady who was concerned about the rumored Microsoft acquisition of WebTV Networks—she was afraid her friendly Internet terminal would turn into a computer. Another user was very adept at using a PC, but he liked the idea of surfing from his recliner. And I love the story of the empty-nester mom who bought each of her kids a WebTV Internet terminal so they could all stay in better touch with her.

Somehow, the WebTV Network has managed to worm its way into all age groups, all income brackets, and all education levels. For every situation, you can find a WebTV Network user who meets the criteria. The same can't always be said for PCs. In that respect, Steve Perlman has really achieved his goal of bringing the Internet to the public at large.

WebTV Classic Versus WebTV Plus—Which Is Best for You?

Those of you who bought a WebTV Internet terminal during its first year are the proud owners of what has become known as WebTV Classic. Now, before you get uptight about your unit becoming obsolete, rest assured that your unit is not obsolete—far from it. In fact, WebTV Classic and WebTV Plus are virtually the same when it comes to Internet surfing functionality. The primary difference lies in the ability of WebTV Plus to interact with your TV. If watching a lot of TV isn't appealing to you, then you have nothing to worry about—WebTV Classic is still for you. But WebTV Plus is a wonderful toy for the true couch potato.

With WebTV Plus, you can surf the Internet for racecar driver statistics while watching Sunday's NASCAR race in a picture-in-picture screen on the bottom right corner of your TV screen (even if your TV doesn't have picture-in-picture capability). While watching a TV ad for a new car, you can jump to a related Web site containing more information about the car featured in the ad; you can even download television programming information, from which you can plan and scan schedules for viewing your favorite shows. All these features are loaded from a secondary home page referred to as TV Home, so the Internet surfing capabilities of WebTV Classic and WebTV Plus remain identical, at least for now.

2: The WebTV Internet Terminal Versus the PC—What's the Difference?

So which is best? Each version has its good points. For TV lovers, WebTV Plus has some wonderful features. (See Chapter 14, "Push Your WebTV Internet Terminal to the Limits" for a closer look.) As I've mentioned, WebTV Classic and WebTV Plus are identical in terms of Internet surfing, but if sending video clips via e-mail using your camcorder is something you'll want to do, you'll have to have WebTV Plus. Printing is also easier with WebTV Plus—all you need is a standard printer cable and a supported printer.

WebTV Classic, on the other hand, has economy on its side. This terminal costs about two thirds as much as WebTV Plus (it costs even less with the rebate), and you have the option of hooking up a cheap PC keyboard to the Classic Internet terminal. When it comes to printing with WebTV Classic, you'll need to purchase a special printer adapter from the manufacturer of your Internet terminal, which sells for around $100 at the time of this writing.

Which is right for you? Given your budget and TV viewing habits, only you can make the best decision, but one thing's certain: you'll be getting a high-quality, economical Internet experience, whichever model you choose.

Chapter 3

Before You Buy a WebTV Internet Terminal

When you make an exciting purchase like a WebTV Internet terminal, you want to be certain you have everything you need to set it up and enjoy it as soon as you get it home. This chapter will tell you what features to look for on your TV set as well as help you prepare a list of things you'll want to have on hand.

Local Access Charges?

One of the first things you'll want to check before buying a WebTV Internet terminal is whether you have local dial-up access to the WebTV Internet Service Provider (ISP) in your area. You can check this by calling 1-800-GOWEBTV or by having a friend with Internet access enter your phone number into the following Web page: *http://www.webtv.net/corp/HTML-/home.retail.html*.

If you live in a rural area not yet served by the WebTV Network, you might want to consider calling your telephone company to investigate getting a foreign exchange. A foreign exchange would eliminate toll charges for Internet access but would require higher monthly phone bills. The exact amount depends on your location and phone company.

Getting Started

> **WARNING** Keep in mind that while getting a foreign exchange might eliminate Internet access charges, it might cause formerly local calls to become toll calls. Check with your telephone company and review your telephone usage habits carefully before making any radical changes.

Perhaps the most practical option in cases where a local dial-up number does not exist is to take advantage of WebTV Network's OpenISP option. These days, Internet Service Providers can be found in even the most remote locations. Using OpenISP, you dial a local number to connect to the WebTV Network, avoiding toll charges altogether. Learn more about using OpenISP in Chapter 5, "Subscribing to the WebTV Network."

Check Out Your TV

Before heading off to buy your WebTV terminal, you'll want to do two things with regard to your TV—locate its owner's manual, and examine the back of the television. WebTV Internet terminal installation may require you to make some adjustments to your TV. While these adjustments won't be major, you'll certainly need the manual to ward off any potential headaches. Examining the back of your TV, however, might be a bit trickier. What you find will determine which installation method you select, which will also determine whether you'll be adding any other items to your list.

In a well-lit area, turn your TV around to get a good view of its back side. Look for groups of round jacks or a single round outlet containing multiple tiny prongs (as shown in Figure 3-1). The plain round jacks will allow you to hook your WebTV Internet terminal directly to your TV with the audio and video cables that came with your unit.

The round outlet with prongs in the center accommodates a super video (S-VIDEO) cable. This cable is not included with the unit since S-VIDEO is most commonly found on newer, high-end TVs. The S-VIDEO installation instructions are only slightly different from those for direct WebTV-to-TV connection. Figure 3-2 shows an example of an S-VIDEO outlet.

If you own an older TV without any jacks or outlets (as shown in Figure 3-3), you'll need to either connect the WebTV Internet terminal through your VCR or purchase an RFU adapter. The bad news, of course, is that the RFU adapter is not included with the WebTV Internet terminal. What's worse is

3: Before You Buy a WebTV Internet Terminal

Figure 3-1. *A TV with standard round jacks. To install your WebTV Internet terminal, you'll use the directions for connecting to a TV or VCR outlined in Chapter 5.*

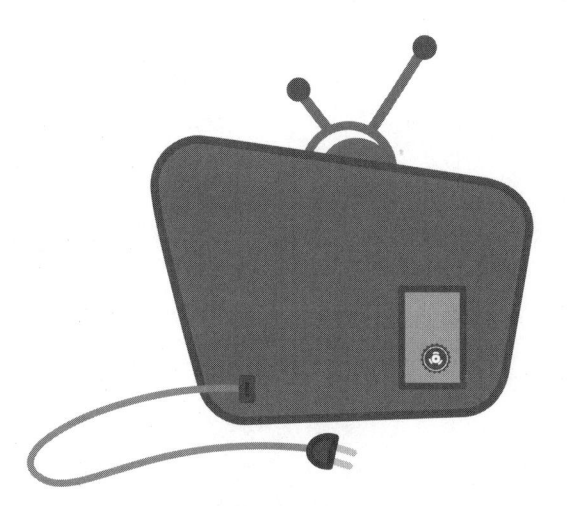

Figure 3-2. *If you have a newer large screen TV, chances are you'll see this outlet. This requires either the direct to TV or VCR installation or the S-VIDEO installation, also described in Chapter 5.*

Figure 3-3. *This TV is an older model requiring an RFU adapter or VCR connection as described in Chapter 5.*

you'll have to part with $50 to get it. The RFU adapter still makes the WebTV Internet terminal a good value, but it's always hard to spend money on add-ons just to get something up and running. I thought you should be prepared; it's better to know ahead of time than to get home and find you don't have everything you need.

Getting 'Board?

In the last chapter, you probably recall me illustrating the importance of getting a keyboard with your WebTV Internet terminal. If you've priced the accompanying accessories, you undoubtedly know that the infrared wireless keyboards cost anywhere from $60 to $80. That's a big chunk of money when you consider it's over half the price of the WebTV Classic Internet terminal and over a quarter of the price of a WebTV Plus Internet terminal. I've got one and I love it, but if the expense puts you way over budget, you do have some alternatives.

If you are buying WebTV Classic, you might want to consider buying a standard AT computer keyboard. It won't be wireless, but it'll cost well under $20 and give you the luxury of having a keyboard. An AT keyboard is essentially any computer keyboard with 12 function keys (F1 through F12) across the top. (See Figure 3-4 for an example.) Most new keyboards have a small plug that will fit the WebTV Internet terminal keyboard outlet perfectly. If you opt to pick up a bargain keyboard at a flea market and later discover its plug is too big, never fear—you can pick up a keyboard adapter for a couple of bucks at your local Best Buy or Radio Shack.

> **TECHNOBABBLE Keyboard Adapter**—To be sure you get the right keyboard adapter, here are the specs: 5 Pin DIN Female to 6 Pin Mini DIN Male. This allows a keyboard with an AT style connector to hook up with a PS/2 style port, like the one found on the back of WebTV Classic Internet terminals.

> **NOTE** Remember that the option to use a computer keyboard is available only with WebTV Classic units, not with WebTV Plus.

Figure 3-4. *When shopping for an economical keyboard for your WebTV Internet terminal, try to get an AT model. This will ensure that all the function key shortcuts will work properly.*

Another thing to put on your list next to the AT keyboard is a keyboard extender cable. This isn't a costly item, and it will give you far greater freedom of movement. You won't have to sit on the floor with your nose pressed against the screen. Just remember to use extreme caution with cables lying across the floor. Someone could trip and get seriously injured quicker than you can say, "Hey, who took my remote control?"

Put It in Writing

The ability to print using a WebTV Internet terminal is a terrific capability, but it's one you don't need the moment you purchase your Internet terminal. Because a printer can cost a couple of hundred dollars (not to mention

Getting Started

the needed cables or adapters), you might want to defer buying a printer to make things easier on your bank account. For more on printing with a WebTV Internet terminal, see Chapter 14, "Push Your WebTV Internet Terminal to the Limit."

Make a List and Check It Twice…

Let's take one last look at everything you'll want to have with you when you install your WebTV Internet terminal:

- The entire contents of your WebTV Network package
- Your TV owner's manual
- S-VIDEO cable if your TV can use it
- An RFU adapter, if needed
- Infrared wireless keyboard, if desired
- AT keyboard, if desired (for WebTV Classic only)
- Keyboard extender cable, if desired
- Keyboard adapter, if needed
- A credit card to complete network registration (don't worry; you can also pay by check)
- A list of login names for each WebTV Network user (have extras in case one is already in use)
- Printer adapter for WebTV Classic Internet terminal owners, if desired (call the manufacturer of your Internet terminal to purchase this)
- IEEE-1284 compliant printer cable for WebTV Classic Internet terminal owners if you wish to print using a WebTV Classic Internet terminal
- Any Hewlett Packard 400 or 600 series DeskJet color printer for WebTV Classic Internet terminal owners, if desired

3: Before You Buy a WebTV Internet Terminal

For those with WebTV Plus, any Hewlett Packard 400 or 600 series DeskJet color printer or any Canon 200, 600, or 4000 series color BubbleJet printer will do. Other options might be available in the future, as WebTV Networks is working closely with printer manufacturers.

Double-check this list before leaving home for any items you might need to buy. Remember, the keyboard isn't necessary to use the WebTV Internet terminal. If you really want the cordless keyboard, consider waiting a month or two until it fits in better with your budget. There's no hurry.

Choosing multiple login names ahead of time is also a wise idea. If your first choice is taken, you'll have a decent backup to count on rather than having to select one on the fly that you'll end up hating later.

Chapter 4

Anatomy of a WebTV Internet Terminal

OK, so maybe exploring the Internet terminal anatomy isn't as exciting as exploring human anatomy, but you'll want to be familiar with all the nooks and crannies of your Internet terminal just the same. Why? Because this familiarity will help you get the most out of this lean, mean, surfin' machine.

This chapter takes a close look at the unit itself, while Chapter 6, "Get with the Program," is devoted to the remote control and optional wireless keyboard. In between, we have Chapter 5, "Subscribing to the WebTV Network," which helps you connect your Internet terminal to the Internet via an Internet Service Provider.

It's What's Up Front That Counts

The following four features all reside on the front panel of the newest incarnation of the Internet terminal (WebTV Plus). Of course, there is one caveat here: as more manufacturers begin making WebTV Internet terminals, the location of these features might vary. For the sake of simplicity, I have described these features as they appear on a Sony WebTV Plus Internet terminal.

Smart Card Slot

In the future, you'll be able to run a credit card or an ATM card through this slot to engage in secure online shopping and banking. Additionally, smart cards will probably be designed to give users belonging to a special group a customized launch page (or home page), presenting them with the resources of the most value and interest to them. For example, a cat lover's smart card might connect them directly to the Cat Fancier's Association, a site containing pet care questions and answers, boutiques offering items with a cat motif, and so on.

Power Indicator

This green light glows when the Internet terminal is plugged in.

Connected Indicator

The Connected indicator blinks yellow when the terminal is attempting to connect to the WebTV Network. The indicator also blinks when information is being transferred between your WebTV Internet terminal and the WebTV Network. At all other times while the WebTV Internet terminal is turned on the indicator glows a solid yellow. (While you're connected to the WebTV Network you can also see an indication that information is flowing between your WebTV Internet terminal and the WebTV Network by looking at the "heartbeat" monitor at the bottom right of your screen. When information is being transferred, the monitor line wiggles around. When nothing is happening the line remains straight.) At times the Net might seem slower than molasses. If the yellow light is blinking (and the green light is wiggling), chances are that large images or blocks of text are being transmitted. If the light glows yellow with no blinking and nothing appears on your screen, the network might be clogged with users. Try browsing another site, or save your surfing for another time.

Message Indicator

When this red light is illuminated, an unread e-mail message awaits you in your mailbox. The light will begin to glow when you've connected to the WebTV Network.

On the Side

While examining your WebTV Internet terminal, you might have noticed a slot-like opening on the side of the unit. This expansion slot is reserved for future growth. Given the many wonders of technology, who knows what this port will house in the years (or even months) to come!

The Flip Side

The back of the Internet terminal is far from colorful, yet the jacks and outlets located there are vital to the operation of the unit. As you've seen in your owner's manual, there are many ways to hook up your WebTV Internet terminal. Rather than waste valuable pages here recapping what you can easily find in your owner's manual, I've opted to briefly introduce you to each of these parts and their corresponding function.

> **NOTE** Again, each manufacturer might place elements in slightly different locations. The description here is based on the locations used by Sony for the WebTV Plus Internet terminal.

Tel Line

If you've ever plugged in a telephone, you'll recognize the shape of the first jack at the left side of the Internet terminal. This jack, labeled Tel Line, is used to connect the Internet terminal to your telephone line using a standard phone cable.

> **NOTE** Technically, a standard phone cable is called an RJ-11 cable. You can find one at just about any discount or electronics store. For the frugal among us (myself included), the dollar store in your local mall often has a good supply of them in varying lengths.

When connecting the Internet terminal to your telephone line, don't forget to make use of the telephone line splitter that came with your unit. It's a great way to keep both a telephone and Internet terminal connected to the phone line at the same time. While both can't be in use simultaneously,

Getting Started

the line splitter prevents the premature destruction of the plastic connector at the end of a phone cable, which can easily snap after repeated plugging and unplugging.

> **TIP** If you have call waiting, remember that you can instruct the Internet terminal to suspend operation while you take the call. To do this, press the Options button, select Hang Up, and then press Go. Your Internet terminal will enable the phone line to take the incoming call while maintaining your current surfing location on screen. To resume Net surfing, verify that the Reconnect box is selected, and then press Go.

IR Out

This jack, immediately to the right of the Tel Line, accepts the connection of something called an *IR shooter* (IR stands for infrared). While an IR shooter might sound like an exotic drink, it's actually a device that enables you to control your cable box with the WebTV Internet terminal remote control. This is a must if you plan to take full advantage of WebTV Plus' TV Home features. Note that this jack is available only on the WebTV Plus Internet terminal.

Printer

WebTV Classic owners needed to purchase a special printer adapter from the manufacturer of their Internet terminal in order to use a printer. This adapter fits into a jack on the back of the unit. WebTV Plus owners, however, now have an actual printer port on the back of their Internet terminals, so no fancy adapter is needed. This printer port uses a 25-to-36-pin parallel printer cable to connect your Internet terminal to a supported printer.

For more information on printing with the WebTV Internet terminal, see Chapter 14, "Push Your WebTV Internet Terminal to the Limit."

MIC

To the right of the printer port is a microphone jack (labeled MIC). Now, imagine the possibilities here. In the future, you will be able to plug in a microphone (with a 3.5 mm plug), and send voice mail to friends and family across the globe. What a great, low-cost way for the grandkids to sing "Happy Birthday" to Grandpa Buck, who lives halfway across the country!

Audio/Video In
If the possibilities of voice mail excite you, hold on to your hat! Toward the middle of the unit are two rows of three jacks. The top row of jacks are audio/video input jacks, which means that someday you might be able to connect a camcorder to your Internet terminal.

Audio/Video Out
The bottom row of jacks is used to connect the Internet terminal to your TV so that you can view your Internet terminal's output.

S-VIDEO Out
If you have a TV with S-VIDEO output, you might want to use an S-VIDEO cable to get the highest quality picture possible. Furthermore, you need only one cable to connect using S-Video, as opposed to the three cables you'd need using the alternate method of installation.

CH 3/4 Switch
In some areas of the country TV stations broadcast on Channel 3 and in others they broadcast on Channel 4. They never broadcast on both in the same area. You want your WebTV Internet terminal to use the channel not being used by a local TV station. This prevents the signal from your WebTV terminal from mixing with the TV broadcast, which would result in a distorted or unclear picture on your TV screen.

ANT In
The ANT In jack, which occupies the highest position on the rear of the Internet terminal, is where you connect your TV antenna, cable TV, VCR, cable box, or other device used to receive a television signal. The TV signal can be used for some of the nifty TV viewing features of WebTV Plus.

RF Out

Many older television sets do not have S-VIDEO or Audio/Video In jacks. In those cases, an RFU adapter can be used to pass the television signal to the TV. For more information about using an RFU adapter, refer back to Chapter 3, "Before You Buy a WebTV Internet Terminal."

AC Input

Finally, the AC Input plug connects your Internet terminal to AC power. This is where the Internet terminal gets its power to function.

Other Cool Bits and Pieces

Those of you who own the Sony Internet terminal will be able to program your remote to control your TV in addition to the WebTV Internet terminal. Follow these steps to program your remote control:

1. Grab your TV owner's manual and locate the chart used for programming your TV's remote control.

2. Find the brand name of your television set, and then look for the three-digit code next to it. If there is more than one number, use the first number in the list.

3. Press the Code Set button on your remote control.

4. Enter the three-digit code you found in Step 2.

5. Press the View button on the remote control.

Your WebTV Internet terminal remote should now be able to control your TV in addition to the Internet terminal.

If you leave your Internet terminal to go fix a sandwich or something, don't be surprised if your Internet terminal has disconnected itself by the time you return. This frees the phone line for incoming calls while maintaining your place on the Internet. A Reconnect box will appear onscreen so you can easily pick up where you left off by pressing the Go button. If the Reconnect box remains displayed for several minutes, a screen saver will activate.

Screen savers were originally used to prevent images from becoming permanently etched onto a monitor's screen. These days, they're used for their decorative and entertainment value. The current screen saver used by WebTV Networks shows the little TV logo bouncing around on your screen. To resume operations with your Internet terminal from screen saver mode, press any button or key and then press Go to reconnect if prompted to do so.

Chapter 5

Subscribing to the WebTV Network

With WebTV Networks providing continual updates to their service, you have even more ways to connect to the WebTV Network than ever. When the WebTV Network first made its appearance in 1996, you had to live in an area with local dial-up access to the WebTV Network if you wanted to connect to the Internet without paying hefty long distance charges. This was because the WebTV Network used only a few predetermined Internet service providers (ISPs), which meant that those people living outside the areas served by the predetermined ISPs couldn't get toll free access to the WebTV Network. Now with WebTV Networks' new OpenISP option, you can use any local ISP to connect to the WebTV Network. This chapter will give you the skinny on which connection option will work best for you and will walk you through the subscription process, whether you plan to use the predetermined WebTV Network's ISP exclusively or whether you need to use the OpenISP option to avoid mortgaging your home to pay your phone bills.

The Lowdown on ISPs

An Internet service provider is a business that provides Internet connectivity. Before the new OpenISP option, WebTV Networks contracted with a variety of ISPs across the country so that people residing in the more populous areas of the U.S. could connect to the WebTV Network without paying for a toll call. As demand for WebTV Network service spread, the number of locations needed to provide toll free access increased.

My parents' situation in rural South Dakota is a good illustration of this point. WebTV Networks hadn't arranged for a local dial-up number in their area, so using a WebTV Internet terminal was cost-prohibitive. But even rural South Dakota has a local ISP. The folks at WebTV Networks realized that this was a common scenario, and swiftly provided the option to choose your own ISP. While I can't be 100 percent certain, it's my speculation that the OpenISP option is the primary reason that WebTV Network subscriber numbers have increased remarkably, even after the holiday rush of its premier year. Think about it—it makes sense!

Here's another situation: Let's say you already have a PC that you use to access the Internet using a local ISP. One day you find that you need to use the PC for word processing at the same time your kids want to surf the Web. What's a parent to do? Simple! Buy a WebTV Internet terminal and set it up to use the OpenISP option so that your kids can use your existing account with your local ISP. This will cost you only an additional $9.95 a month—obviously a whole lot cheaper than buying another PC!

OpenISP: The Whole Truth and Nothing But the Truth

In Chapter 3, "Before You Buy a WebTV Internet Terminal," I showed you how to determine whether you already have local access to the WebTV Network. If you skipped that chapter because you already own a WebTV Internet terminal, you might want to flip back to it now, especially if you are making toll calls to use the WebTV Network. If, in fact, you do not have local WebTV Network access, OpenISP might very well be the option for you.

But before you snatch up your remote control to make the big change to OpenISP, you'll need to do a few things. You'll need to know exactly what you're getting into with the OpenISP option; you'll need to find a good, reliable ISP (sometimes more difficult than it sounds); and you'll need to know what to ask that prospective ISP.

What You Should Expect with OpenISP

Like all great bargains, sometimes OpenISP sounds too good to be true. But there are definitely benefits to using this option, which I'll save until later in this chapter. There's one catch to using OpenISP—while you get the same WebTV Network experience you've grown to know and love (OK, maybe I'm laying it on a bit thick), there's an extra cost attached, and that cost will hit you in the form of an extra bill.

If you access the WebTV Network using your own ISP, you must pay WebTV Networks $9.95 a month because you're still using the WebTV Network's disk storage, software, and content. Sure, it's $10 a month less than regular subscribers pay, but you'll also need to pay your chosen ISP. In general, the cost decreases for an ISP as the amount of competition in a given area increases. How much is this cost? I'll go out on a limb here and say that as of this writing, you should not have to pay more than $20 a month for Internet access with most local ISPs. (That's roughly $30 a month total, in case you're mathematically challenged like I am.) And, if the truth were known, you might be able to get access significantly cheaper from your ISP, since you don't really need disk storage, Web page hosting, or any of the other bells and whistles the ISP might try to sell you.

If $30 a month sounds kind of steep, consider how few toll calls you could actually make with that extra $10 you'd pay for using OpenISP. Even with the ever-popular dime-a-minute rate, you could connect for only a hundred minutes a month. That's just a hair over three minutes a day! I've seen single Web pages that take that long to load. In the long run, the OpenISP option will save you money if your area doesn't yet have local dial-up access to the WebTV Network. And hey, should WebTV Networks expand into your area and provide a local access number, it's as easy as pie to switch back to using of the predetermined WebTV Network ISPs exclusively.

> **CAUTION** You can't use services like America Online or CompuServe as an ISP in this case, so forget about using those free trial disks you get in the mail and in magazines.

The Search for an ISP

Quite frankly, you'd have to be living in a cave to be unable to locate an ISP. Most telephone companies and long distance carriers are offering Internet access, and many small ISPs set up shop when the Internet started becoming so popular. Which one should you pick?

Everyone has his or her preference, but I currently use an independent local provider. Because their existence relies primarily on customer satisfaction, local providers tend to work harder to keep you happy. That means when a rash of busy signals causes an uproar, local providers will bust their rear ends trying to rectify the problem by installing additional modems and phone lines. Larger companies whose primary focus is anything other than providing Internet service (such as most phone companies) tend to let Internet-related problems fester since they're low on their list of priorities. (This is by no means a blanket statement, just my own humble opinion.)

If you're a bit apprehensive about all this Internet connection stuff, you might want to find an ISP with good technical support hours that fit your schedule. The very best tech support means nothing if it's not available when you need it.

If you live in a densely populated area, you'll want to find an ISP that provides several toll free dial-in numbers. This reduces the likelihood that you'll encounter busy signals when you're most eager to surf the Net.

To find one of these local providers, consult your local phone book's Internet section, browse the business section of your local newspaper, or ask a friend who has Internet access. Word of mouth is often the best way to find a good provider.

Ask All the Right Questions

Once you've found a prospective ISP, you'll need to ask a few questions to make sure they have what you need.

First, you'll need to know if the ISP supports Point-to-Point Protocol (PPP). This is a language that computers use to speak with one another. The ISP you select must provide PPP access.

Second, the ISP must use Password Authentication Protocol (PAP). While some ISPs use other protocols, the WebTV Internet terminal needs PAP support to do its job.

I know these terms can seem a little confusing, but don't worry. The people you'll be speaking with at a prospective ISP will know exactly what you're talking about.

> **NOTE** If your ISP seems curious to learn how OpenISP works, give them this URL: *www.webtv.net/corp/openisp/*. This Web page will answer all their questions.

Some information you'll need to get from your ISP before you attempt to use OpenISP on your WebTV Internet terminal includes:

- Login name for your ISP account
- Password for your ISP account (You might want to choose the same password you plan to use on your WebTV Network account to reduce the number of passwords you'll need to remember.)
- Dial-up modem number (Get a second back-up toll free number if you can. Your Internet terminal will try connecting with the second number should you get a busy signal with the first number.)

With this information handy, you're ready to register with the WebTV Network. If you're already using the predetermined WebTV Network ISP exclusively, see the next section, titled "OpenISP: Getting the Best for Less," which will help you start using the OpenISP option.

Getting Started

OpenISP: Get the Best for Less

If you plan to use the predetermined WebTV Network ISP to dial into the Internet, let the surfing begin! Skip to the section titled "Sign Me Up!" starting on page 43 to begin the registration process. If, on the other hand, you want to configure your Internet terminal to use your own ISP, you still have a bit more work to do.

Note that setting up the OpenISP option might initially require a toll call, but if you have all the necessary information handy (the login name, the login password, the modem number, and so on), it shouldn't take long to complete that call and be on your way.

> **NOTE** If you've already accessed the Internet using your WebTV Internet terminal, stop here—you'll need to call 1-800-GO-WEBTV to set up your own ISP. If you just purchased your Internet terminal, follow the steps presented below.

To begin the OpenISP setup process, power up your Internet terminal. From the WebTV Network home page, select Setup and then follow these steps, pressing Go at the appropriate places:

1. Select the Dialing option.
2. Select Use Your ISP, or call 1-800-GO-WEBTV if the Use Your ISP option doesn't appear (for instance, if you've already set up your WebTV Internet terminal).
3. Read each of the information screens, selecting Continue after each one.
4. When instructed to do so, place a check in the appropriate checkbox to activate OpenISP. Select Continue after each step to move on.
5. Enter the name of your ISP.
6. Provide your ISP login name (which might be different from your WebTV Internet name).
7. Supply your ISP password.
8. Enter the dial-in modem number along with a back-up number if available.
9. Select Done.

5: Subscribing to the WebTV Network

The WebTV Internet terminal hangs up and then reconnects using the phone number you provided. Read the information screens to be sure you understand the terms of using your own ISP, select Use ISP, and then press Go.

> **CAUTION** Once you have used your own ISP for a month, you will receive the reduced WebTV Networks fee for service. This might mean you'll have one month of service at $19.95, followed by subsequent months billed at $9.95 each. If, however, you use the predetermined WebTV Network's ISP number to connect at any time, you will be billed $19.95 for that month. Don't worry; you won't inadvertently dial that number. You have to purposely disable the OpenISP option in order to connect using the predetermined WebTV Network ISP exclusively. It's not hard to do, but requires just enough steps to keep you from making a mistake.

As the number of WebTV Network subscribers continues to grow, it's not unthinkable that the WebTV Network will eventually offer a local access number just about everywhere. If it one day offers a local access number in your area, you'll be able to disable the OpenISP option quickly. Just select Setup from the WebTV Network home page, press Go, select Dialing, press Go, select Use Your ISP, press Go, remove the check in the checkbox, and press Go one more time. The next time you power up your Internet terminal, WebTV Networks will find the local access number for you and will store it for future use.

Sign Me Up!

Fasten your seatbelts—you're about to go cruising on the information superhighway! Nestle into your favorite chair, grab the remote or keyboard, and power up your Internet terminal (press the Power button on the keyboard or on the remote control).

At this point, your WebTV Internet terminal dials a toll free number. The computer at the other end of the line uses a technology similar to caller ID to find out where you're calling from and then provides multiple local access numbers to your WebTV Internet terminal, which it uses each time you connect. If no local number is available, a number closest to your vicinity will be used. Your WebTV Internet terminal then hangs up and dials this local number to begin the sign-up process.

Getting Started

Once your WebTV Internet terminal has successfully connected to the WebTV Network, you'll see the WebTV Network logo, followed by the Introducing WebTV screen shown in Figure 5-1. (The fact that this screen has the same title as this book is purely coincidental, I assure you!)

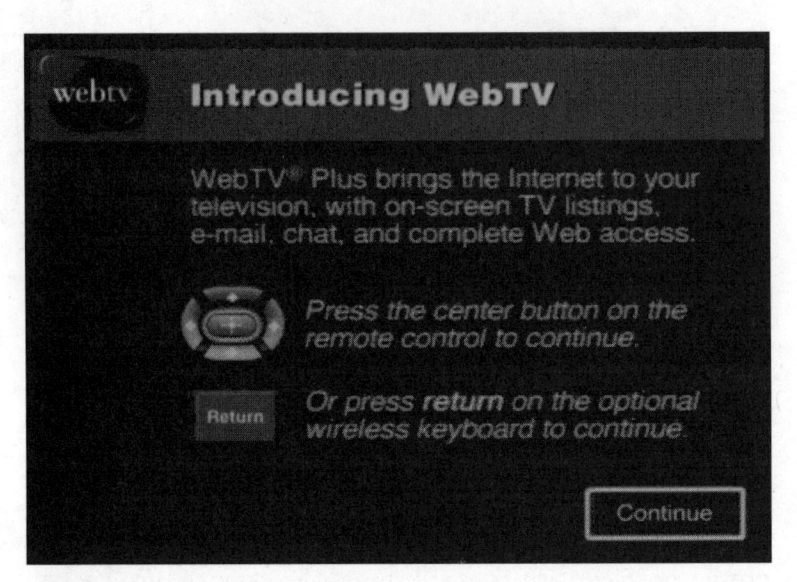

Figure 5-1. *The Introducing WebTV screen acquaints you with the remote buttons and keyboard keys you'll need to complete the registration process.*

> **NOTE** The screens that follow might vary slightly from the ones you see when you sign up. WebTV Classic subscribers might see different screens, but the information requested will be essentially the same. Also keep in mind that because the WebTV Network is constantly changing, the screens might look even better by the time you sign up. The manufacturer of your Internet terminal might also have an effect on the screens you see. The screens in this book were captured using a Sony Internet terminal.

Press the Go button on your remote control or the Return key on your keyboard to move to the next screen. For simplicity's sake, I decided to use Go for all the steps in this book, because everyone will have access to a remote control. The figures, however, show the steps for the keyboard.

The Learn To Choose Items screen illustrated in Figure 5-2 shows you how to use your remote control, but it also asks you whether you want to use the remote or keyboard to complete registration. Simply use the arrow buttons on your remote or keyboard to select the appropriate choice, press Go, and you're set. Select Continue, and press the Go button or the Return key as appropriate to move to the next step.

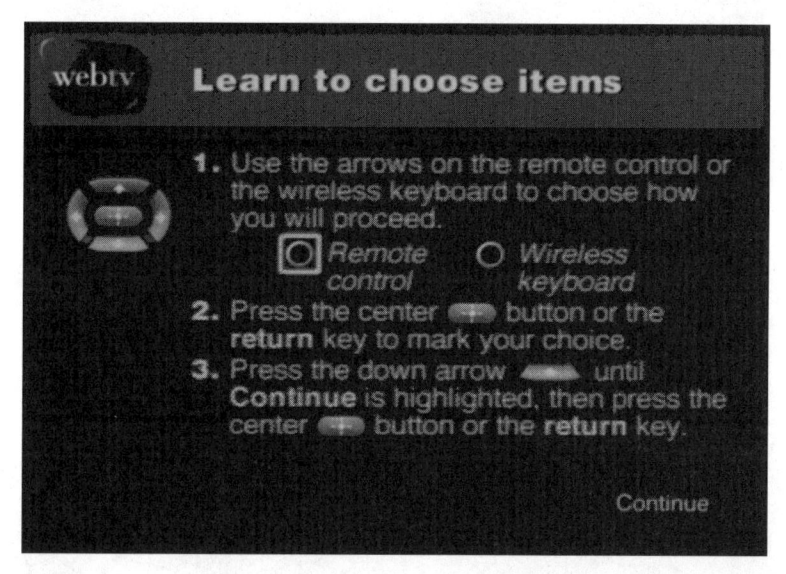

Figure 5-2. *WebTV Networks lets you select your favorite input device to complete registration.*

The Signing Up screen pictured in Figure 5-3 on the following page confirms your selected device, tells you what will be asked of you to complete the registration process, and reiterates the monthly charges and payment methods. Select Continue, and press Go to move to the next screen.

The first bit of information you'll be asked to provide is your first name. (See Figure 5-4.) If you plan to use a credit card to pay for your service, be sure the name you give agrees with the one printed on your credit card. For example, if your name is Katherine and you enter Katie, you might run into some verification problems. So type your name carefully—you wouldn't want to wake up one day and find yourself without WebTV Network access because of some little snag.

Getting Started

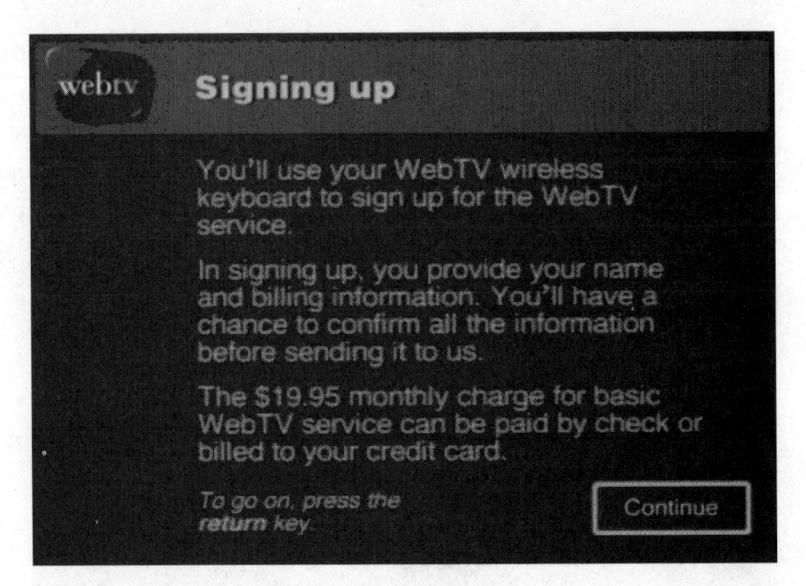

Figure 5-3. *Before you go any further, WebTV Networks gives you up-to-date information on the cost of its service. Keep in mind that the amount will be different if you opt to use OpenISP.*

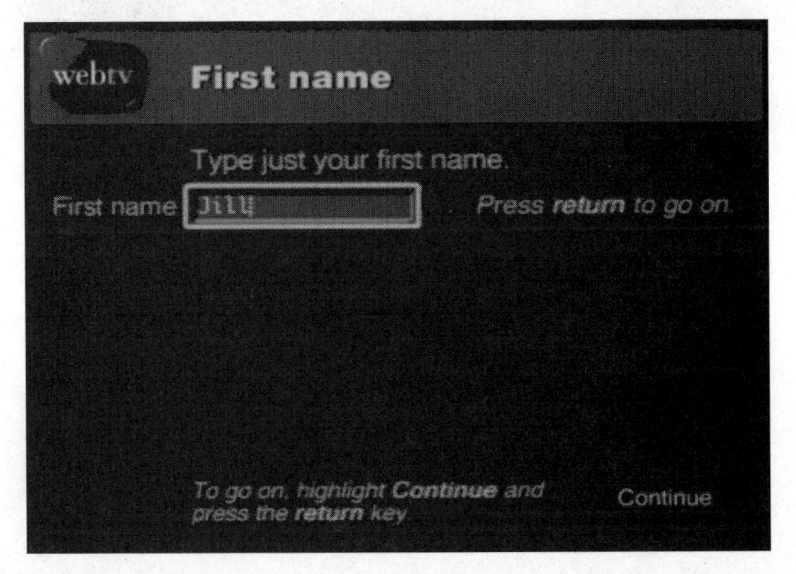

Figure 5-4. *Your first name is the first item you'll be asked to provide in the WebTV Network registration process.*

Next you'll be asked for your last name. Again, you should avoid any discrepancies between the name you give and the name that appears on your credit card, if that's the way you plan to pay. I have one credit card in my maiden name and one in my married name to help keep personal and business expenses separate. Verifying your name might seem like a trivial thing, but it does matter.

Your phone number is next on the list of information you'll need to supply, as shown in Figure 5-5.

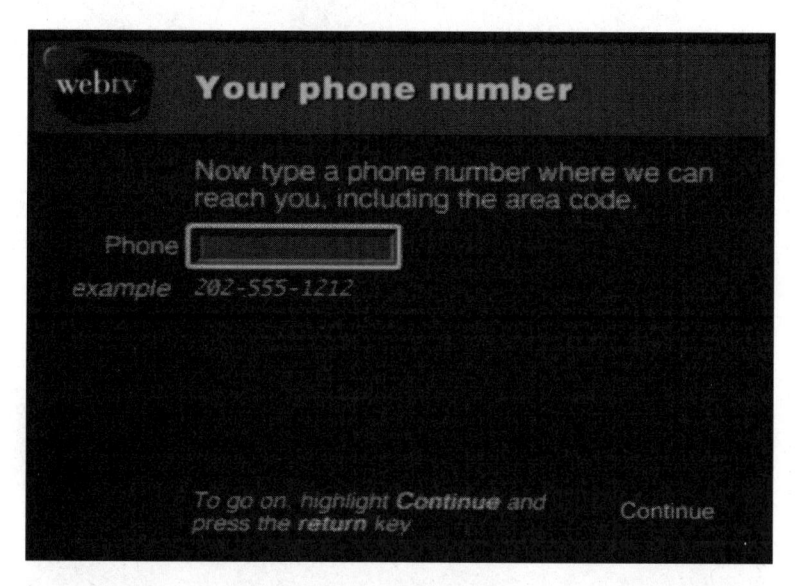

Figure 5-5. *Because phone numbers can be entered in a variety of formats, WebTV Networks gives you an example of the format to use.*

The billing address comes next. (See Figure 5-6 on the following page.) Notice that WebTV Networks has guessed the name of your city and state based on your phone number. While it might save some users the hassle of rekeying this information, in my case the wrong city was displayed because I have a funky phone number prefix. Don't just assume the information is correct; double-check it to be certain. Again, this address must agree with that shown on your credit card statement.

Getting Started

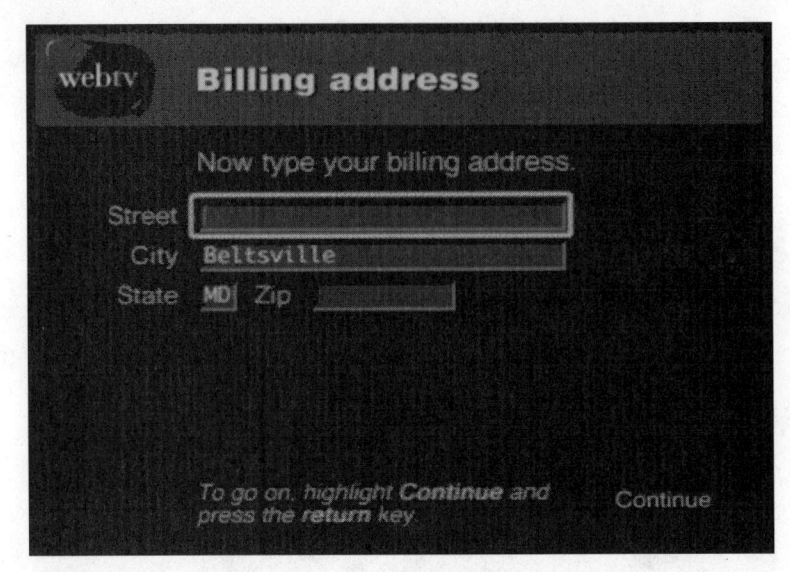

Figure 5-6.   *WebTV Networks uses your phone number to guess your city and state, which can save time in completing your registration.*

The next screen (Figure 5-7) informs you that by signing up for WebTV Networks service, you are agreeing to certain terms. You can either read the terms now (but be prepared to read through a 58-page document), or browse them online anytime. Select Continue to keep the registration process moving.

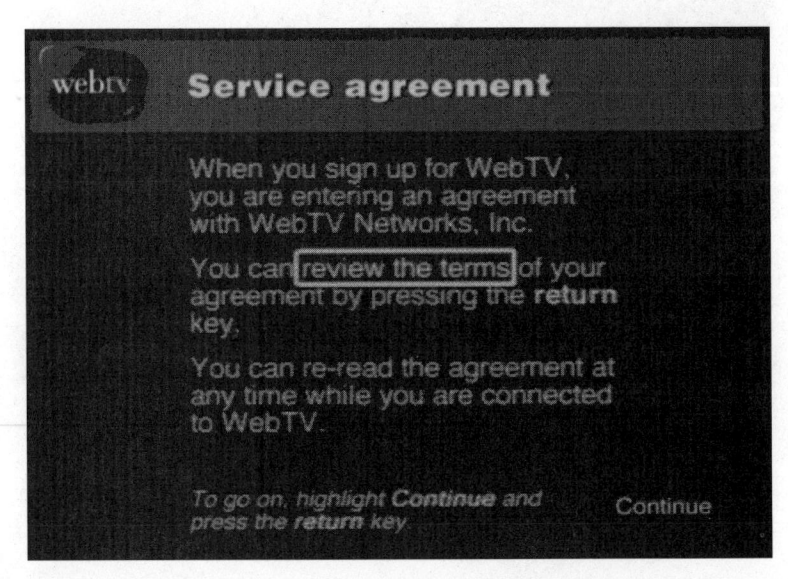

Figure 5-7.   *If you want to save your reading of the nearly sixty pages of legalese for later, select Continue to proceed with registering your WebTV Internet terminal.*

5: Subscribing to the WebTV Network

Your desired method of payment comes next. On the Credit Card Type screen illustrated in Figure 5-8, you'll see pictures of each type of credit card accepted by WebTV Networks. If you'd rather pay by check or if you have some special promotional code to enter, select Payment Options. (See Figure 5-9.)

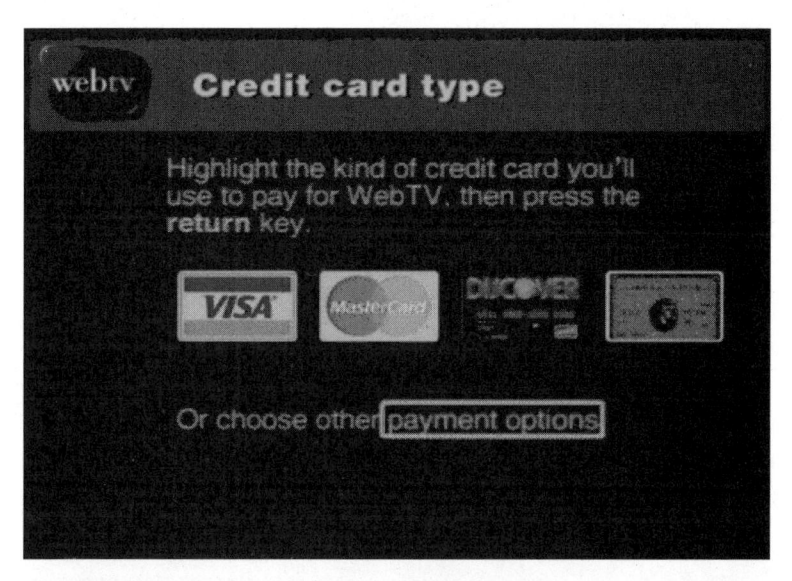

Figure 5-8.   *WebTV Networks offers a variety of payment options to meet your needs.*

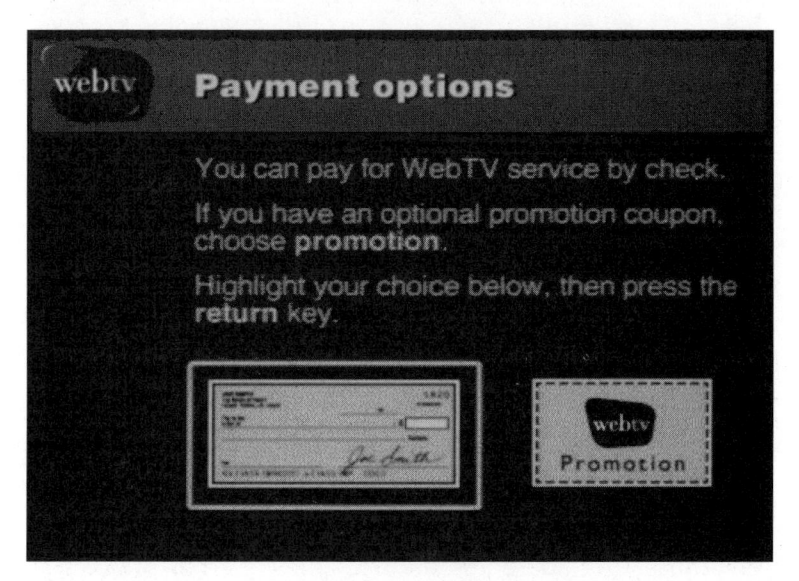

Figure 5-9.   *Use this screen to pay by check or to take advantage of special promotional offers.*

49

Getting Started

Select the desired method of payment, and then enter the necessary information. Never fear, this is a secure transaction, so all the information you've provided is safe.

For those paying by check, WebTV Networks will tell you exactly how much you'll be billed, as shown in Figure 5-10.

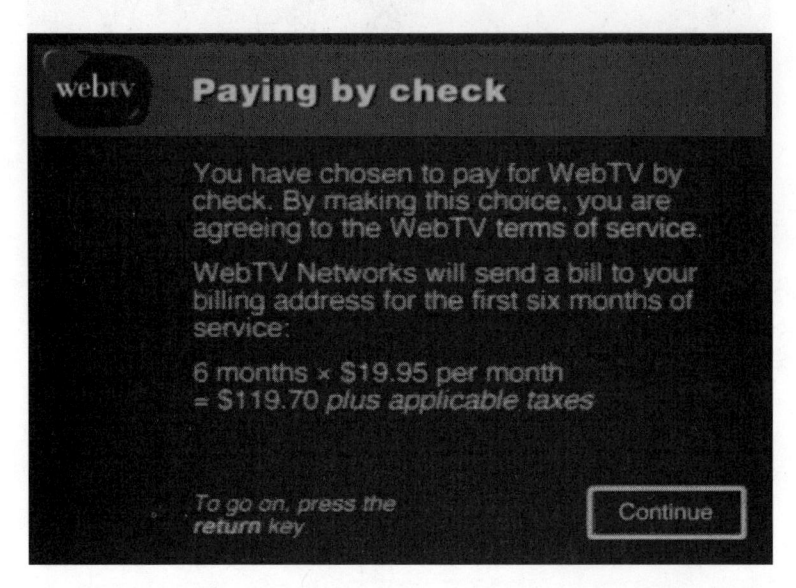

Figure 5-10. *And of course the appropriate sales tax will be added to your bill.*

Now comes the fun part—choosing your Internet and e-mail name. Whatever you select as your Internet name will be added as a prefix to *@webtv.net* to form your e-mail address. The Internet And E-mail Name screen shown in Figure 5-11 gives you a space for entering your desired Internet name. Keep in mind that this name can have any combination of letters and numbers, although no punctuation or spaces are allowed. Your name cannot exceed 15 characters, the length of the box on the screen. Be creative! Let this name reflect your true personality or a special interest. It isn't often that you get to name yourself.

Once you've chosen your Internet name, select Continue, and then press Go. If the name is already in use, the WebTV Network will ask you to try again. If the name is available, you'll see a Review screen that recaps all of the information you entered during the registration process. If you need to change any of the items, select the desired item, and then press Go.

5: Subscribing to the WebTV Network

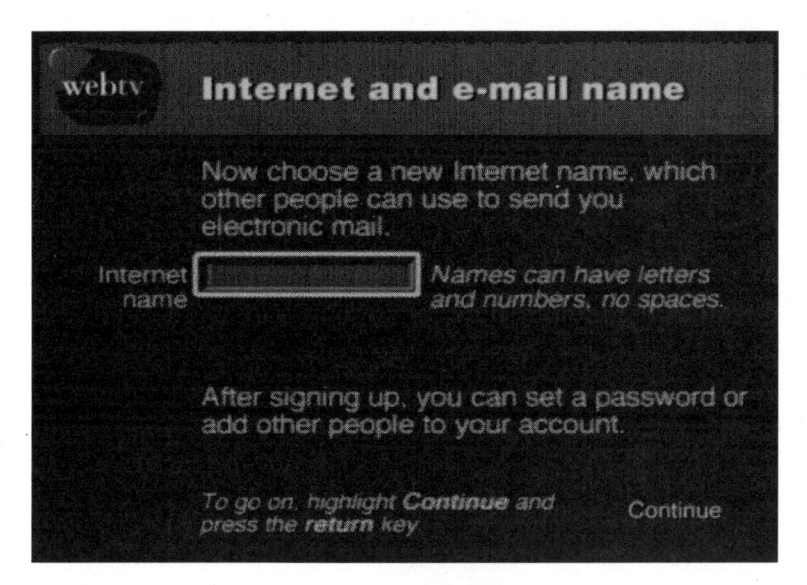

> **webtv** | **Internet and e-mail name**
>
> Now choose a new Internet name, which other people can use to send you electronic mail.
>
> Internet name [_____] Names can have letters and numbers, no spaces.
>
> After signing up, you can set a password or add other people to your account.
>
> To go on, highlight **Continue** and press the **return** key.   Continue

Figure 5-11.   *Any combination of numbers and letters can form your Internet name as long as it contains no spaces or punctuation. It must also fit into the box provided.*

Finally, you'll get the welcome news that you're finished registering. (See Figure 5-12 on the following page.) WebTV Networks invites you to begin your surfing safari from the WebTV Network home page, which will appear each time you power up your Internet terminal.

> **NOTE**   WebTV Networks sometimes refers to the first page you see as your home page, which I find a bit confusing. In my mind, your home page would be something you've created and would be at least somewhat personalized. While the launch page does say "Home to (fill in the blank)" on the title bar, I'd prefer to reserve "your home page" for a self-constructed Web page, and refer to this launch page as the WebTV Network home page. For WebTV Plus users, this launch page might be referred to as Web Home as opposed to TV Home. But just so you know, I'm sticking with "WebTV Network home page" so we don't have a million terms for one concept. If you had read the introduction to this book, you'd already know this. Gotcha! Hey, I skip my share of introduction chapters, too, so you're in good company.

Getting Started

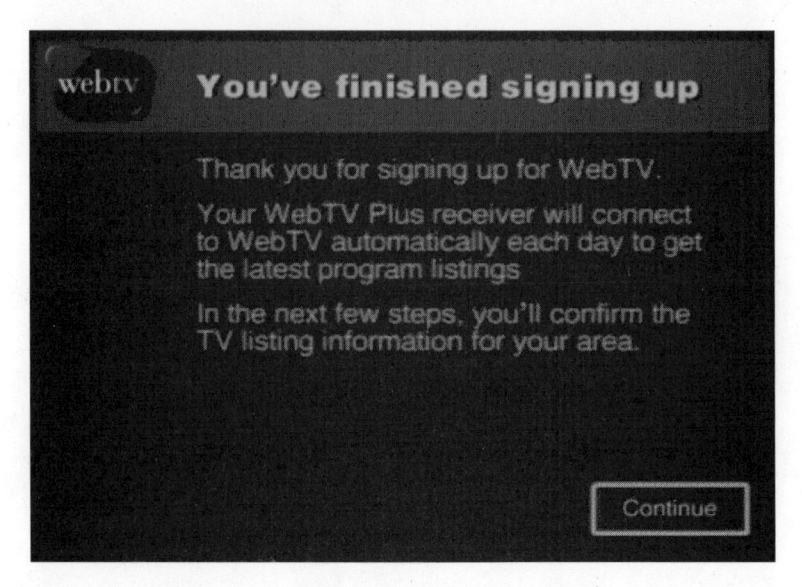

Figure 5-12. *Once all the virtual paperwork is completed, you're invited to begin surfing the Net and sending e-mail.*

Because the WebTV Network is in a constant state of evolution, there's a high likelihood that you'll see the Update Available screen shown in Figure 5-13.

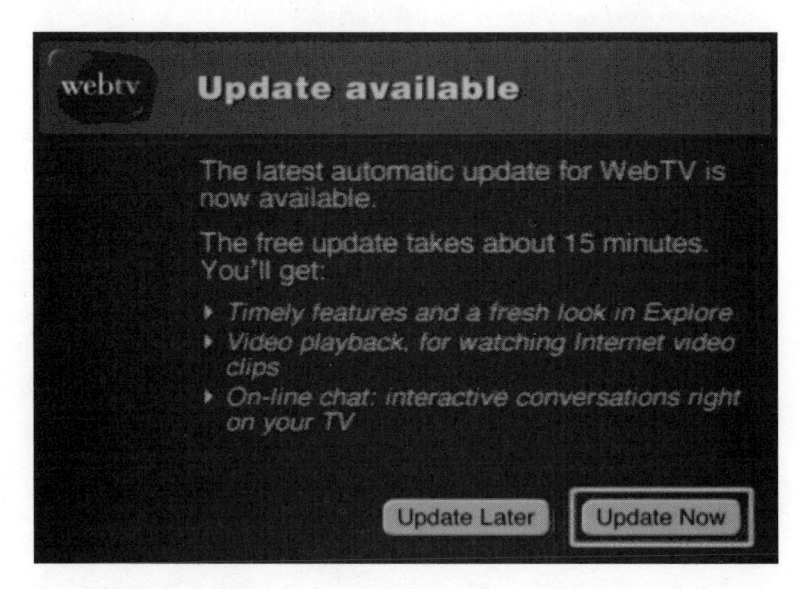

Figure 5-13. *This screen gives you the opportunity to download the latest and greatest WebTV Network updates instantly.*

5: Subscribing to the WebTV Network

The Update Available screen presents the highlights of the latest update, tells you approximately how long the update will take to load, and gives you the option to do it now or later. If you choose not to update on the spot (who wants to wait fifteen minutes to do a quick check for an e-mail message?), the screen will reappear the next time you connect. But don't wait too long to load your update—they're designed to make your Internet experience more pleasant, so get them while they're hot. The onscreen status bar (see Figure 5-14) lets you know once the latest update is complete, so there's never any second-guessing about whether it's done. Just turn off your Internet terminal and start it again to enjoy the best that WebTV Networks has to offer.

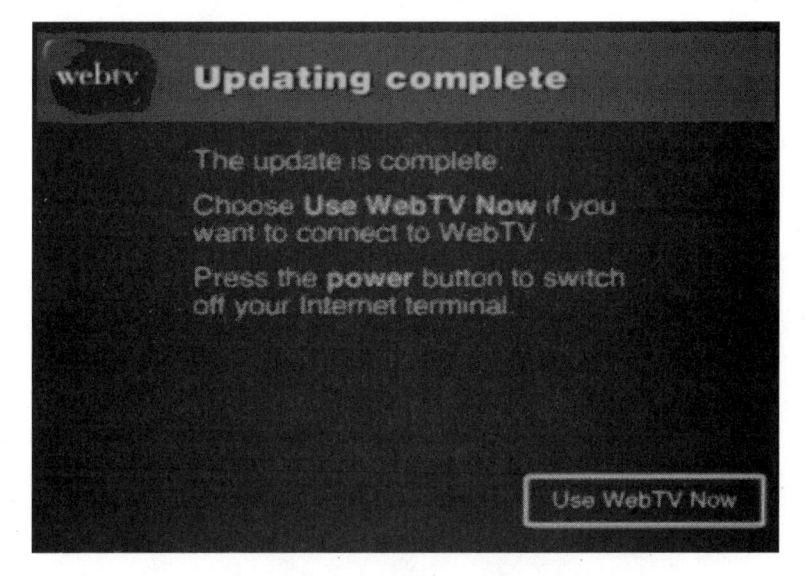

Figure 5-14. *When the update is finished installing on your system, you'll need to turn your Internet terminal off and on to begin surfing with all the newest goodies.*

53

Chapter 6

Get with the Program

When you signed up for your WebTV Network account, you fiddled with the remote control a bit. Now it's time to take a closer look at that remote control and at the keyboards you can use with your WebTV Internet terminal. You'll learn many of the shortcuts available for each device. By the time you finish reading this chapter, you'll be a WebTV Internet terminal navigation expert.

Thumb-Surfing Basics

With three different companies (Sony, Philips Magnavox, and Mitsubishi) manufacturing the WebTV Internet terminals, you're bound to see slight differences in the remote controls supplied with them (see Figure 6-1 on the following page). These companies have produced televisions for years, and they've undoubtedly thrown gobs of money into designing user-friendly remote controls. It only makes sense that they would try to incorporate this design wisdom into their version of the WebTV Internet terminal remote control.

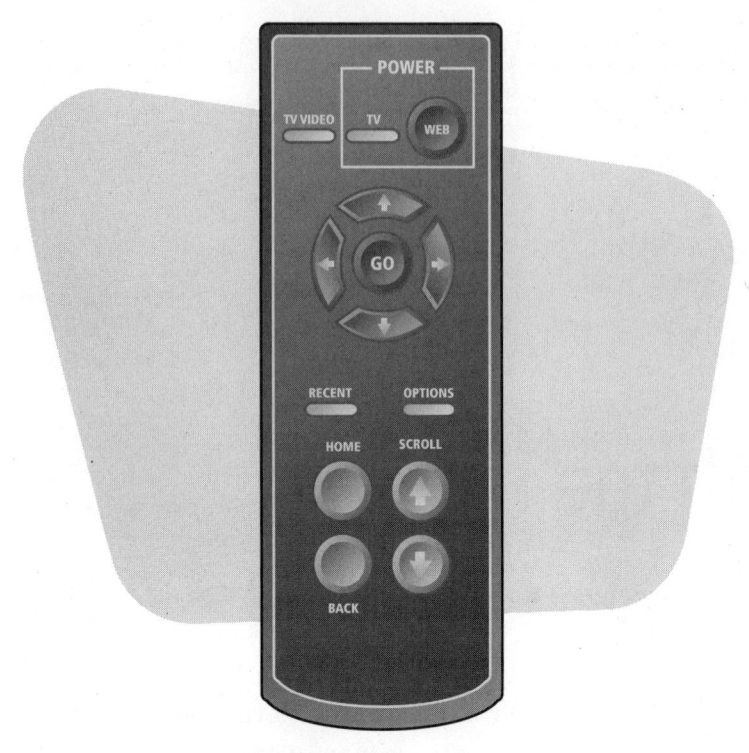

Figure 6-1. *This remote control designed by Philips Magnavox is just one of the three produced for the WebTV Internet terminal.*

Some buttons will be the same no matter who designed the remote. See Table 6-1 for a list of the most typical buttons along with a description of their functions.

One of the variations between the remotes is different button placement. Sony has omitted some buttons and has added a number pad that allows you to access Web sites shown in their companion Web-surfing site directory by entering a three-digit number. Some WebTV Network users argue that the number pad makes the remote control too cluttered, while others like the simplicity of using short numbers to visit Web sites.

> **TECHNOBABBLE Thumbnail**—A small picture. Your WebTV Internet terminal can display a tiny image of the Web page so that you can select the page to visit by name or by picture. (You'll see this term in Table 6-1.)

6: Get with the Program

Table 6-1. **Remote Control Buttons and Their Functions**

Button	Function
Arrow	Helps you jump from one link to another by moving the highlighted box frame. The up and down arrows move you up and down the page one line at a time.
Back	Takes you to the previous page.
Code Set	Sony's WebTV Internet terminal remote controls come with a Code Set button, which is used to program your remote to work with your TV. Simply press this button and enter the applicable code as found in your TV owner's manual.
Favorites	Accesses your Favorites folders, from which you can revisit some of your favorite Web sites.
Go	Executes a command. This button is commonly placed inside the circle of arrow buttons. It also opens and closes the onscreen keyboard when you are working with forms.
Home	Returns you to the main WebTV Network page.
Options	Brings up the Options panel from which you can enter a Web URL, reload a Web page, search for a word on the current page, add a page to your Favorites folder, and perform a number of other functions. The WebTV Network folks wisely left some buttons blank for future expansion.
Recent	Brings up thumbnails and titles of all the pages you recently viewed so that you can instantly hop from one to another.
Scroll	Moves the current Web page up and down.
Search	Use the Excite search engine to search the Web for the word or phrase of your choice. See Chapter 21, "Become a Virtual Bloodhound," for other search options.
TV/Web	Toggles back and forth between watching TV and surfing the Web if you've used an RFU adapter to connect your WebTV Internet terminal to your TV.
View	Press this button once (available for WebTV Plus only) to see a small TV picture in the bottom right corner of your screen. Press it twice to toggle between the WebTV Network's home page and TV Home.
Volume	Once you've programmed your remote to control your TV, you can adjust the sound using the remote control that comes with your WebTV Internet terminal. (Not all remotes may have this function. The availability may vary by manufacturer.)

One-Finger Typing

Now, I'll be the first to admit that my typing speed stinks, but even I can type with more than one finger. With the WebTV Internet terminal, however, you don't have to be a speedy typist. In fact, if you plan to rely on the remote control and onscreen keyboard, you're almost better off if you can't type at all. Typing with the remote might drive some fast typists batty because each letter must be painstakingly selected using the arrow buttons. For those of you who are hunters and peckers, however, you'll feel right at home with the speed at which you can enter text with the remote control. It's actually not as tedious as I'd anticipated.

When you select a text box that needs to be filled out, press Go to call up the onscreen keyboard (see Figure 6-2).

Use the arrows to select the letter you want, and then press Go. Repeat this process for each letter, space, or punctuation mark you want to place in the active text box. (This process sounds a lot slower than it really is. You

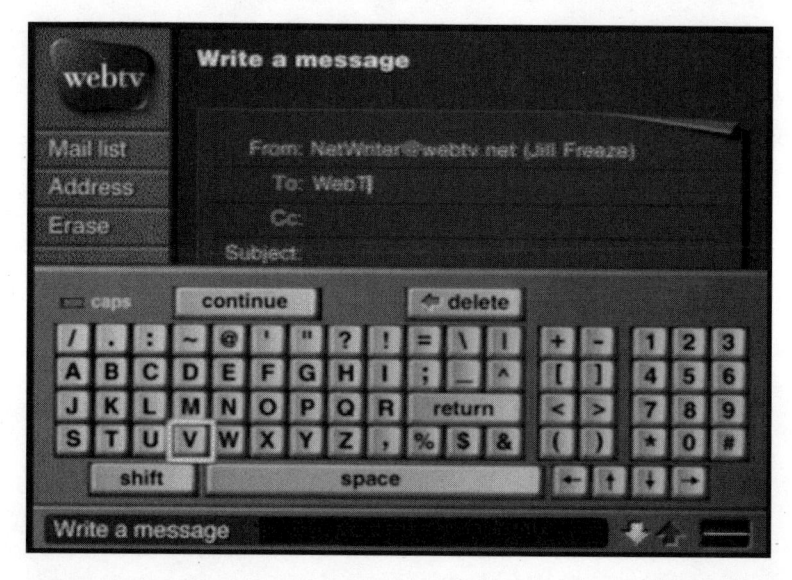

Figure 6-2. When you've selected a text box, pressing Go brings the onscreen keyboard onto the screen.

eventually get into the rhythm.) If you need to capitalize a letter, select the Shift button, and then press Go. A little red light will glow on the onscreen keyboard to let you know you're in shift mode. Deleting letters is as simple as selecting Delete, and then pressing Go until the letters you want to delete are gone. To exit the onscreen keyboard either to move to the next text box or to continue surfing, select Continue, and then press Go. For even quicker response, press the Back button.

Get Attached

If you've had enough of typing with the remote control but don't want to pay for a wireless keyboard, you might want to connect an AT-style computer keyboard to your WebTV Internet terminal. You can find these for less than half the price of the wireless keyboards, and they're a practical solution for limited budgets and smaller rooms where you might sit in closer proximity to your TV.

> **TIP** Many keyboards use the smaller PS/2-style connector instead of the older but larger AT-style connector. If you try to connect a PS/2-style keyboard to your WebTV Classic Internet terminal, you'll need an adapter, which you should be able to find at any computer store.

> **NOTE** You cannot attach a computer keyboard to a WebTV Plus Internet terminal; only the remote control or optional wireless keyboard can be used. I've mentioned this before, but felt it was important to include in this chapter as well in case you're skipping around the book.

Because these computer keyboards were built for computers and not for WebTV Internet terminals, the shortcut keys aren't as obvious as those you'll see on wireless keyboards in the next section. Table 6-2 lists the shortcut keys you'll find on attached computer keyboards.

Getting Started

Table 6-2. **Shortcut Keys for Using a Computer Keyboard with the WebTV Internet Terminal**

Key	Function
F1	Turns the WebTV Internet terminal on and off.
F2	Moves you to your Favorites folders.
F3	Searches the Web using Excite.
F4	Brings up your main e-mail screen.
F5	Searches for any word or phrase on the current Web page.
F6	Displays information about the current Web page, such as its URL, date last modified, and so on.
F7	Allows you to enter a URL manually.
F8	Adds the current Web page to your Favorites folder.
F9	Sends the URL of the current Web page you're browsing or the letter you're writing to the desired recipient.
F10	Brings up the thumbnails of recently viewed pages so that you can jump to them instantly.
F11	Slides the Options panel into view.
Insert	Toggles the current insert mode.
Home	Returns you to the WebTV Network home page.
Page Up	Moves the current Web page up.
Page Down	Moves the current Web page down.
End	Returns you to the previous page.

TECHNOBABBLE Insert mode—This is a behavior of your WebTV Internet terminal when you type text in a text box. When insert mode is on, any text you type is inserted in the text box where the cursor is currently blinking. When insert mode is off, the new text overwrites the old text.

Look, Ma, No Cords

If only the best will do, the wireless keyboard is the way to go. You can type normally without being tied down by a cable, you have the benefit of special shortcut keys, and you can even assign shortcut keys to seven of your favorite Web sites.

When you first look at the wireless keyboard, you'll notice some special keys that are not available on any other keyboard (see Figure 6-3).

Figure 6-3. *The wireless keyboard sports a number of special keys designed to simplify your surfing.*

Like a computer keyboard, the wireless keyboard has a series of function keys across the top. These are the keys you will use to access the Web site shortcuts you will define in Chapter 10, "Everything You Always Wanted to Know About the Web." To the left of the function keys is a Power key, which you can use to turn on your WebTV Internet terminal. To the right of the function keys are special keys designed exclusively for using your WebTV Internet terminal. You'll recognize them instantly because their names appear in a different color than the rest of the keys. These special keys include those presented in Table 6-3 on the following page.

Getting Started

Table 6-3. **Wireless Keyboard Keys Unique to the WebTV Internet Terminal**

Key	Function
Arrow	Changes what is selected on the current page.
Back	Returns you to the previous screen.
Edit	Lets you edit the contents of a highlighted text box.
Favs	Moves you to your Favorites folders.
Find	Lets you search for any word or phrase on the current Web page. (The Find key searches the entire Web page, not just the part in view on your screen.)
Go To	Allows you to enter a URL manually.
Home	Returns you to the WebTV Network home page.
Info	Displays information about the current Web page, such as its URL, date last modified, and so on.
Mail	Brings up your main mail screen.
Options	Slides the Options panel into view.
Recent	Brings up thumbnails and titles of the last few pages you viewed.
Save	Adds the current Web page to your Favorites folder.
Scroll Down	Moves the current Web page down.
Scroll Up	Moves the current Web page up.
Search	Allows you to search the Web using Excite.
Send	Sends the URL of a Web page or the e-mail message you're writing to the desired recipient.

With the introduction of WebTV Plus and its host of new features came the need for a new wireless keyboard. This keyboard is equipped with several new buttons across the top to make your TV viewing more pleasurable. See Table 6-4 for a listing of these special WebTV Plus buttons and their functions.

Table 6-4. Wireless Keyboard Buttons Unique to WebTV Plus Keyboards

Key	Function
Channel –/+	Changes the channels up or down.
Code Set	Programs the keyboard for universal TV control.
Mute	Turns the TV volume on and off.
Power (TV)	Turns the TV unit on and off.
Power (WebTV)	Turns the WebTV Internet terminal on and off.
TV/Video	Switches between video inputs to your TV.
TV/WebTV	When set to TV, the channel buttons on the keyboard will change TV channels. If WebTV is selected, the channel buttons will change the channel in the small TV window.
View	Moves between Internet and TV viewing. Can also be used to open a small TV viewing window in the bottom right corner of the screen.
Volume –/+	Adjusts the volume down and up.

> **TIP** If your wireless keyboard isn't working like it used to, try replacing the batteries. A keyboard with low battery juice can be extra finicky, so if you use yours a lot you'll want to stock up on batteries.

Command Performance

In addition to the obvious shortcut keys described in the previous table, there are several less commonly known shortcuts that you can take with your wireless keyboard. These involve pressing and holding down the Command key (two keys to the left of the space bar), and then pressing a second key. Some of the more interesting shortcuts are presented in Table 6-5 on the following page.

Table 6-5. **Shortcuts Using the Command Key**

Press this...	To do this...
cmd+left arrow	Moves the cursor to the beginning of the line of text you're editing.
cmd+right arrow	Moves the cursor to the end of the line of text you're editing.
cmd+delete	Deletes an entire line of text.
cmd+F	Finds some text on the current page you're viewing.
cmd+G	Looks for the next occurrence of the text you searched for.
cmd+R	Reloads the current page so that you can get the latest information available.
cmd+P	Prints the page displayed on your screen (if you are equipped to do so).

Chapter 7

It's a Setup

OK, maybe the goodies tucked into this chapter aren't as exciting as the title implies, but they're pretty cool just the same. You'll learn how to customize your Web surfing environment, and you'll be introduced to some additional setup options available through the primary subscriber's account.

Customize Your Web Surfing Environment

There are several things you can do to customize your WebTV Network environment for greater surfing enjoyment.

Open Sesame: Create or Change a Password

Say you've been e-mailing a fellow collector to locate something special for your wife's collection as a surprise, but you don't want her reading the e-mail and finding out about it. Consider creating separate accounts for the two of you, and consider creating a password for your account to keep her from sneaking a peek at your e-mail.

To create a password, follow these steps:

1. From the WebTV Network home page, select Using WebTV, and then press Go.

2. A list of Additional options appears. Select WebTV Users under the "Your WebTV Account" section, and then press Go.

Getting Started

3. Select your name on the screen containing the user names for your account, and then press Go.

4. If you do not have a password, select No Password, and then press Go.

5. You will be asked to type your chosen password into the first text box. (See Figure 7-1.)

6. To verify that the password you entered was the one that you intended, you'll be asked to type the password again into a second text box.

7. Select Continue, and then press Go to complete the setup.

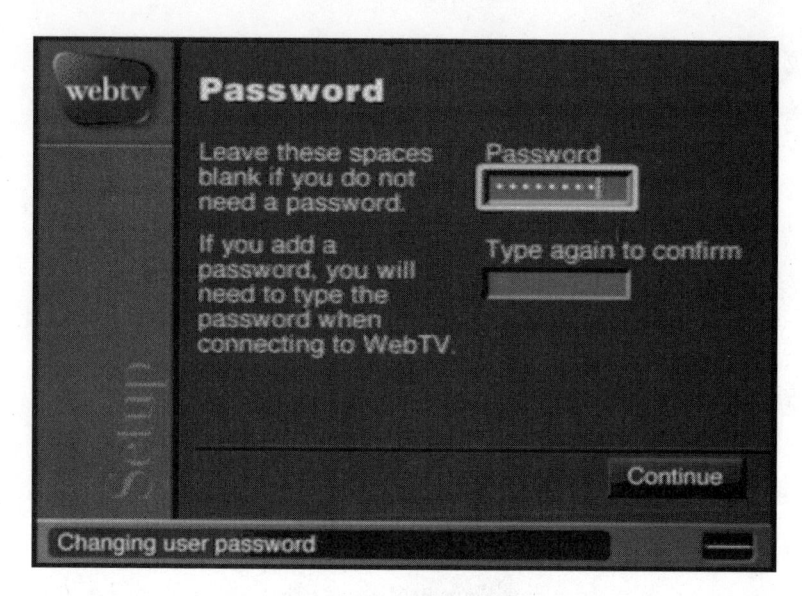

Figure 7-1. *You can set up your password by using this screen.*

Now each time you attempt to access your account, you'll be prompted for your password.

To change your password, follow the steps above, but select Password rather than No Password in Step 4. Simply leave the boxes blank to remove the password.

Put Things in Order

If you'll be using the onscreen keyboard for any length of time, you might want to specify the order of the keys. You can display the keys either alphabetically or in traditional QWERTY order.

7: It's a Setup

> **TECHNOBABBLE QWERTY**—This is the common order of keys on typewriters and computer keyboards, as well as the default setting on the optional wireless keyboard for your Internet terminal.

To set this option, follow these simple steps, pressing Go after each one:

1. From the WebTV Network home page, select Using WebTV.
2. Select Customize WebTV from the list of Settings options.
3. Select Keyboard from the list of options.
4. On the Keyboard Setup screen (see Figure 7-2), select the keyboard layout you want.
5. Select Done, and then press Go to save your selection.

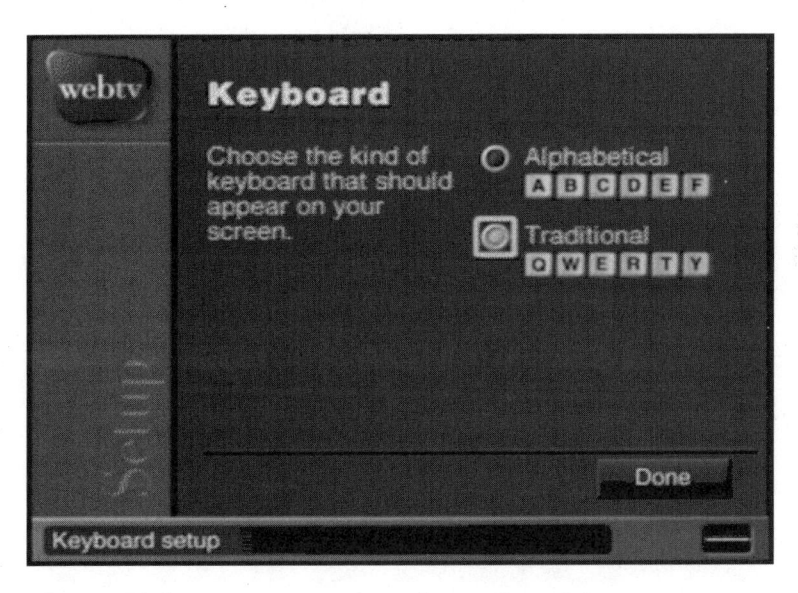

Figure 7-2. *Choose the layout you want from this Keyboard Setup screen.*

The next time you use the onscreen keyboard, the keys should appear in the order you specified on the Keyboard Setup screen.

Small, Medium, or Large—It's Up to You

If your eyesight is less than perfect (like mine), or if your easy chair is simply too far away from the screen, you'll find it comforting to know that the size of screen text can be increased or decreased.

67

> **NOTE** Keep in mind that this setting does not affect text presented as graphics or WebTV Network pages, such as the home page or the online documentation.

Follow these steps (pressing Go after each one) to select the screen text size that best meets your needs:

1. Select Using WebTV on the WebTV Network home page.
2. Select Customize WebTV from under the Settings heading.
3. Select Text Size from the list of Settings options.
4. Confirm that the gray drop-down list box is highlighted.
5. Select one of the three options (see Figure 7-3).
6. Select Done to continue surfing with the new size of text.

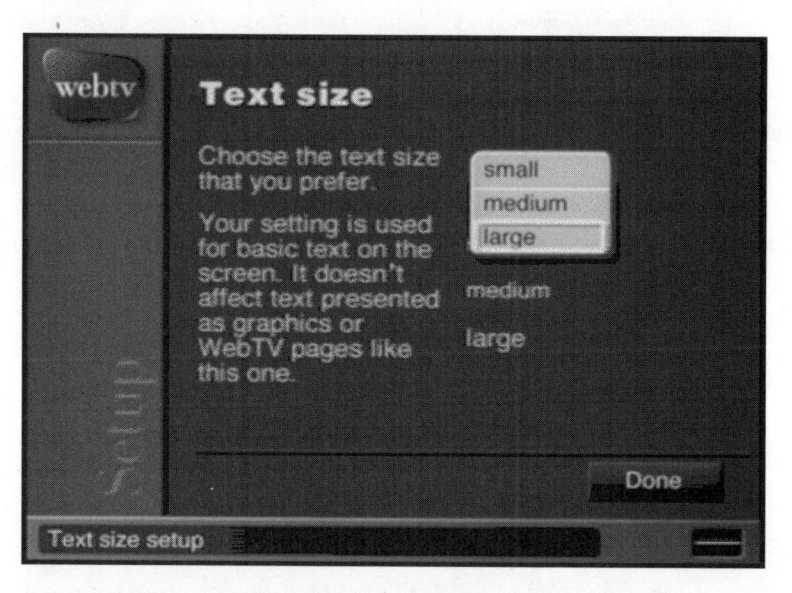

Figure 7-3. *Select the text size that is best for you from this screen.*

> **NOTE** By default, Small is the selected size, so there's no need to bother fiddling with this setup unless you need bigger text.

Want to see how much of a difference these settings make? Take a look at Figure 7-4 (small text), Figure 7-5 (medium text), and Figure 7-6 (large text) on page 70.

7: It's a Setup

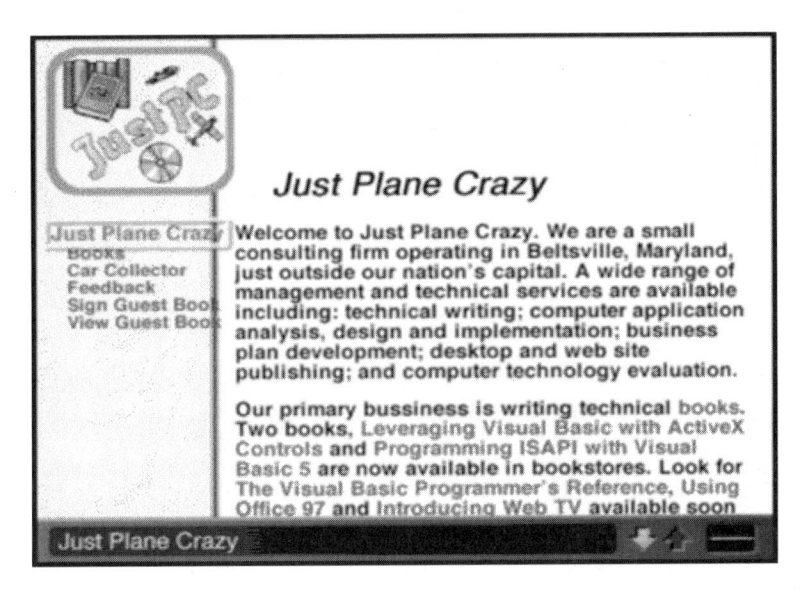

Figure 7-4. *The default text size setting, Small, maximizes the amount of text seen on each screen.*

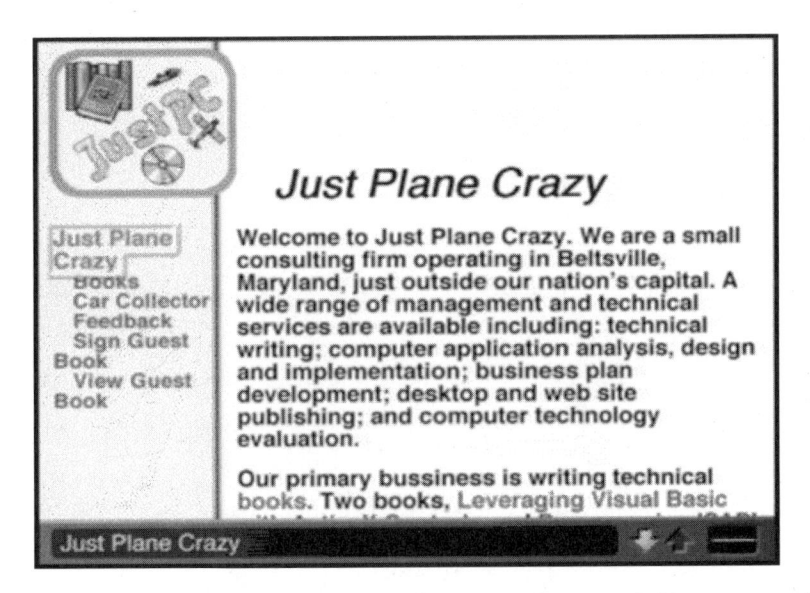

Figure 7-5. *Notice how the Medium text size increases the size of the text just a hair.*

69

Figure 7-6. *This is as big as it gets.*

Sing While You Surf

Well, you won't be singing these songs exactly, but you might find them to be a nice addition to your surfing experience. Or they might start to grate on your nerves after a while—you be the judge.

Start by selecting Setup on the WebTV Network home page, and then pressing Go. Select Customize WebTV from the list of Settings option. Select Music from the list of Settings options, and then press Go. You can toggle the background music on and off by selecting the Background Music box and then pressing Go. A glowing red light means you'll hear music as you surf.

Now for the fun part—you can actually choose the type of music you want to hear. Select Choose Music Styles, and then press Go. The Background Songs screen shown in Figure 7-7 appears.

Choosing your favorite musical style is as easy as placing a checkmark into the box next to the kind of music you want to hear. Do this by selecting the box and then pressing Go. The same technique can be used to remove a checkmark as well. To save your selections, select Done, and then press Go.

Figure 7-7.   *You can choose from any number of musical styles.*

Master Controls

In addition to the setup options presented in the previous sections, there are a few settings you can tweak only if you are the primary subscriber. Some of these include changing billing information, adding users to the account, or instructing your Internet terminal to automatically connect each day to check for e-mail (which will be discussed in detail in Chapter 14, "Push Your WebTV Internet Terminal to the Limit").

The More, the Merrier

Adding a user is probably the setting you'll tweak most frequently. The reasons why you'd want to add a user are endless, and with the WebTV Network, you can make certain that young Web surfers in particular have a safe environment in which to experience the Internet.

Follow these steps to add a user to your account (press Go after each selection):

1. From the WebTV Network home page, select Using WebTV.
2. Select Additional Users.
3. Select Add User.

Getting Started

4. Enter the user's first and last name into the appropriate text boxes, and then select Continue.

5. Type in an Internet name for the new user. If the selected name is already taken, keep trying until you find one you can use. Once your choice has been approved, select Continue.

6. You will be asked if you want to create a password. Leave the boxes blank if one is not needed, or refer to the section titled "Open Sesame" for more details on creating a password. Select Continue.

7. Setting user restrictions is the next step involved in adding a user (see Figure 7-8). You can choose from three levels of access—Unrestricted, where anything goes; SurfWatch, which filters out access to mature material; and Kid-Friendly, which provides a safe surfing environment and a special kids' home page. When you've selected the desired level of restriction, select Continue.

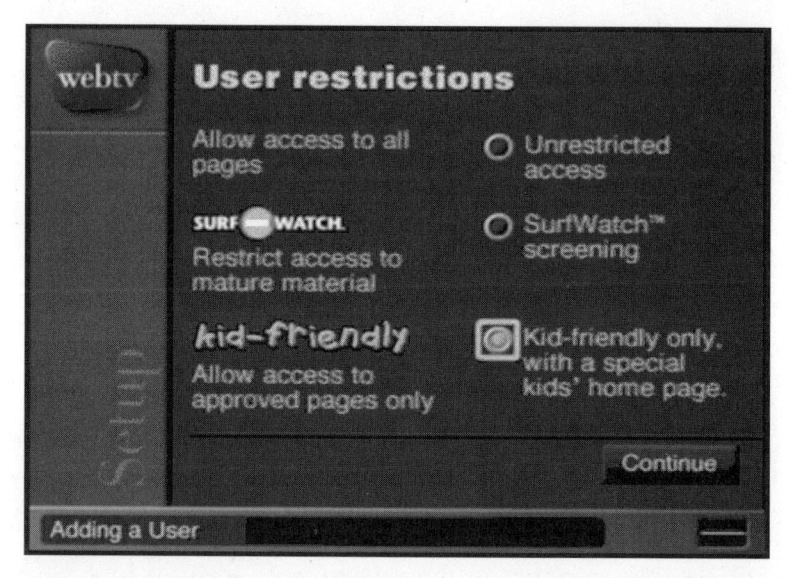

Figure 7-8. *Use this screen to choose from three levels of access restrictions.*

> **NOTE** With new Web sites popping up every day, it's still a good idea to monitor your youngster's Web surfing to make certain he or she isn't accessing inappropriate material. Even setting user restrictions won't filter out everything.

8. The next screen you'll see allows you to block incoming and outgoing e-mail for the account. Select Block E-Mail and press Go to block e-mail, or simply select Continue, and then press Go.

9. You'll see a screen summarizing the account you have just created. When you've verified that the information is correct, select Done, and then press Go.

10. You'll see a list of all the WebTV Network users you have defined. Select Done, and then press Go to continue surfing.

Each user can customize their Web surfing environment as described earlier in this chapter. If a user has been restricted to Kid-Friendly sites, the special home page shown in Figure 7-9 will appear.

Figure 7-9. *If you choose the Kid-Friendly restriction for your junior surfer, this colorful home page designed especially for kids will appear.*

Bills, Bills, Bills

You know what a pain it is to change billing information on a magazine subscription or credit card account, right? You might spend what seems like hours on hold while your ears are assaulted by Muzak versions of your most despised songs. Well, never fear—the WebTV Network has made changing your billing information a breeze.

Getting Started

Start by selecting Using WebTV from the WebTV Network home page (remember, you must use the primary subscriber's account), and then pressing Go. Select Billing from the list of options in the "Your WebTV Account" section, and then press Go again. You'll see a screen displaying all of your account information, including your method of payment (but not the actual credit card number). Select any of the sections you want to change, and then press Go. Each chunk of information will be presented in easy-to-edit text boxes. Simply change it as needed, select Continue, and then press Go. Once all the fields have been updated, select Done, and then press Go. It's as easy as that, and you don't even have to listen to any elevator music.

Call the Shots

Not all phone lines are created equal, which is why WebTV Networks gives you flexibility when it comes to configuring your dial-up options. To enter the Dialing Setup area, select Using WebTV on the WebTV Network home page, press Go, select Dialing from the list of options, and then press Go again.

You'll see a Dialing options menu with the following choices:

- **Basic.** By selecting Basic and then pressing Go, you can define a dialing prefix. For example, many hotels and large corporations require you to press 9 before dialing out of the building. If your WebTV Internet terminal happens to be set up in such a building, simply enter the number 9 in the designated box. If your phone line requires pulse dialing, you can select that option by placing a checkmark in the necessary box. Note that the WebTV Network defaults for these options are touch-tone dialing and no special prefix.

- **Call-Waiting.** If you have call-waiting on your phone line, use this screen to set one of three options: My Phone Line Does Not Have Call-Waiting (WebTV Networks assumes no call-waiting); Accept Calls By Disconnecting From The WebTV Network; and Block Calls Using The Following Prefix (you enter the prefix used in your area to shut off call-waiting). If you choose one of the call-waiting options, you can even adjust the sensitivity of incoming calls' detection. For example, you might want to increase the Internet terminal's sensitivity to call waiting if call waiting doesn't always kick in as it should. Likewise, noisy phone lines that result in repeated interruptions to your connection might warrant reducing the Internet terminal's sensitivity to call waiting. Select Adjust Sensitivity, press Go, and choose your options according to the guidelines presented.

- **Access.** If you should ever have trouble with your WebTV Internet terminal, the WebTV Customer Care staff may ask you to dial in using a special phone number. Use this screen to enter it as directed.

- **Advanced.** This option is the catch-all category for the dialing options you can't find elsewhere. You can tell your WebTV Internet terminal to wait for a dial tone before it attempts to dial out (you might want to disable this if you have voice mail). You can also set the audible dialing option, which might come in handy for troubleshooting problems with your Internet terminal. Setting this option enables you to hear the Internet terminal connect to the Internet—extremely useful for verifying that your unit has access to a usable phone line. And finally, you can set the speed at which your Internet terminal dials out— choose from Slow, Medium, or Fast.

- **Reset.** If you've been fiddling with all the dialing options and aren't sure what you did or didn't change, use the Reset screen to return all the Dialing options to their default settings. Since the WebTV Internet terminal is configured to work with the most common settings, this should get you going again in most cases.

Picture Perfect

While I'd like to say that the pages you see using your WebTV Internet terminal will look perfect right out of the box, that might not always be the case. Television sets can vary radically when it comes to their displays and adjustment options, so you might find yourself playing with all kinds of knobs and buttons before you achieve the crisp display you desire.

To help you meet this goal, WebTV Networks gives you a couple of screen setup options to move you in the right direction. Start by selecting Using WebTV from the WebTV Network home page, and then pressing Go. Select Settings, and then select Screen from the Settings list of options. (WebTV Plus users will find this option by selecting Settings from the TV Home page.)

Getting Started

To center the image on your television screen, select Center, and then press Go. Select the arrow pointing in the direction you want to move the image, and then press Go until the image is in the center of the screen.

Select Picture from the Screen page to begin working your way through a series of steps designed to produce the best image output possible from your television set.

While following all these steps might seem like a time-consuming endeavor, your work will pay off in the form of crisper, cleaner images.

Anatomy of Your Home Base

Wouldn't traveling be more exciting if you could wander the streets of a foreign country without the fear of getting lost? WebTV Networks gives you the security of always knowing you can find your way home, no matter how far away you go. Your friendly WebTV Network home page (see Figure 7-10) is a mere push of the Home key away.

Figure 7-10. *The WebTV Network home page helps you get your bearings in an instant.*

This home page has a few elements you'll want to be familiar with. The four icons across the top of the screen (Mail, Favorites, Explore, and Search) help you jump to four of the main WebTV Internet terminal functions. (In my opinion, there should be a fifth icon for Discussion groups, rather than having it buried under Explore.)

> **TECHNOBABBLE ICON**—This is a picture that represents a certain object (or in this case, function). For example, WebTV Network's use of binoculars for the Search function seems perfectly logical.

You'll see some important buttons down the left side of the screen. The first, Using WebTV, is one you've probably worn out by this point. I don't think there's a need to explain any more about what this button does, because if you don't know by now you've been asleep for the entire chapter and explaining it again would serve no purpose!

> **NOTE** WebTV Plus owners will also have a TV Home button on the left side of the screen.

In addition to leading you to all the setup options, Using WebTV leads you to the Club WebTV News (the online monthly newsletter), provides instructions on how to use your WebTV Internet terminal, and provides a link to a WebTV-specific discussion group.

Another button, Switch User, is used to switch from one WebTV Network account to another. Just select Switch User, press Go, select the account you want to access, and then press Go again. Soon you will see the WebTV Network home page for that account. You'll see this button only if you have more than one user associated with your account.

The Community button takes you to the Around Town section, which presents local weather, movie listings, classified ads, and so on, based on the ZIP code you provided during the sign-up process. The Community button is also the quickest way to begin chatting or browsing discussion groups.

Finally, at the bottom of the screen is a black title bar that holds the name of the current page you are viewing. To the right of this title bar is a heart monitor look-alike. When a page is loading, the monitor comes to life. (Does anyone else feel like they've stepped into an episode of *ER* yet?) A flat green line means that the entire page has been loaded and your link to the Internet is still active. A flat red line means your connection is, uh, dead. Either your connection timed out or the terminal's operation was suspended to accept or place a phone call. You'll need to reconnect before you can do anything else.

> **TECHNOBABBLE TIMED OUT**—If ten minutes pass and you haven't done anything on your WebTV Internet terminal, the unit will disconnect from the WebTV Network. Your terminal will remember where you were, however, so you can easily resume your online travels when you reconnect.

If a page is too big for the screen, up and down arrows will appear between the title bar and the connection monitor to let you know there's more to see. The arrows will be green if that area has been loaded and is ready for viewing, or the down arrow will be yellow if there's more data to load. Use your Scroll Up or Scroll Down buttons to view material in these areas.

PART 2

WebTV Basics

Chapter

8   E-Mail 101   81

9   Reading, Writing, and E-Mail Management   91

10   Everything You Always Wanted to Know About the Web   101

11   A Nose for News (or Gossip?)   117

12   Virtual Chatrooms and Cybercommunities   125

13   Traffic Jams and Other Roadblocks   139

14   Push Your WebTV Internet Terminal to the Limit   149

Chapter 8

E-Mail 101

Once you start sending e-mail to a friend or to a family member, you're not going to want to stop. The convenience, simplicity, and affordability of it all will spoil you forever.

Throughout this book, you'll learn how your WebTV Internet terminal works to bring you all of the goodies you've heard so much about. But how does e-mail work specifically? Here's an oversimplification since the grungy details don't really concern us anyway.

E-mail isn't much different than snail mail (mail delivered by the U.S. Postal Service). You supply an address, and then rely on someone else to get the message to its destination. When you send e-mail, the animated mailbox on your screen (shown in Figure 8-1 on the following page) lets you know that your WebTV Internet terminal and the worldwide network of computers are moving the message on its way. With snail mail, you rely on machines and dozens of people to do the work. Each method has its advantages, but at least with e-mail there are no yucky-tasting envelopes or stamps to lick.

As for which is quicker—no contest. Grab your WebTV Internet terminal remote control or keyboard and try this little experiment. Connect to the WebTV Network as usual, and then follow these steps:

1. Select Mail on the WebTV Network's home page, and then press Go.

2. Select Write, and then press Go.

3. On the "To" line, type *netwriter@justpc.com*. That e-mail address is set up to automatically respond to any message it receives.

4. Press the down arrow key until the blinking cursor reaches the Subject line.

> **TECHNOBABBLE Cursor**—Someone who sits around shouting obscenities all day. Just kidding! (That would probably be spelled "curser" anyway.) A cursor is the blinking box that appears on screen to let you know where any text you type will appear. You'll see it while working with e-mail, performing online searches, or using Web pages with forms.

5. Enter the subject of your choice, although something like "Introducing WebTV is the Best Book Ever Written" works extremely well.

6. Press the down arrow key until the cursor reaches the area where you enter your message, and then type in some text. You can also not enter anything for the sake of this experiment.

Figure 8-1. *You know that your letter is being sent when the mailbox appears onscreen and then closes. Once you've executed this step, there's no turning back; it's just like dropping a letter into a real mailbox.*

7. Select Send, and then press Go. A mailbox containing a letter appears onscreen and then closes to let you know that your message has been sent.

8. For the most accurate results, press the Power button, select Power Off, and then press Go, as you do when you normally disconnect from the network.

9. Connect to the WebTV Network as before. If all has gone as planned, you should have a new message waiting for you.

Think about that for a minute. In the time it took to send your message, disconnect from the WebTV Network, and then reconnect, your message reached a computer in the middle of Maryland, and that computer sent you a note back! I don't care if you're as close as Pennsylvania, that's still pretty darned impressive.

> **NOTE** "Hey, how come I didn't get anything?" If you connected to the WebTV Network during peak hours (10 a.m.–1 p.m. EDT when people all across the country are checking their mail, or 7 p.m.–10 p.m. EDT when families want to go for their nightly surf), chances are the Internet was just slow and bogged down with traffic. Or that computer in Maryland may have been down for maintenance. You might want to repeat the experiment at another time.

What Happens to My E-Mail When I'm Offline?

Unless you deliberately discard a message, it will stay on a WebTV Network server until you delete it or until you have too many messages. This system is much more forgiving than many PC e-mail programs because it's next to impossible to accidentally delete something. I'm not saying it can't happen, but you'd have to be pretty preoccupied not to notice that you're about to delete a message.

Even if you save a message, it will be stored on a WebTV Network hard drive. The downside to this is that if you're overly sentimental and want to keep every piece of e-mail you receive, you'll quickly meet your 150 message limit. You'll either need to be more discriminating about the mail you save or print paper copies of the messages. See Chapter 14, "Push Your WebTV Internet Terminal to the Limit," for more information on printing.

> **NOTE** While 150 messages might seem like a lot of e-mail, you might not be able to store even that many if a large percentage of the messages are oversized or contain attached files, which eat up a lot of space. WebTV Networks gives you two megabytes of storage on its servers, so once that space is filled, it's time to clean house!

Set the E-Mail Stage

Before you begin using e-mail frequently, you'll want to be sure you're getting the most out of all the available options.

From the WebTV Network home page, select Mail, and then press Go. Select Setup, and then press Go. You'll see the Mail Setup screen shown in Figure 8-2.

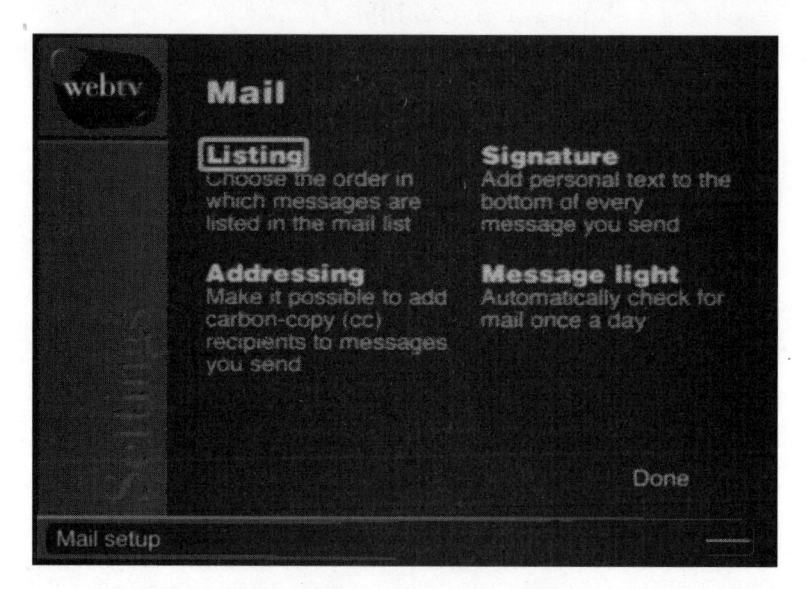

Figure 8-2. *The Mail Setup screen is the home base for setting all your e-mail options.*

Put Your E-Mail Ducks in a Row

From the Mail Setup screen, select Listing, and then press Go. The Listing option allows you to specify how you want to see the mail in your inbox—from newest to oldest, or from oldest to newest.

The Newest Mail First option enables you to scan an overflowing inbox more quickly for the newest arrivals, whereas the Oldest Mail First option gives you incentive to clear the clutter, because you have to keep scrolling down to see the newest entries. The choice is yours, although the most commonly used option is Newest Mail First. In fact, if you never touch this option at all, the WebTV Network will sort your mail from newest to oldest by default.

To set the Listing option, select the Newest Mail First or Oldest Mail First button as desired, and then press Go. Select Done, and then press Go. Your chosen Listing option will now be in effect.

Create Your Virtual Signature

You can tell a lot from a person's signature. From the stereotypically illegible scrawl of a doctor's signature to the crooked print of a preschooler's name, each signature says something unique about the person behind it. Just because e-mail is produced by typing doesn't mean individuality has to fall by the wayside, however. WebTV Networks gives you multiple ways to make your electronic signature an original work of art.

From the Mail Setup screen, select Signature, and then press Go. You'll see the Mail Signature Setup screen shown in Figure 8-3.

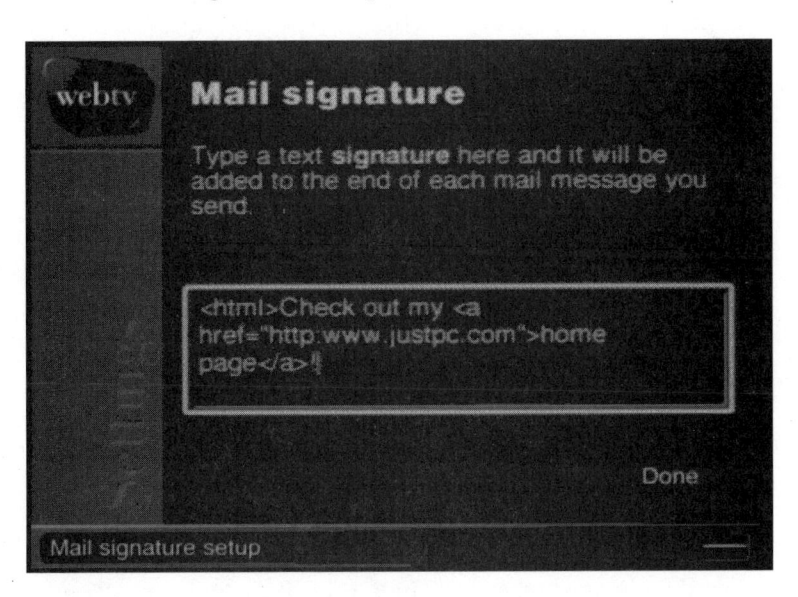

Figure 8-3. *The Mail Signature Setup screen gives you a large box in which to place your signature, an image, or even a link to a favorite Web page, as shown here.*

An electronic signature may not seem as unique as a handwritten one, but you can do a lot to make it stand out. Try adding a favorite quote, designing some ASCII art, or including a link to a favorite Web site. Once you've created your signature, it will automatically be appended to all your e-mail messages. Not all mail readers will be able to see your work of art the way you do, so don't be disappointed if your cousin doesn't notice that cool animated cat picture and "meow" sound file you attached to your signature.

> **TECHNOBABBLE   ASCII Art**—Pronounced "askee art," this involves making shapes or designs out of the letters and punctuation symbols on the keyboard. For example, you can design a rose by typing the following: @-->->--. You can even create larger images like the outline of your state or a picture of the starship *Enterprise*. The possibilities at your fingertips are endless.

To add the following elements to your signature, follow the steps in Table 8-1.

Table 8-1.   Adding Elements to Your Signature

To add this...	Do this...
Your name	Simply type your name in the Signature box.
ASCII art	Create the image in the Signature box.
A link to your e-mail address	In the Signature box, type *<HTML><A HREF="mailto:youraddress@webtv.net"> Click here to send me e-mail!</A>*
A link to a favorite Web page	In the Signature box, type *<HTML><A HREF="http://www.nascar.com"> Click here to get the latest NASCAR news </A>*. Obviously, the Web address and the text following the URL can be edited as desired.
An image stored on the Web	In the Signature box, type *<HTML><img src="http://www.justpc.com/jpclogo1.gif">*. You can also follow the right angle bracket (>) at the end of the URL with your name without additional formatting. Insert the desired URL and image name in place of the one shown here.
A sound file played when your message is opened	In the signature box, type *<HTML><bgsound src="http://www.justpc.com/cool.wav"></HTML>*. (Obviously, you'll need to edit the URL and file name to point to the sound file you want.)

> **TIP** Looking for a good source of free images and sound effects? Try one of these for starters: Draac's Free Gifs 123 at *members.tripod.com/~gifs123/index.html* or 100,000 FREE Cool Graphics at *www.geocities.com/SiliconValley/Heights/1272/index.html*.

> **TECHNOBABBLE** **HTML**—is a language that dictates how text should appear when displayed by a Web browser. (It stands for Hypertext Markup Language.) It can alter text appearance or incorporate links to e-mail addresses or Web pages but only if the environment supports HTML as WebTV Network's e-mail program does.

Once you've finished designing your signature, select Done, and then press Go. You can see how your new signature looks by returning to the main mail screen, selecting Write, and then pressing Go. The signature as you designed it will appear at the bottom of the message.

More Power to You

From the Mail Setup screen, select Addressing to gain access to two advanced e-mail functions: a CC line and a Reply All button. Unfortunately, both functions are treated as one advanced addressing option, so you can't take one without the other, but you'll probably find you'll want them both anyway.

To enable these options, select Advanced Addressing from the Mail Addressing Setup screen (see Figure 8-4 on the following page), select Done, and then press Go. Note that these two additional features will not appear unless you set them specifically.

So what do they do? The CC line is pretty basic—it allows you to send a message to one person while sending copies to others for their information. Say, for instance, you think that your phone company changed your long distance service without your permission. You can send the primary message to the phone company while sending copies to the state's attorney general, the Federal Communication Commission, and so on. Copying someone simply means you're passing along the message for their information while the primary recipient is expected to act on it.

WebTV Basics

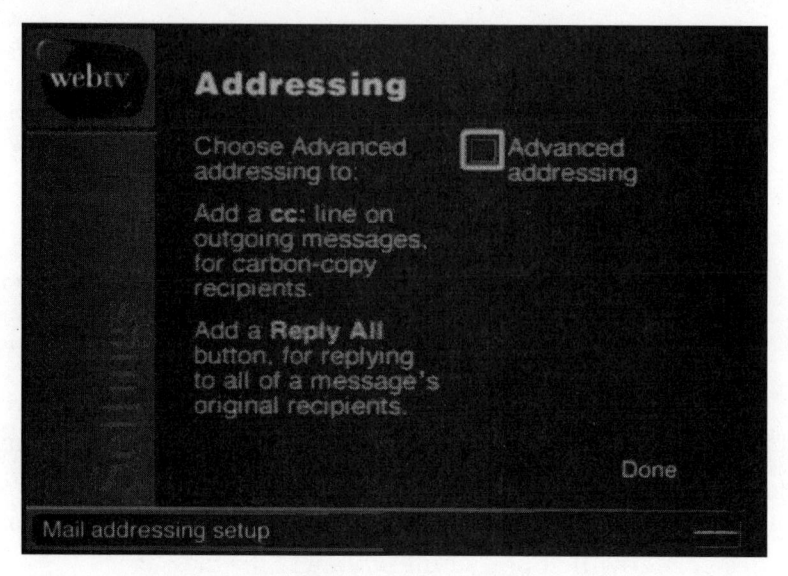

Figure 8-4. *Adding the advanced addressing options is as easy as checking a box, selecting Done, and then pressing Go.*

The Reply All button will come in handy for group discussions, since it'll allow you to reply to all of the original message's recipients at once, not just to the sender.

Fill Up Your Address Book

Maintaining an address book with commonly used addresses can save you a bundle of time rooting through old messages, searching for addresses on the Internet, or rekeying them each time you want to send a message.

To add a new address to your virtual black book, select Mail on the WebTV Network's home page, and then press Go. Select Addresses, and then press Go to see the list of addresses contained in your book. (See Figure 8-5.)

From this screen, select Add, and then press Go. You will be prompted to enter the name and e-mail address of the desired contact in the boxes provided. (See Figure 8-6.)

8: E-Mail 101

Figure 8-5. *Notice that the WebTV Network has already entered their Customer Support address into your address book.*

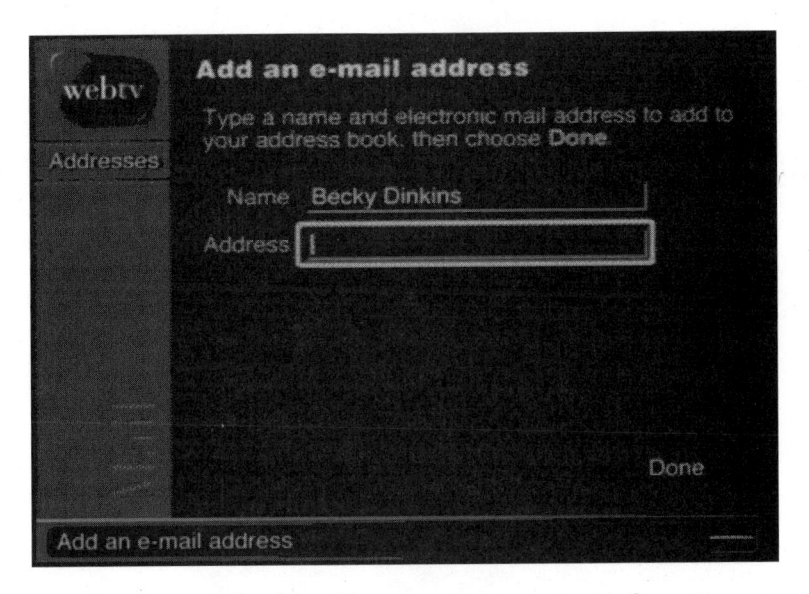

Figure 8-6. *Use the Name and Address boxes to enter contact information.*

89

To edit the information at a later date, select Addresses, as described above, select the entry you want to edit, and then press Go to make the necessary changes.

You can also look up an e-mail address by selecting Look Up from the Addresses menu (refer to Figure 8-5) and then pressing Go. You will be linked to 411, an online e-mail directory that you can search to locate the desired address based on the person's name.

Chapter 9

Reading, Writing, and E-Mail Management

Now that your WebTV Network's e-mail environment is set up to do things the way you want it to, you can get to the meat of e-mailing—reading, sending, and managing your messages.

Read Your Messages

When you see your Mail List for the first time, you'll find a note or two from the fine folks at WebTV Networks, Inc. The note might welcome you to the WebTV Network, or it might describe the newest features of the most recent software upgrade. Whatever the case, all new messages are presented in a dark-colored font, whereas previously read messages will appear in a light-colored font (see Figure 9-1).

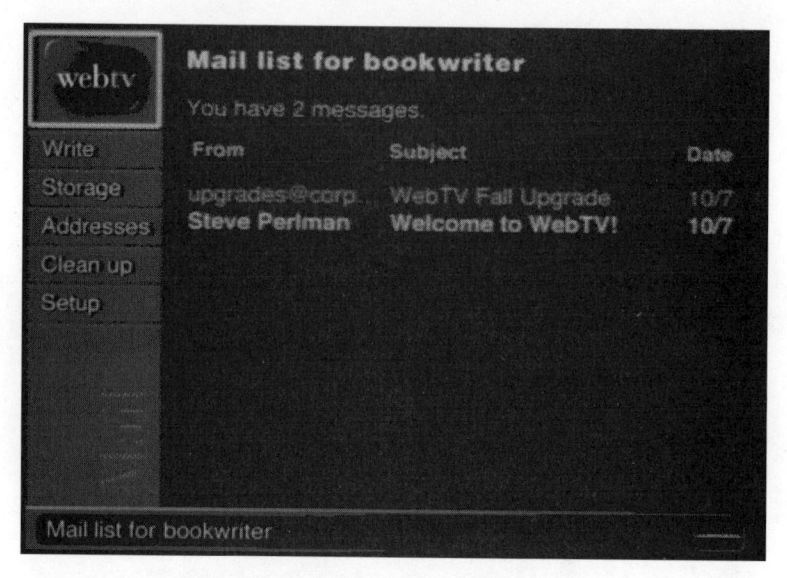

Figure 9-1. *New messages appear in a dark-colored font, while previously viewed messages appear in a light-colored font.*

To read a message displayed in your Mail List, select it, and then press Go. The message appears as shown in Figure 9-2.

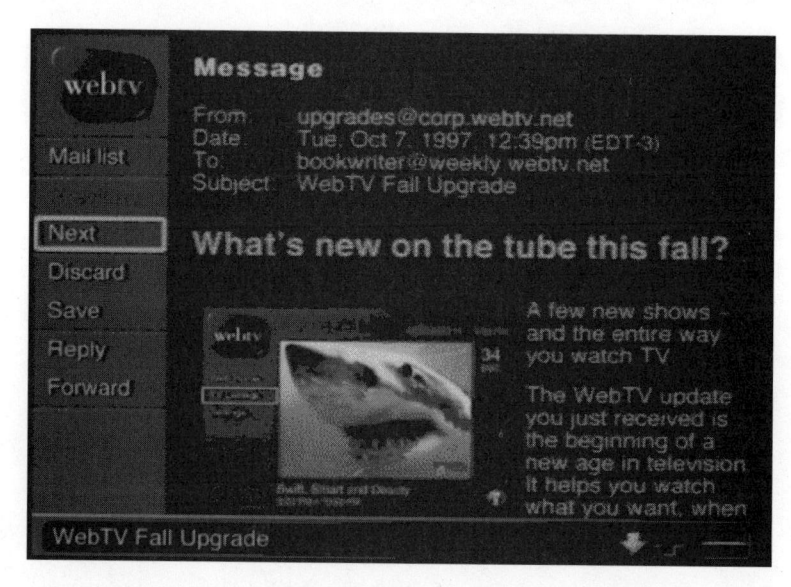

Figure 9-2. *Choose the desired option from the left side of the screen, or simply press the Back key to return to your Mail List.*

9: Reading, Writing, and E-Mail Management

From this screen, you can execute a number of options on the message displayed. Do this by selecting one of the options listed in Table 9-1, and then pressing Go.

Table 9-1. **Actions you can take on a message**

Select this...	To do this...
Mail List	Return to your Mail List.
Previous	Move to the previous message in your Mail List when the option is available (not grayed out).
Next	Move to the next message in your Mail List when the option is available.
Discard	Permanently delete a message. Once electronic junk mail starts arriving, you'll use this option more than any other!
Save	Remove a message from the Mail List and save it until you explicitly say to delete it.
Reply	Respond to the sender of the e-mail message. Keep in mind that none of the original message will be attached to the note, which can make it hard to keep your comments in context.
Forward	Send a message you've received on to someone else, which is a great option to use when someone has shared a funny joke with you. Why not continue to share the fun? You can also forward the message along with your comments to the original sender of the note, since forwarding attaches the original message to any comments you choose to make. But be careful about what you're forwarding and to whom you forward it. Unless you're sure your intended recipient wants to get this stuff, you might make enemies by continuing to forward urban legends around the Internet.

Revisit Saved Messages

If you've chosen to save any of your messages, they will appear in your Storage area. Just as you can pull a dusty letter out of a dresser drawer, you can retrieve old messages to be read again. You read stored mail the same way you read messages in your Mail List—simply select Storage from the Mail List screen, and then press Go. You'll see a Saved Mail screen like the one shown in Figure 9-3 on the following page.

WebTV Basics

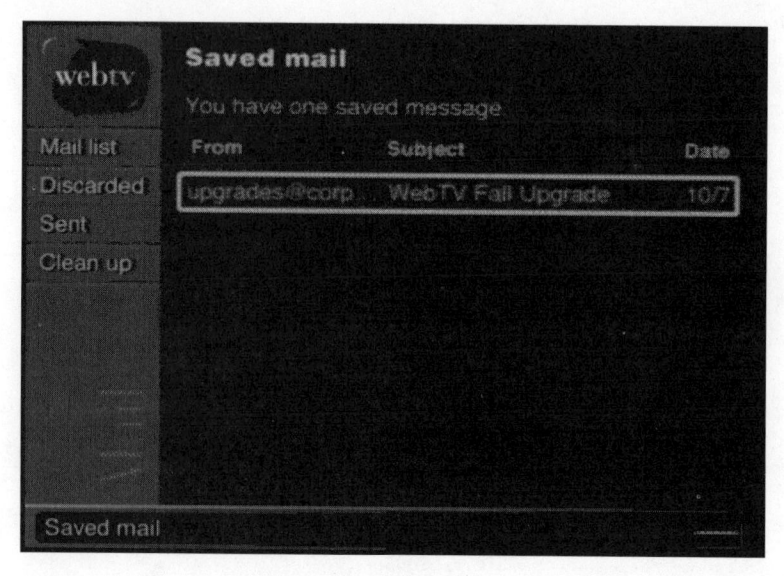

Figure 9-3. *Messages appear on the Saved Mail screen just as they do in the Mail List.*

The messages will appear just as they did originally in the Mail List, but the options you might select on this screen are slightly different. You will notice this list of four options on the menu down the left side of the screen. (Execute them the same way you do any other option—select the desired button, and then press Go.)

- **Mail List.** Select this option to return to the Mail List.

- **Discarded.** Use this option to view messages you've deleted within the last week. After one week, they disappear for good.

- **Sent.** Use this option to look at any messages you have sent over the past week, but get 'em fast—after one week they, too, disappear.

- **Clean Up.** Use this option to display your entire saved message list with check boxes for easy group discarding. See more about this option in the section titled "Clean Up, Clean Up…" later in this chapter.

After opening a saved message, you can move through all the saved messages using the Previous and Next buttons, or you can choose to discard the message.

Write to Others for Free

I admit it; I used a slimy gimmick to get you to read this section of the book—I used the word "free" to draw you in. Not many people can resist that word. It's right up there with "sale," which can make grown people (myself included) salivate and break into a mad dash for the store. While sending e-mail is a feature included in your WebTV Network subscription, you still have to pay the monthly service fee to use it. But it's quite a deal just the same when you consider that the monthly fee covers all the surfing you and your family can handle, chatrooms, discussion groups, plus unlimited e-mail. The point of all this is don't be afraid to e-mail liberally. Hear a funny joke? Jot it down and fire it off to a friend.

You've probably already experimented with it, but in case you haven't, here's how to send an e-mail message using your WebTV Internet terminal:

1. From the WebTV Network home page, select Mail, and then press Go. You'll see the Mail List screen shown in Figure 9-1 on page 92.

2. Select Write, and then press Go. You'll see the Write A Message screen pictured in Figure 9-4. Notice that any signature you might have added in the last chapter is also visible.

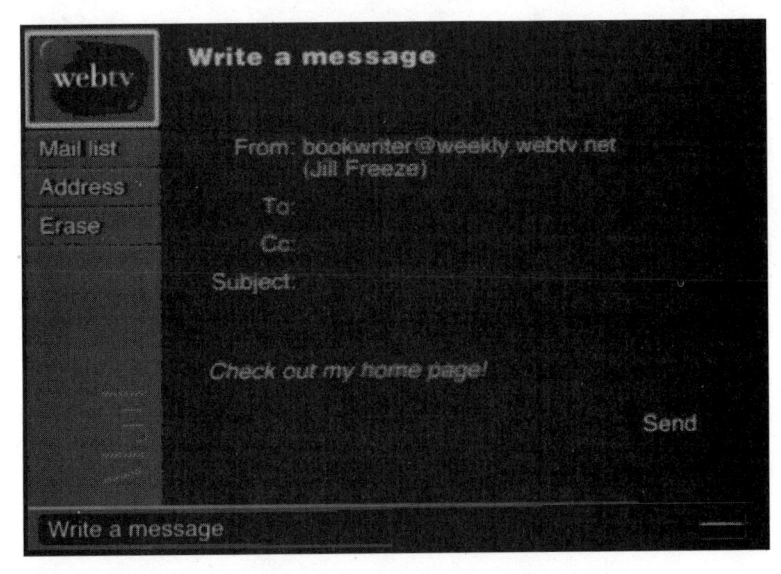

Figure 9-4. *This figure shows a blank message. You can tell by the presence of the CC line that the advanced addressing options are enabled.*

WebTV Basics

3. In the To line, enter the person's address. If the person's address has already been entered in your online address book, select Address, and then press Go. The Choose An Address panel shown in Figure 9-5 will appear on the screen. If you need to make some changes to the entry, select Edit Addresses, press Go, and then edit to your heart's content.

   Select the desired name, and then press Go. The address for the name you selected will appear in the To line. If you're done entering addresses, select Continue, and then press Go.

> **NOTE** If the person you're writing to has a *webtv.net* address as well, you need only supply the person's user name (the stuff before the @ sign), because WebTV Network assumes the *webtv.net* extension automatically if no other is specified.

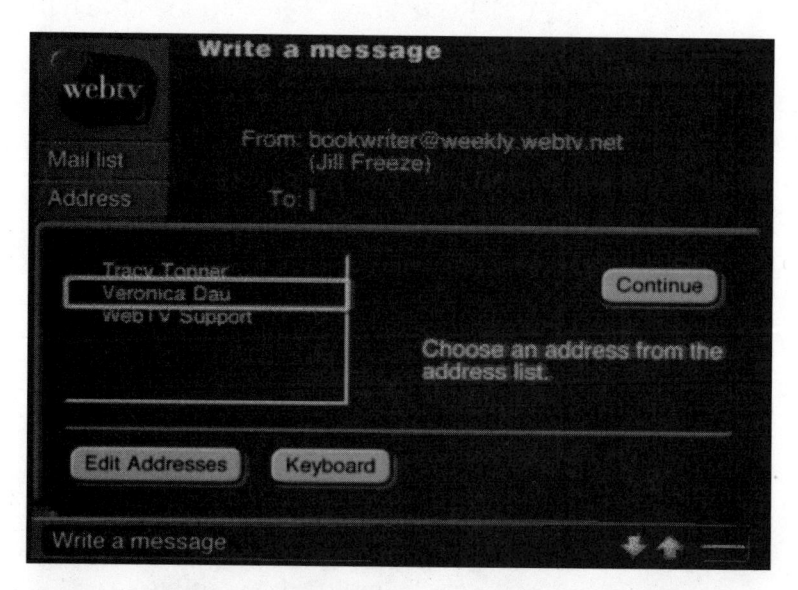

Figure 9-5. *Use this panel to insert a predefined address into an e-mail note.*

4. Enter a title for your message in the Subject line so that the recipient can determine the general subject of the message.

> **NOTE** If you really want to make things simple, send e-mail to the people at WebTV Networks, Inc., asking them to support nicknames in e-mail. This means that you could just enter the person's name in the To line, and WebTV Networks would furnish the full address from your address list. Sure, selecting the name from the list as you do now is pretty quick, but you could probably have entered the person's name in the time it takes to pull up the address panel and scroll to the person's name.

5. Type the text of the note.

6. When you've finished writing the note, select Send, and then press Go. The closing mailbox animation will appear to let you know that the message is on its way.

> **NOTE** If an e-mail message can't get to its recipient, it might bounce back to you. This means an error message along with the original note you sent will appear in your Mail List. E-mail can bounce for any number of reasons: the address may have been mistyped; the recipient's mail server could have been down for more than a couple of days; or the recipient's account might no longer exist. In any case, the reason the e-mail message bounced should be contained in the error message, although such error messages aren't always easy to understand. If you entered the address manually or are using the address book entry for the first time, verify that the information in the To line of the message is correct, and then resend the message. If you used an address book entry that's worked fine in the past, simply resend the message.

Unfinished Business

We've all started lengthy e-mail messages that we haven't had the time to finish. But what do you do when you're using your WebTV Internet terminal and have no local disk space on which to store unfinished, unsent messages? Here's a good trick: send the message to an invalid address like *yourself@webtv.ne* (deliberately drop the last "t" in *.net*). That way the message will bounce back to you and remain in your inbox for editing and sending at a later date.

97

Clean Up, Clean Up...

Is anyone else hearing the purple dinosaur's clean up song? I'm sorry, but when you have two preschoolers, you get immersed in this stuff, like it or not. Anyway, the whole point of this is that in order to keep your sanity, you'll need to clean out the messages in your Mail List from time to time. It's sort of like the clutter that accumulates around your house—it'll grow until it becomes overwhelming.

To clean out the messages in your Mail List, select Mail from the WebTV Network home page, and then press Go. From this Mail List screen, select Clean Up, and then press Go. You'll see each of the messages displayed with a checkbox in front of them. (See Figure 9-6.)

From this screen, you can select any number of messages to be saved or discarded by placing a checkmark next to them, selecting Save or Discard, and then pressing Go. The saved messages will be moved to storage, and the discarded messages will remain available for a week before they are permanently deleted.

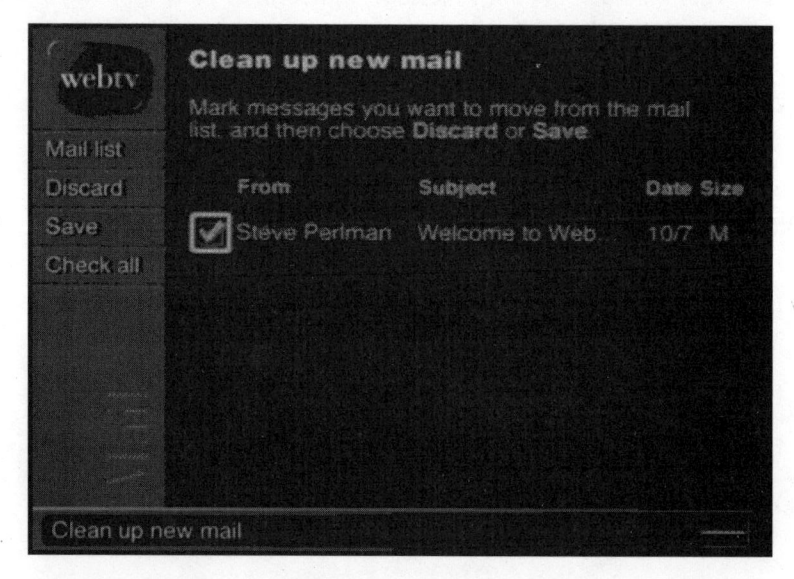

Figure 9-6. *Mail List messages are displayed with checkboxes in front of them.*

You can clear the clutter from stored messages the same way. Select Storage from the Mail List screen, and then press Go. Select Clean Up, and then press Go. The messages will appear just as they do in Figure 9-6.

> **CAUTION** Clean out your Mail List and storage area regularly, because once you hit the 150-message (or two megabyte) limit, the WebTV Network bounces messages intended for you back to their sender. Don't worry, you don't have to count the messages yourself; the WebTV Network will display a note telling you that your Mail List is full. (I can hear Elvis singing "Return to sender...")

Retrieve Your E-Mail Daily

We get so busy at times that we might forget to check our e-mail. The WebTV Network gives us a simple solution to this problem. You can now instruct the WebTV Internet terminal to connect to check your e-mail once daily.

To do this, connect to the WebTV Network in the normal way and use the subscriber's account (this is the only account that can set this option). Then follow these steps, pressing Go after each one:

1. From the WebTV Network home page, select the Mail icon.
2. On the Mail List screen, choose Setup.
3. The Mail Setup screen will appear. Select Message Light.
4. You will see a gray box with an arrow pointing down. (See Figure 9-7 on the following page.) This is known as a drop-down list box. Select the gray box.

WebTV Basics

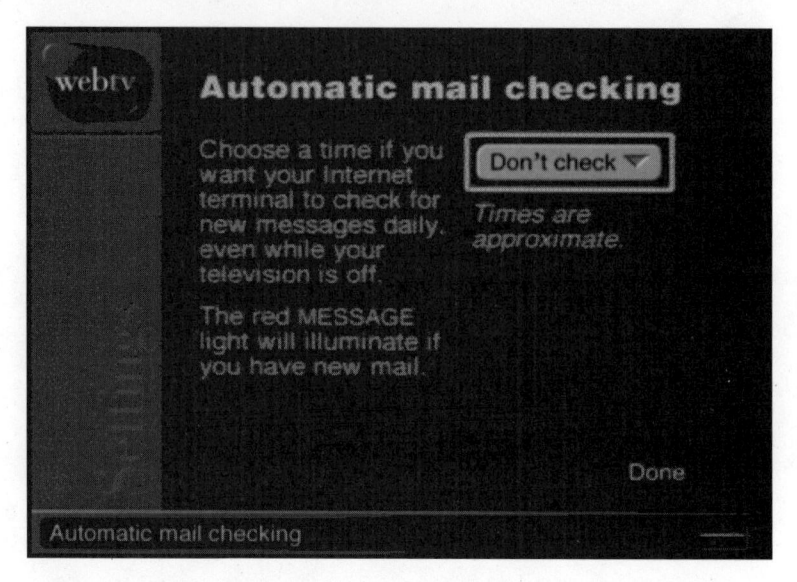

Figure 9-7. A drop-down list box makes it easy for you to see your options.

> **TECHNOBABBLE Drop-Down List Box**—A box that expands when you select it to present a list of options from which to choose.

5. Use the arrow keys to scroll to the time you want the WebTV Internet terminal to connect and check your e-mail each day.

> **TIP** The time you select will be approximate, but for the best results and minimal hassle, pick something in the middle of the night so that you won't interfere with anyone's phone call.

6. Select the Done button.

Your WebTV Internet terminal will check for messages each day, and the red message light on the front of the WebTV Terminal will glow when you have new e-mail.

Chapter 10

Everything You Always Wanted to Know About the Web

I made an interesting observation about the World Wide Web a while back. Companies and organizations now include Web URLs in their television ads. The Internet and its related terms have become household words, and you're among the first to make your TV actually do something other than broadcast *Married...With Children* reruns. With the Web so accessible, you can check out the lyrics to the theme song of lead character Al Bundy's favorite TV show, skim the biographies of the show's stars, even check out when the show will air next. Whether you watch the prime-time shows or one of the daytime soaps, you'll find a wealth of related information on the Web.

What Is the Web and How Does It Work?

The World Wide Web is a collection of some 80 million Web pages, some of which are connected by hyperlinks. The hyperlinks appear in a different color from the surrounding text to let you know that you can select that word or phrase and then be transported to a related Web page by clicking on the selected area. You can literally click your way around the world in a matter of minutes.

You can start with one Web page and keep following links as they appeal to you (the virtual Sunday drive in the country), or you can use a search engine's subject index to hone in on exactly what you want. For more about using search engines and subject indexes, see Chapter 21, "Become a Virtual Bloodhound."

To access a Web page using your WebTV Internet terminal, press the Options button, select Go To, and then press Go. (Or if you have a wireless keyboard, just press the GoTo key.) You'll see a panel slide up from the bottom of the screen, like the one shown in Figure 10-1.

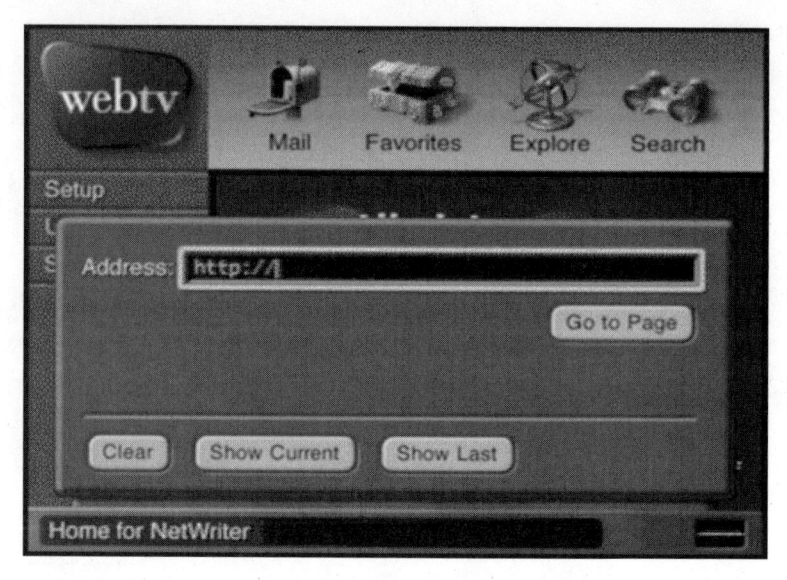

Figure 10-1.   *Use the Go To panel to visit your favorite Web pages.*

You'll notice that the WebTV Internet terminal already provides the *http://* prefix for the address. This prefix tells your WebTV Internet terminal what kind of information you're seeking. Should you forget to add the *www* to the beginning of a URL, the WebTV Internet terminal will supply it for you. The same goes for the *.com* extension. Because a majority of the Web pages you visit will contain the *.com* extension in their URLs, the WebTV Internet terminal will provide it if no other extension is specified. To display the desired URL, type the URL in the Go To panel, select Go To Page, and then press Go to display the new location.

10: Everything You Always Wanted to Know About the Web

Form Opinions on the Web

A number of Web pages allow you to supply personal data by using forms. These forms might be part of a simple guestbook for the Web site, or the company might use the data to send you more information on its products or services.

You'll encounter two kinds of form boxes on the Web—text boxes and drop-down list boxes. Text boxes are basically empty boxes (see Figure 10-2), which you select and fill in as appropriate. Once all the fields are filled in, select Done or Submit and then press Go to send the data back to the Web site.

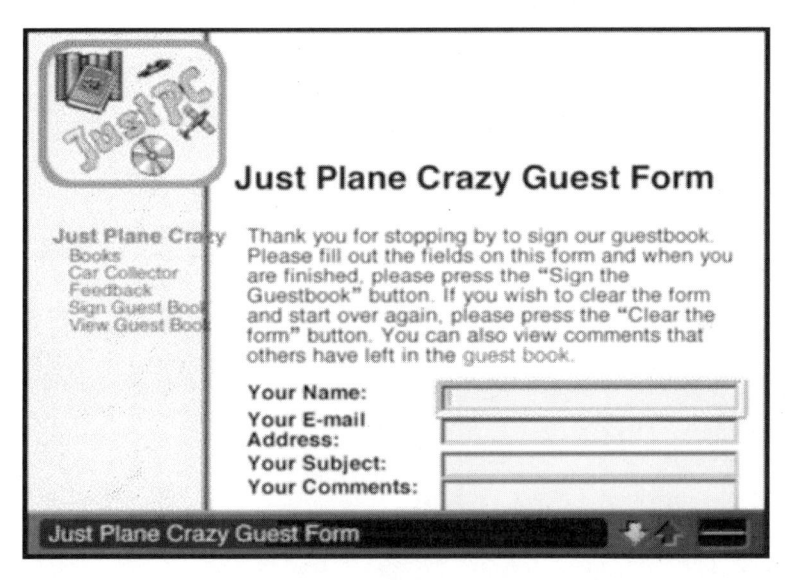

Figure 10-2. *The most commonly used forms are made up of a collection of simple text boxes. The green arrow on the title bar at the bottom of the page lets you know that there are more boxes to fill in.*

The second type of form box you'll see is a drop-down list box. (See Figure 10-3 on the following page.) This box enables you to choose from a variety of predefined options. Select the box, and then press Go to see a list of options. (See Figure 10-4.) Use the up and down arrows to move from one option to another. When the option you want is selected, press Go, and the option's name will appear in the same gray box. If you've made an error, you can repeat the previous steps to view the list of options and select the one you want.

103

Figure 10-3. Drop-down list boxes are easy to spot with their downward-pointing arrows.

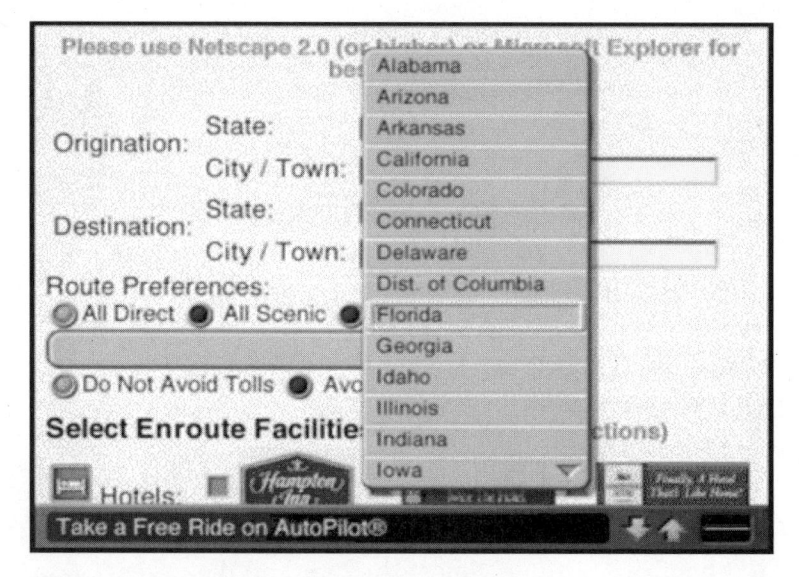

Figure 10-4. Once the drop-down list box has been selected, you can use the arrows to select the option you want.

> **NOTE** Just because a Web page displays a note saying "View with Netscape Navigator or Microsoft Internet Explorer for best results," that doesn't mean you'll have trouble seeing it with your WebTV Internet terminal. In fact, the page in Figure 10-3 suggests that you use one of these Web browsers, yet everything looked fine when I viewed the page using my WebTV Internet terminal.

Once all the boxes have been filled in, select Done or Submit and then press Go to complete the transaction.

Play Favorites

The more familiar you become with the Web, the more likely you are to find a few pages you'll want to visit regularly. For example, my husband makes a daily visit to a Web page dedicated to tracking NASCAR rumors and I go to a site dedicated to my favorite soap opera for sneak peeks at upcoming story lines, cast changes, and so on. Do you want to be bothered with remembering and rekeying a URL each time you want to visit your favorite page?

These frequently visited pages are known, aptly, as Favorites. Your WebTV Internet terminal gives you a number of ways to specify, manage, and access your favorite Web pages, as you will see in the sections that follow.

Add a Web Page to Your Favorites List

If you find a Web page that you think you'll want to visit in the future, consider adding it to your Favorites list. With the ability to hold 680 URLs (up to 36 in each of 20 folders), you'll have plenty of room to store anything that strikes your fancy.

To add a Web page's URL to your list, do the following:

1. View the Web page you want to add to the list.
2. Press Options.
3. Select Save, and then press Go. Select Save Page, and press Go to confirm the addition. The gold-bearing treasure chest (see Figure 10-5 on the following page) will appear, letting you know that your selection has been added to your Favorites list.

Figure 10-5. *The treasure chest animation lets you know that your selection has been saved successfully.*

View a Favorites List

You can configure your WebTV Internet terminal to display your Favorites list by name only or to display the Web page's name accompanied by a thumbnail image of the page.

The WebTV Internet terminal will automatically display the Web page names with the corresponding thumbnail. If your Favorites list is long, you might want to display more of the Web page names at one time. You can do this by telling your terminal to display the page names only. You won't have the tiny pictures to go by, but you will have the Web page names, which are more useful anyway.

To specify a name-only display, follow these steps:

1. Press the Favs key (or select Favorites on the WebTV Network's home page), and then press Go.

2. When your Personal folder (the folder your Internet terminal will put everything in unless you tell it otherwise) is displayed, select Organize and then press Go.

3. From the Organize Favorites screen, select Listing and then press Go.

4. In the With Pictures check box, place a checkmark if you want a thumbnail of the Web page to appear with its name, or remove the checkmark if you want to see the page's name only. (See Figure 10-6.)

To go to a Web page stored in a Favorites folder, simply highlight the page's picture or name and then press Go. Within a few seconds, the page will appear on your screen.

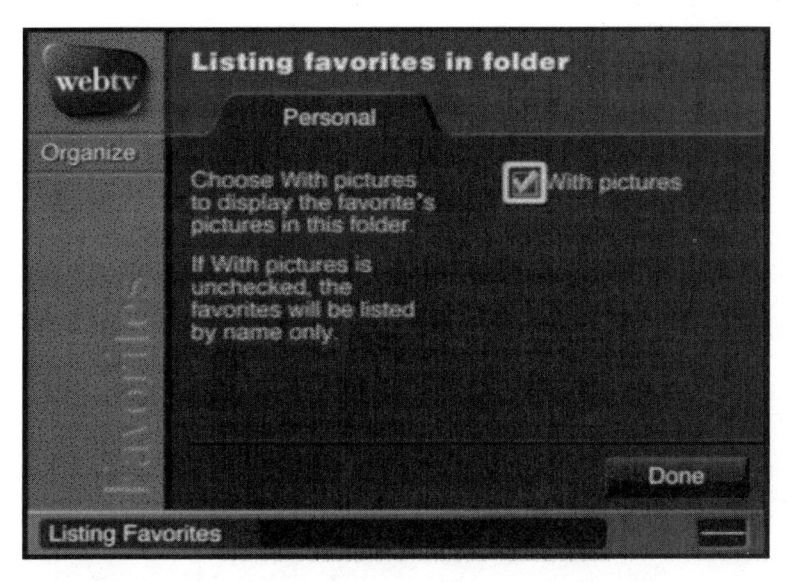

Figure 10-6. *Changing the display of your Favorites list is as easy as selecting the With Pictures box and then pressing Go to add or delete the checkmark.*

Manage Your Favorites List

Of course, finding one page buried in your Favorites list among 680 others could be challenging, which is why the WebTV Network gives us the ability to store our Favorites list in folders. You can keep a folder for personal favorites, for work-related pages, or for those dedicated to your favorite hobbies or television shows.

Before you can add pages to a given folder, you'll obviously need to create the folder. (You'll learn how to move pages from one folder to another later in this chapter.) To create a folder, do the following:

1. Select Favorites, and then press Go.

WebTV Basics

2. Select Add Folder on the left side of the screen, and then press Go.

3. The Add A Folder screen will appear with a text box, into which you will enter the desired name for the new folder.

4. When you've finished naming the folder, select Add and then press Go.

5. The new folder will appear in alphabetical order among the other folders you've already created. (See Figure 10-7.)

To add more folders, select Add Folder and then press Go to cycle through steps 2 through 5 as many times as needed.

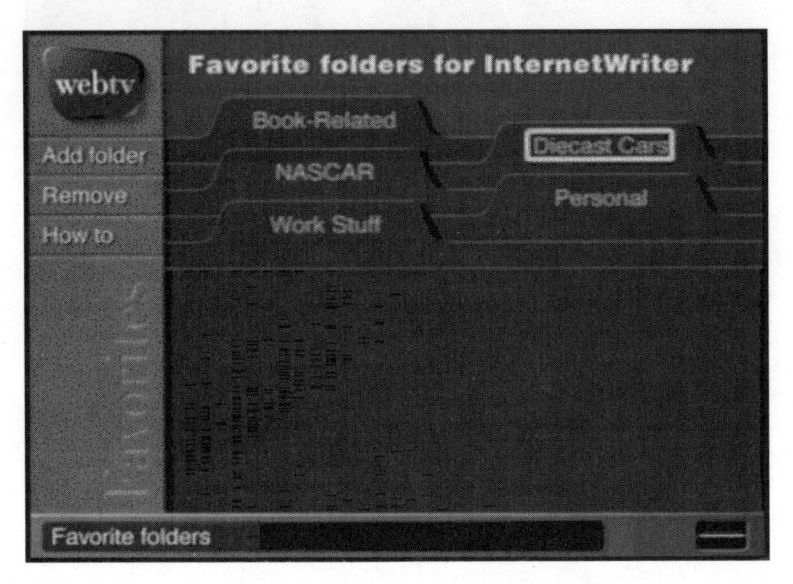

Figure 10-7. *The folder you've just added will appear highlighted among all the other folders you've created.*

Delete a Folder

As your interests change, you might want to delete one of your folders. You might even decide to do away with your Personal folder once you've moved all of the pages in it to other more specific folders. To delete a folder, first make sure all of its contents have been moved elsewhere (described in the next section). Then starting from your WebTV Network home page, select

10: Everything You Always Wanted to Know About the Web

Favorites and then press Go. Now select Remove on the left side of the screen. You'll see each of your folders on screen with a Remove button on each folder. (See Figure 10-8.)

To delete a folder, select Remove on the folder you want to delete. The WebTV Network will whisk the folder away for good.

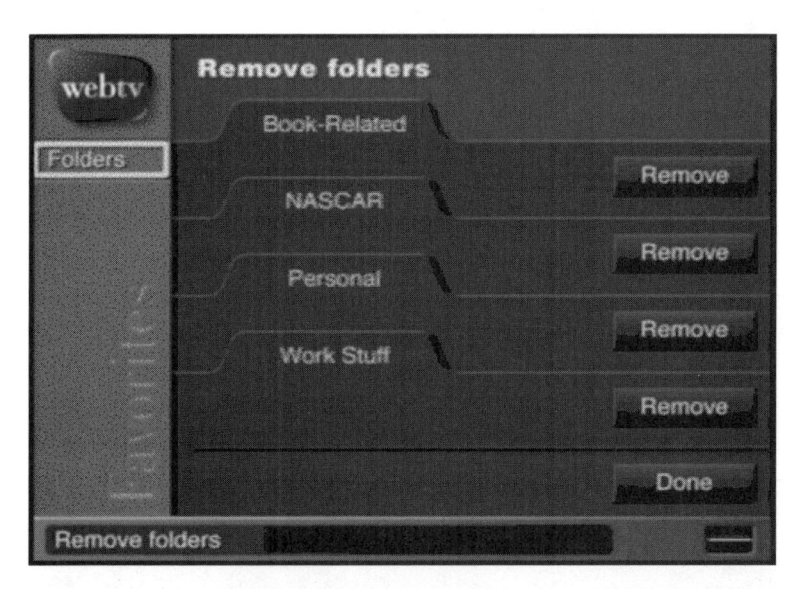

Figure 10-8. *The Remove Folders screen makes it easy to see which folder you're about to delete.*

Delete Unwanted Pages

Adding pages to your Favorites list can quickly get out of hand. It's sort of like keeping your teenager's favorite baby clothes in her dresser drawers—there isn't room for them, and she sure doesn't need them anymore.

With the WebTV Internet terminal, you have two options for cleaning up the clutter: you can delete unwanted pages from your Favorites list or you can reorganize the pages into more specific folders, making them easier to find.

To discard unwanted Web pages from your Favorites list, do the following:

1. Press the Favs key.

2. Select the name of the folder from which you want to discard pages, and then press Go.

3. Select Organize on the left side of the screen, and then press Go.
4. Select Discard, and then press Go. All the pages will appear in a list with a Discard button next to each page (as shown in Figure 10-9).
5. Select Discard next to the Web page you want to delete, and then press Go.
6. You can also choose Discard All, but use it with caution since the folder might contain some pages you searched long and hard to find.
7. The selected page will be permanently removed from your list.

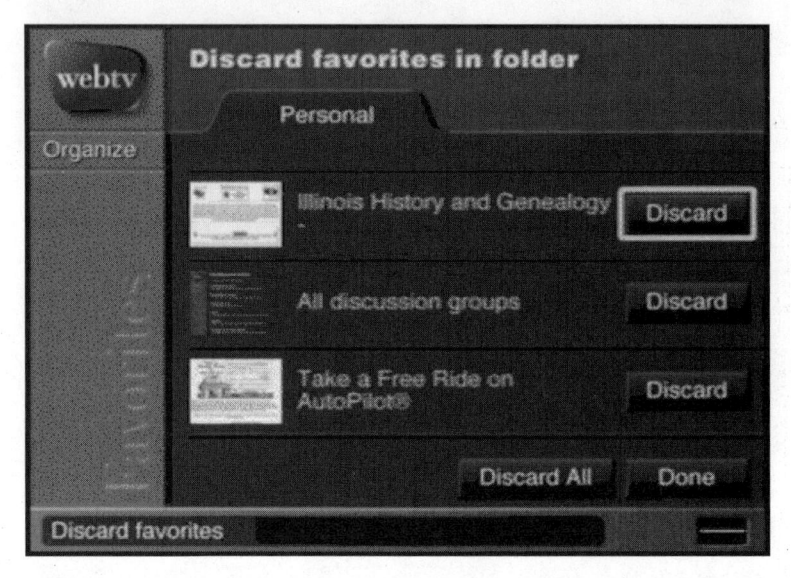

Figure 10-9. *The Discard Favorites screen makes it easy to see which pages you're about to delete.*

Move Without Lugging All Those Heavy Boxes

If you're like me, you dread moving anything. It usually means chaos, followed by a lot of work that makes you sweaty and sore. Well, there's good news when it comes to moving your favorite Web pages between Favorites folders—it's virtually foolproof, you won't break anything, and you can do it sitting on your duff sipping your favorite beverage.

10: Everything You Always Wanted to Know About the Web

Most likely you'll decide to place all those pages that have been gathering dust in your Personal favorites folder into other more appropriate folders. To do this, follow these steps:

1. Press the Favs key.
2. Select the folder containing the pages you want to move, and then press Go.
3. Select Organize, and then press Go.
4. Select Move To Folder, and then press Go. You will see a list of all the pages contained in the folder, with a gray drop-down list box next to each page. (See Figure 10-10.)
5. Select the drop-down list box next to the item you want to move, and then press Go. You will see a list of folders that you have already defined on the following page. (See Figure 10-11.)

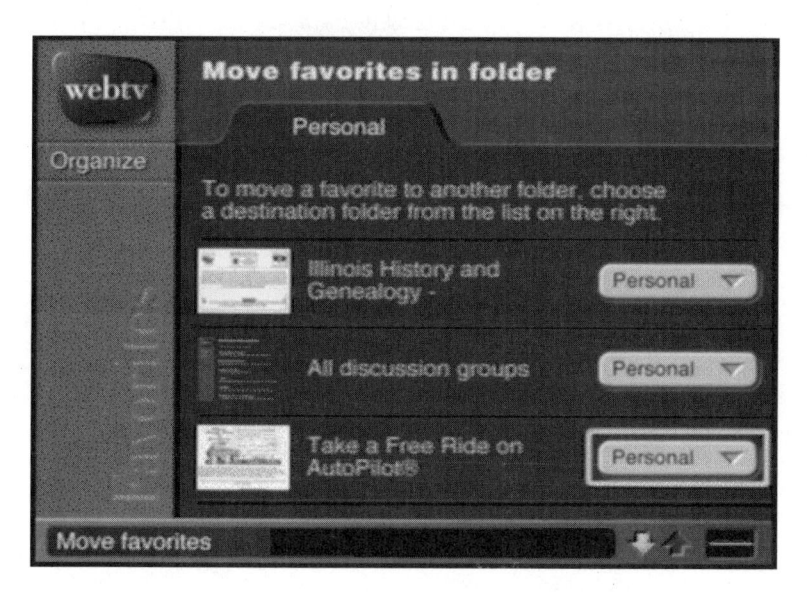

Figure 10-10. *This list of pages is ready to be moved to other folders.*

111

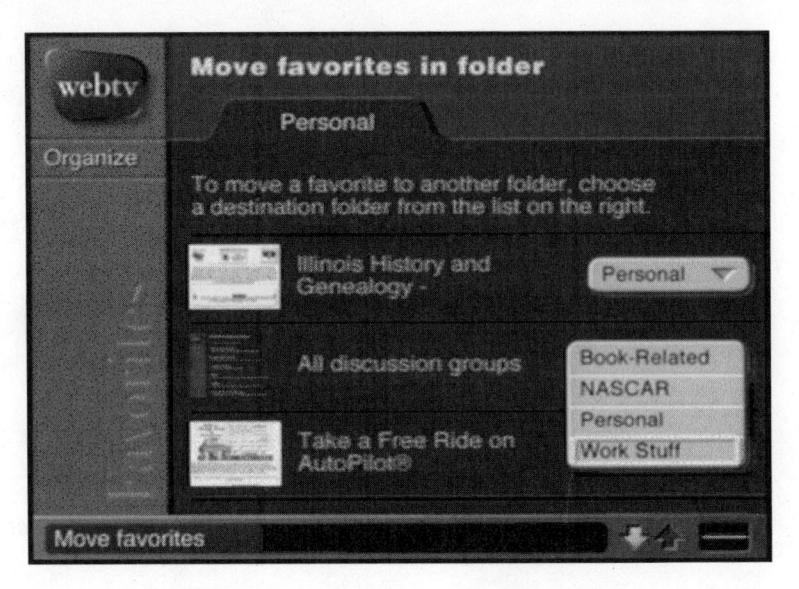

Figure 10-11. *Here is a list of predefined folders to which the pages can be moved.*

6. Use the arrows to highlight the name of the folder to which you want to move the page, and then press Go. The Web page listing will be transferred to the designated folder.

Assign Shortcuts to Your Favorite Web Pages

How would you like to be able to access one of your top seven most frequently visited Web pages by pressing a single key? It's simple with your WebTV Internet terminal. Just follow these steps to put the function keys at the top of your keyboard to work:

1. Press the Favs key.

2. Select the folder containing the page to which you want to create the shortcut, and then press Go.

3. Select Organize, and then press Go.

4. Select Shortcuts, and then press Go. You will see a list of pages with a keyboard key next to each one. (See Figure 10-12.) In some cases, the WebTV Network will have assigned a shortcut for you. In other cases, you'll see a gray key without a label.

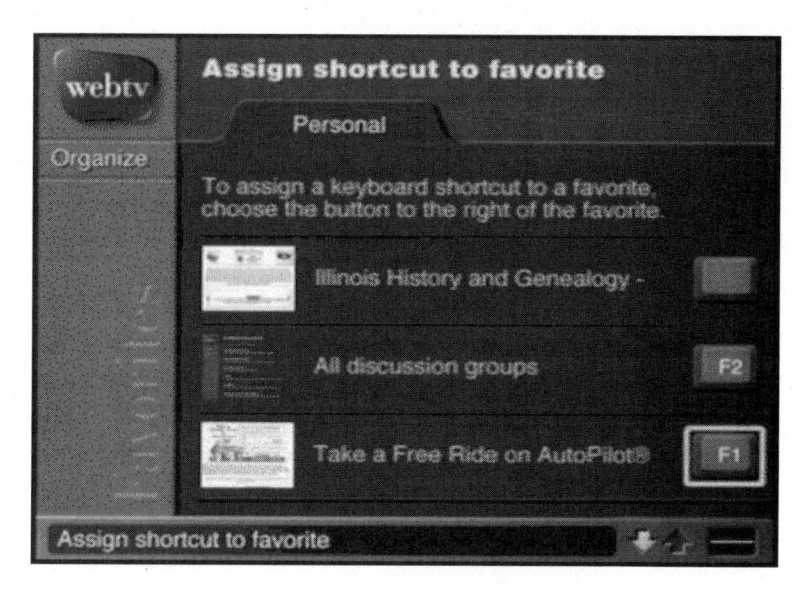

10: Everything You Always Wanted to Know About the Web

Figure 10-12. *You can create shortcuts to your favorite Web pages by using the screen shown here.*

5. To assign a shortcut key, select the gray key next to the page for which you want to create the shortcut and then press Go.

6. Select the button next to the function key name you want to use for the shortcut, and then press Go. If you select a function key already in use, your current selection will override the previous selection. When you're finished assigning shortcuts, select Done and then press Go.

7. To access a page with a shortcut, simply press the applicable function key from anywhere within the WebTV Internet terminal screens and you will immediately be taken to the page.

Web Surfing Tricks

Now that you know how to organize your favorite Web pages, it's time to get to the fun part—the surfing itself. The next sections show you how to make the most out of some of the keys on your remote control or keyboard.

Back, Back!

The Back key lets you move backward through the screens you recently accessed, one by one. This key comes in handy when you're using a search engine and want to refine the search. All you have to do is press Back to return to the search screen, where you can tweak your search parameters.

> **TECHNOBABBLE** **Tweak**—A term often used to refer to a small adjustment to almost anything.

Information, Please

Web page information can quickly become stale, so when you're looking at information that could potentially change significantly over time (like sports scores or stock quotes), you might want to take a peek at the information panel of the Web page to see when it was last updated.

To view the information panel, press the Options key while looking at the Web page you want to learn more about. Select Info on the Options panel, and then press Go. You'll see a panel such as the one shown in Figure 10-13.

Figure 10-13. *Use the information panel to see how recently the Web page was modified.*

Get Loaded

This is a family book, so don't get all excited! If the information on a Web page is older than you anticipated, you can try one last thing to make sure you're viewing the most current information available.

From within the Web page, press the Options key. Select Reload, and then press Go. (Those using the optional wireless keyboard can simply press cmd+R.) Your WebTV Internet terminal will reload the most current version of the Web page, which might be more current than the version you already saw.

How is this possible? Your Internet terminal uses something called a cache (pronounced "cash," as in something we could all use more of) to store Web pages and such for quicker access. That way your WebTV Internet terminal doesn't have to fetch the page from halfway around the world each time you want to view it.

To illustrate this point, press Back a few times after you've been surfing awhile. The first few pages (which the Internet terminal can store locally using its own cache) pop up almost instantly. If you're keeping an eye on live stock quotes or the World Series scores, you'll definitely want to get acquainted with the Reload button.

> **TIP** Here's how to get a Reload button on your Options screen if you missed it earlier in the book. Press the Home key, select Setup, and then press Go. Select Options, and then press Go. Select the Advanced Options box, and press Go until a checkmark appears in the box. Select Done, press Go, and you will be advanced-option enabled.

Recent History

Recent history might sound like an oxymoron, but it's actually a very useful feature of your WebTV Internet terminal. No matter what you're doing, you can press the Recent key to see a list of all the Web pages you recently visited on the following page. (See Figure 10-14 on the following page.)

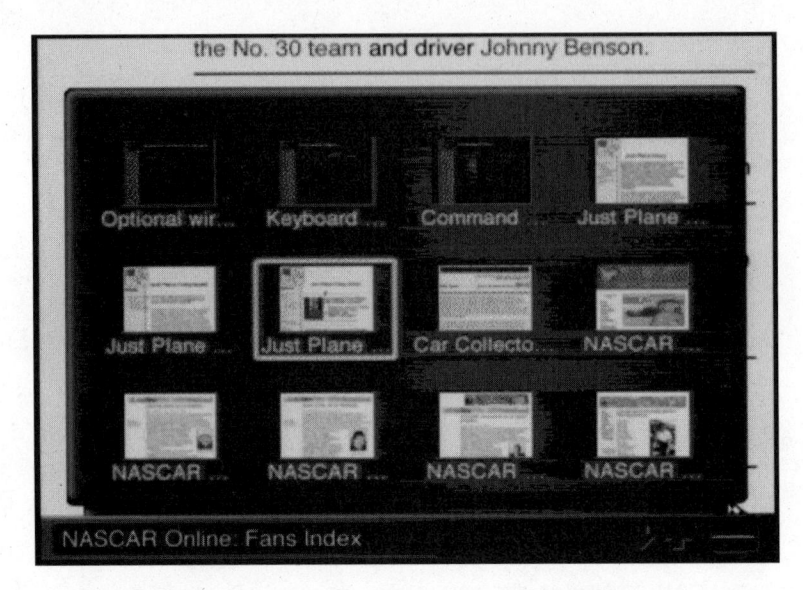

Figure 10-14. *Jump back to any page listed on the screen by selecting it and then pressing Go.*

To jump to any of the pages listed, use the arrows to select the desired item and then press Go. The desired page will appear.

Chapter 11

A Nose for News (or Gossip?)

Most of us have a healthy dose of curiosity whether we care to admit it or not. Likewise, many of us like to flaunt our knowledge, and we feel good when we can inform others or set the record straight on rampant, inaccurate rumors. Newsgroups (called discussion groups by WebTV Networks) are the perfect place to get the most up-to-date information available. News of upcoming products leaks out for the world to see; trade show attendees share what they saw with others who couldn't attend; people trade advice about products not worth buying or steer you to reputable dealers and coach you on fair pricing...it's an interesting experience.

Of course, the medium also lends itself well to misinformation and mischief. Wait until you experience your first April Fool's Day on the Internet—you'll see all kinds of crazy rumors and announcements generated for the sole purpose of a good laugh.

The key is to use your judgment before jumping to any conclusions. Remember, you have the World Wide Web at your disposal now, so you can easily verify much of what you hear by poking around a bit.

TIP Want to determine the accuracy or credibility of news you've heard on the Net? Start on the WebTV Network home page. (Press the Home key if you need to.) Select Explore, and then press Go. You'll see a list of available topics. Select News, and then press Go. Select your desired news category from the options on the left side of the screen, and then press Go. The Etcetera category gives you access to some of the best newswire services on the Web, and the Newspapers section links you to some of the premiere publications. Either way, you'll get reliable information to substantiate or refute some of the claims you might see in your favorite discussion group.

So How Do the Groups Work?

You might be wondering how people all over the world can post articles to the same discussion group. When somebody originates a message, whether a new article or a response to an existing article, that message is given a unique message ID. All the computers linked to the Internet use that identifying number to make sure the message is sent to all the other computers that need to view it. This number also keeps the message from appearing on one computer multiple times, because the computers that store news articles are designed to reject duplicates.

NOTE Given the way messages are transmitted over the Internet, it's possible for you to see a response to a message before you see the original message. Don't worry, you haven't slipped into a time warp; your machine might simply have a more direct link to the respondent's computer than to the message originator's. This is one good reason why you should always include critical parts of the original message in your response, so others have a frame of reference or context for your remarks.

Because there are literally thousands of discussion groups to choose from, these groups are organized in a hierarchical fashion. For instance, there are groups with a *rec* (recreation) prefix, a *misc* (miscellaneous) prefix, a *comp* (computer) prefix, and so on. As an example, take the discussion group *misc.kids.pregnancy*. Moving within the hierarchical structure of discussion groups, you'll find a large number of groups starting with the *misc* prefix

11: A Nose for News (or Gossip?)

and a smaller number starting with the *misc.kids* prefix, until you reach the stand-alone group *misc.kids.pregnancy*. The hierarchy tree (see Figure 11-1) can always grow. In this case, *misc.kids.pregnancy* could eventually contain related groups such as *misc.kids.pregnancy.multiples* or *misc.kids.pregnancy.highrisk*.

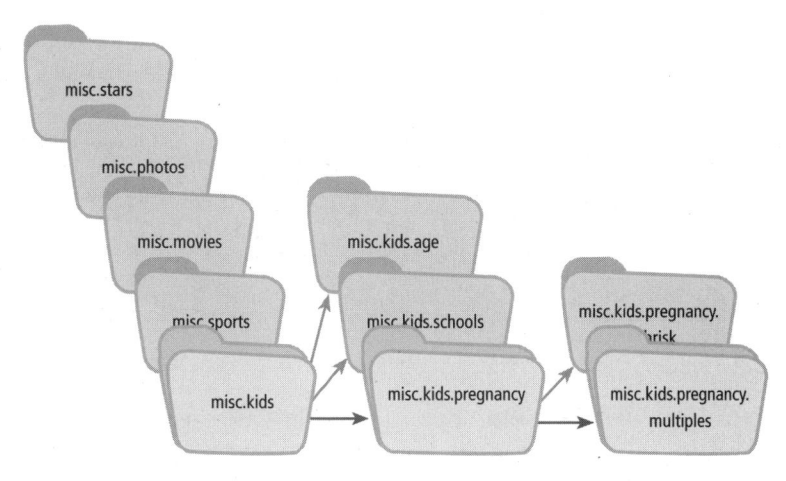

Figure 11-1.   *The group hierarchy is dynamic, always growing and changing.*

Get to the Goodies

Now that you're excited about checking out some discussion groups, here's how to get there. From the WebTV Home page, select Explore, and then press Go. Under the Features section of the Explorer Main Menu screen, you'll see the Discuss icon. Use the arrow keys to select it, and then press Go. The first time you do this, you'll see some introductory information about groups. You'll then see the Featured Discussion Groups screen shown in Figure 11-2 on the following page.

WebTV Basics

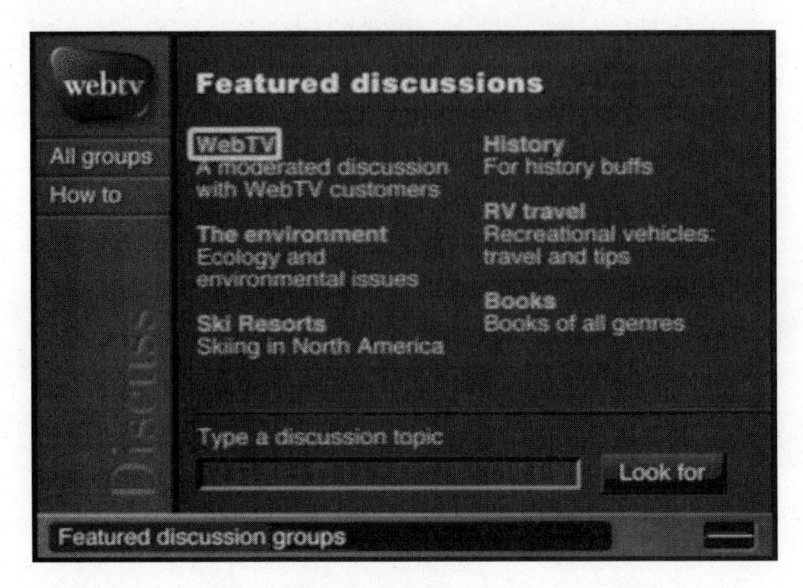

Figure 11-2. *Use this screen to select a discussion group.*

Each day, WebTV Networks selects a few discussion groups to spotlight for the day. If one of these groups grabs your attention, select it and press Go to take a peek. The discussion group titles are also searchable. To look for a group dedicated to a favorite hobby or other interest, follow these steps:

1. From the Featured Discussion Groups screen, select the Type A Discussion Topic text box at the bottom of the screen.
2. Enter the topic you want to search for.
3. Select Look For, and then press Go.
4. WebTV Networks will return a list of groups meeting your criteria. (See Figure 11-3.)
5. To view one of the groups, use your arrow keys to select the group name and then press Go.

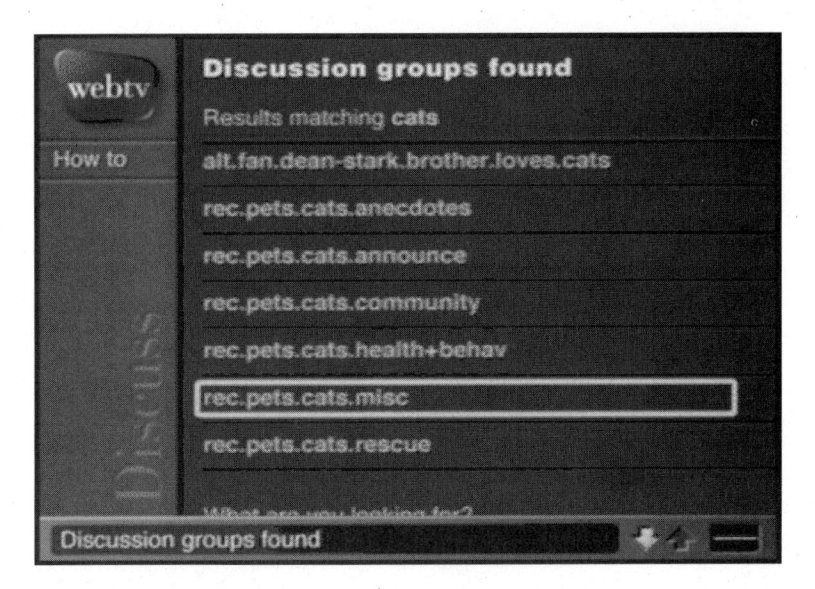

Figure 11-3. *When I searched on my favorite animal, cats, WebTV Networks returned a number of possibilities.*

You can also browse the list of available groups by selecting All Groups and then pressing Go. You'll see a list of the primary discussion group hierarchies. Select one, and then press Go to see all the groups within that category. Keep selecting the categories you like until you get to the group you want to view. Because the discussion group hierarchy can get incredibly complex, use the search facility to locate specific groups; otherwise, you could end up selecting buttons for what seems like days. Browsing through the hierarchy is a great way to see the true scope of what's available, however.

Get Involved in the Discussion Groups

Sure, you can read all the discussion group articles, but what fun is that if you can't participate in the excitement? In the sections that follow, you'll learn how to view articles, how to post your own articles, and how to respond to others.

Read Up on the Latest Information

To view the articles in a chosen discussion group, select the article you want to read and then press Go. You'll see the article along with a new set of buttons on the left side of the screen. Use these three buttons to read the articles recently posted to your chosen discussion group:

- **Group.** This button moves you back to the list of articles in the group. You'll want to use this button to avoid discussion threads that don't interest you. Simply skip ahead to the next article you want to view, and then select it. (Alternatively, you can select Back to return to the main listing of discussion group articles.)

> **TECHNOBABBLE Threads**—A series of articles pertaining to the same subject make up what is known as a thread.

- **Previous.** Select this button and then press Go to move to the article previous to the one you are currently viewing.
- **Next.** This button moves you to the next article in the thread or, if there isn't a follow-up, to the next new subject.

If you encounter an article with a GIF (an image file format) buried in it, your WebTV Network software will automatically decode it so that you can see the image. Search the discussion groups for the word "pictures" to see a list of groups dedicated to posting images.

> **CAUTION** You're bound to see some phenomenal art on the Internet, because many commercial photographers share their work in these groups. If you have young children in your home, however, you might want to view these groups with them. People will occasionally post inappropriate images in groups like *alt.binaries.pictures.animals*.

Post It Yourself

Posting an article to a discussion group is a breeze. With the group's main page on the screen, select Post and then press Go. The first time you do this, you'll see information about posting. You will then see a screen like the one shown in Figure 11-4.

11: A Nose for News (or Gossip?)

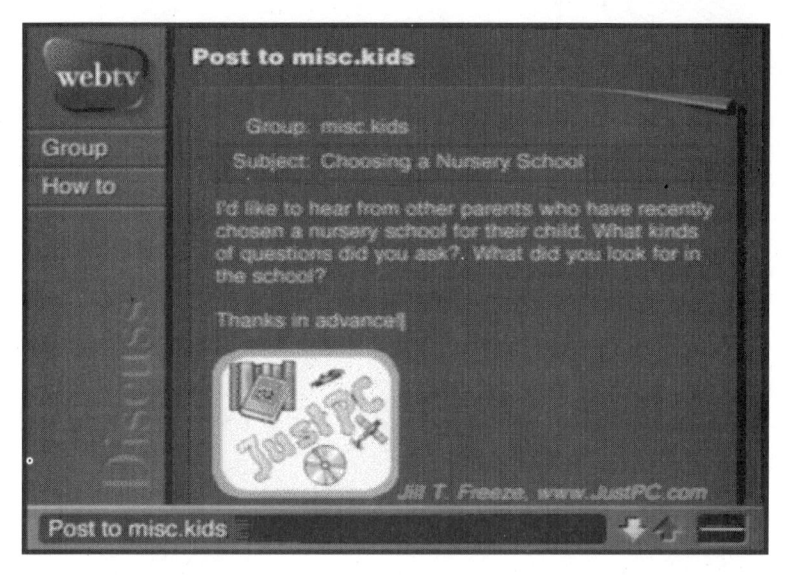

Figure 11-4. *Note that the fancy signature file you created on the WebTV Network might not appear to everyone as you'd expect, since their software might display HTML as plain text.*

Fill in the subject line and the body of the message, select Send, and then press Go. Your message is on its way for the world to see. If you want to abort the mission, simply select Back (before you press Go, of course).

> **TIP** Before you send your article, double-check the spelling and content to make sure it's an appropriate topic for the chosen group.

Action!

When it comes to responding to an article in a discussion group, you have two options—you can e-mail a response directly to the person originating the message, or you can post a response to the group for all to see.

By selecting Mail To and then pressing Go, you will get a screen similar to the one in Figure 11-4, but the poster's address and the subject line will already be filled out for you. Use the Mail To option when your response deals with a sensitive issue or when the response may not be of interest to everyone in the group.

The Respond option, on the other hand, lets you share your wisdom and insight with the entire discussion group. Select Respond, press Go, fill in your response, select Send, and then press Go.

Posting and following up to articles in discussion groups is arguably the most fun you'll have on the Internet because it's truly interactive as opposed to being entirely passive. It's a terrific way to make new friends too.

Chapter 12

Virtual Chatrooms and Cybercommunities

If you wanted to meet someone new these days, how would you go about it? You could try the old standby of joining a club or a group of people who share your interests, but these days you have a lot more options. Whether you're looking for the love of your life or trying to find a buddy to trade collectibles with, chatrooms and cybercommunities are a couple of ways to expand your circle of acquaintances.

Let's Chat a Moment

Chatrooms are places you can go to converse in real time with people who share your interests. Many corporations host online chats about their products, while professional entertainment or sports associations might invite celebrities to interact with their fans in chatrooms. Likewise, there are countless chatrooms dedicated to various interests. Chatrooms are a fabulous medium because they allow a larger number of fans to get closer to their favorite celebrities than ever before. Now fans can ask famous rock stars how they got their start or can tell a favorite soap opera star how much her work is appreciated.

How Do Chatrooms Work?

Chatrooms usually consist of screens similar to the one shown in Figure 12-1. Each person's username is followed by their questions or comments. If you're like me, you'll find it almost impossible at first to locate the answers to questions asked, or to match the comments to the reactions they elicit. Your screen will look like a random mish-mash of unrelated conversations. Never fear—a little time and experience will change all that. You'll be a pro before you know it!

Figure 12-1. *Learning to spot which responses go with which comments might take a while, but knowing what to look for in a particular chatroom can really speed up the process.*

Two different types of chatrooms exist—bulletin board style, where you must refresh the chat screen when you're ready to read the next block of text, and IRC (Internet Relay Chat), where new text flows into view as it's entered. Each has its advantages. The bulletin board style gives you the time you need to soak up the conversation, while IRC can put you into sensory overload with its rapid scrolling of input. With IRC, however, you see virtually no delay in the conversation, so you have a better feel for the tempo of the dialog. This format also lends itself well to witty comebacks and other banter.

WebTV Networks makes it simple for you to engage in either type of chatroom. Given the WebTV Network's arrangement with Talk City, all you have to do to enter an IRC chatroom is to select Community from the WebTV Network home page, press Go, select Chat, and then press Go. For bulletin board–style chatrooms, consult your favorite Web sites, use your favorite search engine to look for chatrooms on desired topics, or browse your preferred subject index for leads.

Know What to Look For

Before you jump into an online chat, you might want to sit a spell and scope out the scene. See what kinds of topics the group tends to discuss, and get a feel for how well a certain brand of humor will or won't be received.

It's also important to get adjusted to the chatroom's rhythm. Does the group have many participants or just a few regulars? Do people use any special headers or identifiers to make finding related comments easier? Obviously, if a chatroom has many participants, it'll take longer for people to respond to questions or comments because there's a higher volume of input to read through and react to. Using headers or putting the username of the person whose comment you're responding to at the beginning of your reply can greatly simplify the lives of chatroom participants.

Now That I'm Ready to Participate…

Finding a chatroom that fits your personality and interests is the first step. Try a few of these suggestions to get started:

- From the WebTV Network home page, select Community and then select Chat. Skim the "What's On Now" listings to see if anything piques your curiosity.

- Watch your favorite discussion groups for pointers to chatrooms dedicated to related topics.

- While visiting Web sites of particular interest, watch for notices of celebrity chats, chatrooms related to the Web site's topic or content, and so on.

- Use your favorite search engine to locate possible chatrooms of interest. (For more information on using search engines, see Chapter 21, "Become a Virtual Bloodhound.")

IRC on the WebTV Network

The quickest way to participate in an IRC is to go to the WebTV Network home page, select Community, press Go, select Chat, and then press Go again. You'll see a screen like the one shown in Figure 12-2, which introduces you to the concept of online chatting.

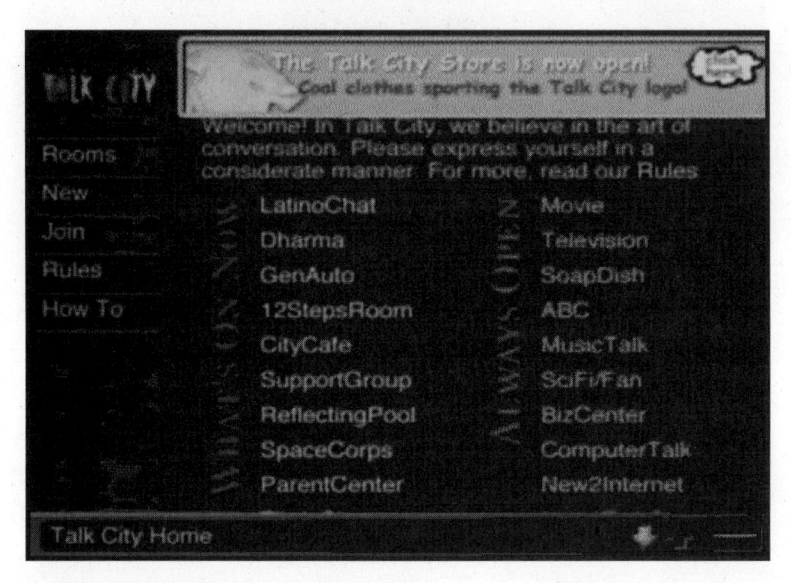

Figure 12-2. *The first time you enter the Talk City chat area, a screen like the one illustrated here shows you what to expect.*

Once you've worked your way through the screens containing the introduction, you'll reach the WebTV Network chat area. (See Figure 12-3.)

On this screen, you'll see a sampling of open chatrooms under "What's On Now At Talk City." The New2WebTV room never closes, so you'll always be able to find other WebTV Network users to chat with. If none of these rooms looks interesting to you, select the Talk City icon at the right side of the screen, and then press Go. You'll see an extended listing of the Talk City chatrooms, and you'll gain access to a number of new menu options.

12: Virtual Chatrooms and Cybercommunities

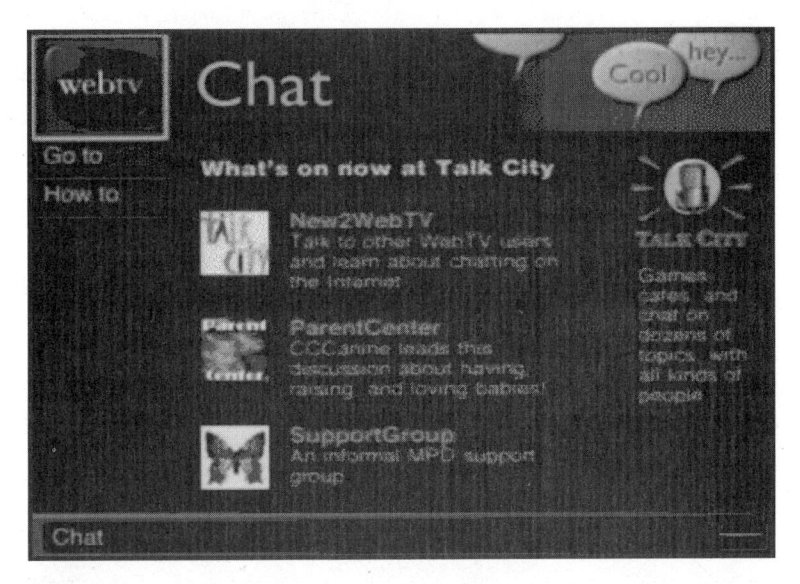

Figure 12-3. *Consult the "What's On Now" section to see if any of the active chatrooms strike your fancy.*

Still can't find anything you like? Select Rooms from the menu on the left side of the screen, and then press Go. A seemingly endless list of active chatrooms appears along with a description of what topics are being discussed and the number of people currently in each room. (See Figure 12-4 on the following page.) Select More at the bottom of the screen to proceed through the list. When you find a room you want to join, select the room and then press Go.

Upon entering a room, you'll see scrolling comments with a text box at the bottom of the screen. To participate, simply enter your comment, select Send, and then press Go. Your comment will appear onscreen for all the chatroom participants to see and respond to.

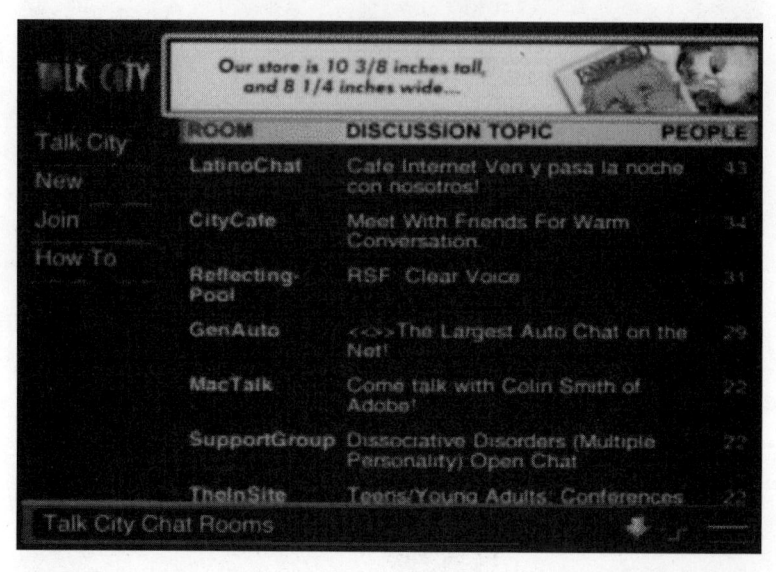

Figure 12-4. *By selecting Rooms from the Talk City home page, you'll see a list of all active chatrooms, the topics being discussed, and the number of people currently participating.*

Show, Don't Tell

For anyone who's ever taken creative writing in school, this phrase will sound all too familiar. Believe it or not, you can actually "show-not-tell" when participating in online chats, too. In the text box at the bottom of the chatroom screen, enter "/me" before whatever action you want to perform. The "/me" will be replaced by your WebTV Network name. For instance, if I entered the following, "/me flashes an evil grin," other chatroom participants would see, "Netwriter flashes an evil grin." To further distinguish talk from actions, actions are displayed in a different color (gray) than standard "spoken" messages, which appear in green.

12: Virtual Chatrooms and Cybercommunities

If You Want to Capture Someone's Attention, Whisper

Talk City has a cool feature that lets you "whisper" (talk one-on-one) to another chatroom participant with minimal hassle. While visiting a chatroom, select Whisper from the left side of the screen and press Go. A panel such as the one shown in Figure 12-5 will slide into view. Use the arrows to select the person you want to whisper to, and then press Go. Highlight the Write A Private Message box, and then type your text. When you're ready to send the message, select the Whisper Message button, and then press Go.

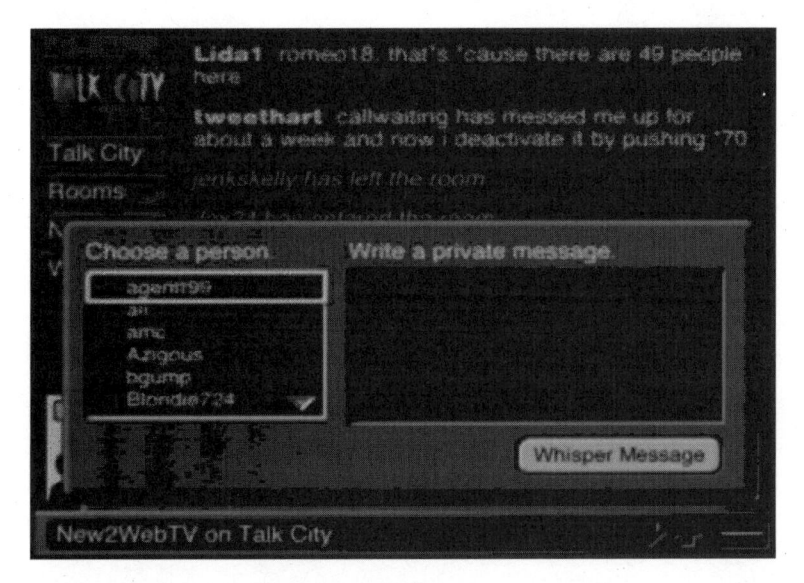

Figure 12-5. *Choose the person you want to whisper to, enter the message, select Whisper Message, and then press Go.*

Using Whisper is a safe way to exchange e-mail addresses with one other chatroom participant at a time. (Just remember the tips for safe chatting presented throughout this book and later in this chapter.)

Hop to It!

If you frequent a particular chatroom, you can join in anytime by simply entering the group's name without having to weed through the names of dozens of chatrooms. From the Talk City home page, select Join from the menu on the left side of the screen. A panel such as the one shown in Figure 12-6 slides into view. Enter the exact name of the chatroom you want to visit, select Enter Room, and then press Go to be instantly transported.

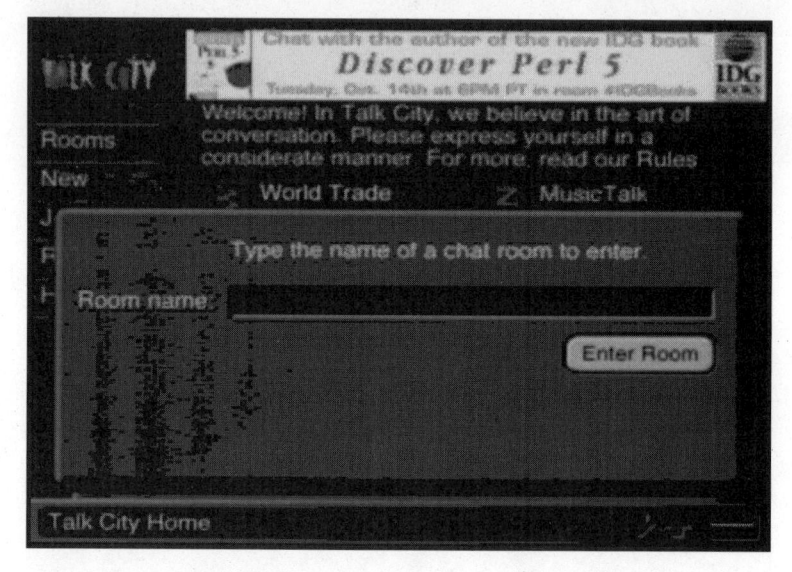

Figure 12-6. *Type in the name of the chatroom you want to enter, select Enter Room, and then press Go to move directly to it.*

The Do-It-Yourself Chatroom

Do you want to discuss a controversial topic pertaining to current events? Would you like to meet with new e-pals to engage in a real-time chat without the cost of long distance phone calls? Talk City makes it easy to create your own chatroom. From the Talk City home page, select New, and then press Go. A screen like the one pictured in Figure 12-7 will appear.

12: Virtual Chatrooms and Cybercommunities

Figure 12-7.   *Use this screen to create your own chatroom, which you can make public or private.*

Select the Room Name text box and give your room a name that reflects the topic you plan to discuss. Use the arrows to move to the Room Topic box, into which you should enter a description of what will be discussed in the room. (You might not want to create a description for the room if you plan to restrict the access to the room.) Next you'll need to decide whether the group should be open to anybody who's interested, or whether you should restrict the room for just you and a few select friends. If you want to make the room private, place a checkmark in the Set Up As Private Unlisted Room box. When you're ready to create the room, select Create Room, and then press Go. You're ready to begin chatting about the topic of your choice.

Go Directly to the Source

As you roam through various discussion groups, you might come across a post mentioning an online chat. In fact, the discussion group covering my favorite soap opera hosts a weekly IRC. Thanks to the WebTV Network, you can easily participate in any IRC as long as you know the name of the server, the port number, and the name of the chatroom. Sound complicated? Not at all—just select Community from the WebTV Network home page, press Go, select Chat, and then press Go again. The WebTV Network chat area appears. Select Go To from the menu on the left side of the screen. The screen shown in Figure 12-8 on the following page appears.

133

WebTV Basics

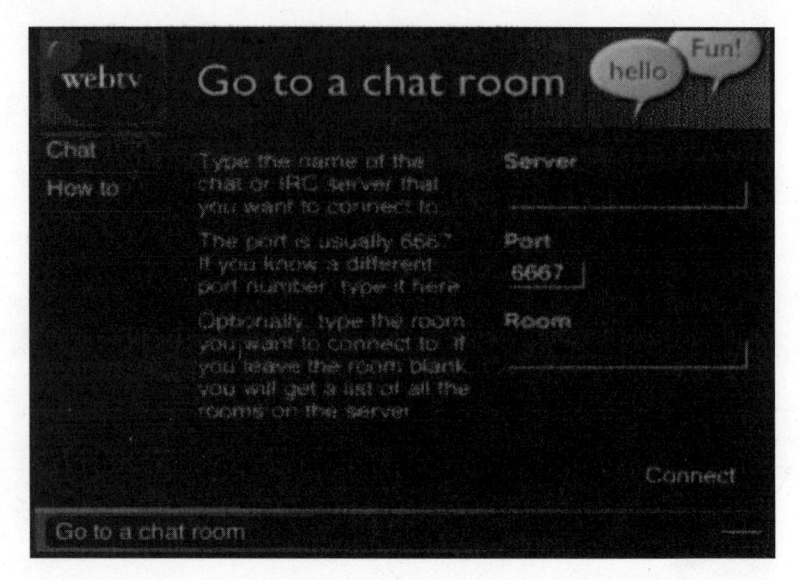

Figure 12-8. *With this easy-to-understand screen, it's a snap to find that IRC you read about in your favorite discussion group.*

The first thing you'll need to provide is the server's name in the box provided. Next you'll need to enter a port number. The WebTV Network provides the most common port number, which will work in a majority of cases, so you shouldn't need to worry about this. Finally you have the option of entering the chatroom's name. Don't worry if you've forgotten it—most chat servers will provide you with a list of room names upon connecting. When you've entered all the known information, select Connect, and then press Go.

When you enter one of the chatroom sites hosting multiple topics, you'll see a menu of broad topics, from which you can make selections to narrow the number of choices. In general, once you've chosen a chatroom to participate in, you're asked to sign in with your userID.

Some chatrooms require you to sign up for an account. Although there's rarely a fee, signing up does give the hosts a way to check that you really exist. They might verify the e-mail address you gave them by sending you a password or some other piece of e-mail thanking you for signing up. But most important, this gives the hosts a way to find you should you misuse your account privileges.

You might need to select a password to fully participate in many online forums and Web sites. Consider using the same password everywhere. This might not sound like the most secure thing to do, but it might be the best way for you to remember your password. If the password is chosen with care and is not something others could easily pick out (like the name of a spouse, your birth year, and so on), it most likely will not pose any problems. Interestingly, some Web sites allow you to set up a password hint so that if you forget your password, the site can jog your memory with a key piece of information.

> **TIP** Most chatrooms allow you to select a user name that is different from your WebTV Network userID. So even if you couldn't get your preferred user name for your WebTV Network account, you might be able to use it in chatrooms.

Cybersense: Things to Keep in Mind While Chatting

I'll elaborate on more of these issues in some later chapters, but here are a few chatroom-specific things to keep in mind:

- Be sure to use people's usernames, even if you know their real names. It's an issue of privacy. If somebody elects to use a particular username for their online activities, it's up to you to respect their wishes.

- Use caution when telling others about yourself. Much like you might look around before using an automatic teller machine to withdraw cash, you might think twice before revealing a lot of information about yourself, especially in chatrooms and discussion group forums where hundreds—if not thousands—of people have access to the information.

- If a dialog turns into a two-way debate, "take it outside," as they say in old western movies. There's no need to take up everyone else's time and system resources if the conversation has turned into a two-person shouting match. You can continue the discussion using the Whisper function or by exchanging e-mail with one another.

- Remember that what is written is not always what is meant. A fair amount of meaning relies on inflection and body language. It's best to clarify a person's intentions before jumping to conclusions or getting defensive.

Tales of Friendship and Camaraderie on the Internet

Admittedly, this is one of those touchy-feely sections of the book that contains no tangible information. On the other hand, making new friendships and helping others are two of the most rewarding aspects of getting involved with the Internet. Allow me to indulge in sharing a few personal experiences.

When I first heard of the WebTV Network, I thought about some of the most important people in my family (besides my husband and children, of course)—my parents and my 90-year-old grandmother.

My parents live in rural South Dakota and have enjoyed surfing the Internet each time they visit our house. My mom used the Internet to trace her family roots, and my dad went house-hunting online (they've been wanting to move closer to the grandkids for years). Both parents often found using the mouse on our computers frustrating and intimidating and would give up after a short time. Since I installed WebTV Network and its easy-to-use remote control, however, I've been able to leave my mom alone to surf into the wee hours of the morning. Now she can't wait to start surfing from her own home, and thanks to WebTV Network's OpenISP option (described in chapter 5), she'll be able to connect without all the long-distance phone charges. (Mom will be finding a WebTV Internet terminal under her Christmas tree. Shh!) And I'm betting that within a month she'll be conversing regularly with other cat lovers around the world using e-mail.

Ask people who have been surfing for a while whether they've helped or been helped by someone they met on the Net. Or ask them if they've made any new buddies. If they've been surfing for six months or more and say no to both of these questions, I'd be greatly surprised. In my years on the Internet, I've helped a new friend in Oklahoma incorporate the nonprofit organization she founded; exchanged childbirth stories with an e-pal in Australia; talked about kids and diecast cars with a fellow mom in New Zealand; kept up with old high school and college friends in Minnesota and Massachusetts; traded collectibles with collectors across the country; even received articles for my son and daughter's nursery school newsletter, which I edit.

I make no secret of it; I'm a big supporter of the wonders of the Internet. Do you have a favorite story about your involvement with the WebTV Network and the Internet? I'd love to hear it! Send an e-mail note to *netwriter@webtv.net* and tell me all about it. Maybe I'll even post your story on my Web page dedicated to this book at *www.justpc.com*.

So What Is a Cybercommunity, Anyway?

Cybercommunity is a fancy word for a relatively simple concept: A cybercommunity can be any of a number of things. It can be a discussion group whose culture and personality have evolved over time. It can be a group of people who meet regularly in a chatroom. It can even be a number of people who contribute to an online magazine.

A cybercommunity isn't much different from the neighborhood you live in—you have a group of people that you get to know over time, and you form a bond based on your interests or values.

How do you find cybercommunities? If you're willing to get involved, they sort of find you. The communities come about naturally, and being a member can only happen if you're willing to take part in the group. As you get deeper and deeper into the Internet, you learn the attitudes of the groups you participate in and you become adept at conversing within the groups, even if you don't agree with the attitudes.

Chapter 13

Traffic Jams and Other Roadblocks

Sometimes surfing the Internet bears a great resemblance to driving in a huge metropolitan area during rush hour—it's slow going and, yes, unfortunate things can happen. When bad things do happen, standard Web browsers display cryptic error messages. Often the information in these messages doesn't tell you what to do next or how to fix the problem. Luckily, the WebTV Network demystifies the error messages by showing on-screen guidance for rectifying the problem. (See Figure 13-1 and Figure 13-2 on the following page.)

In this chapter, you will see some of the problems that might occur while using your WebTV Internet terminal. While the WebTV Network's WebTV Customer Care staff is always available to help, these pages might just save you a phone call.

WebTV Basics

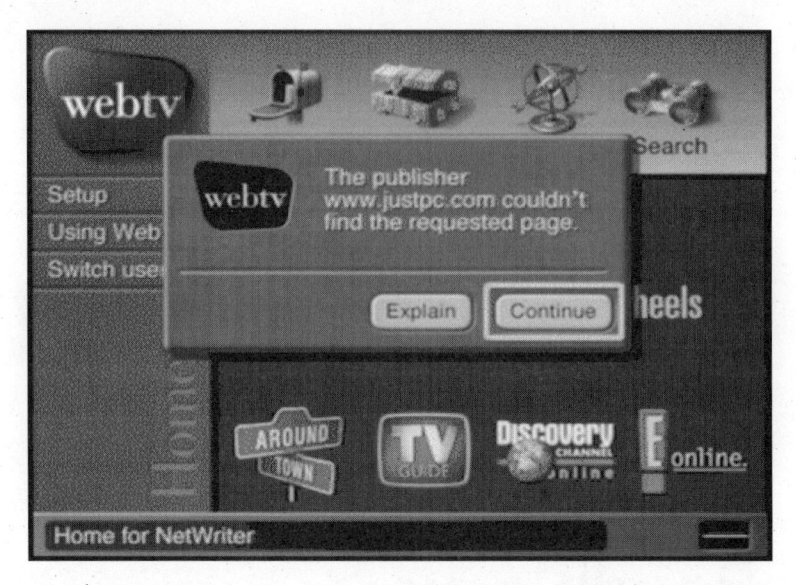

Figure 13-1.   When a problem occurs, a message like the one shown in this figure appears. You can either request an explanation or go back to the previous screen.

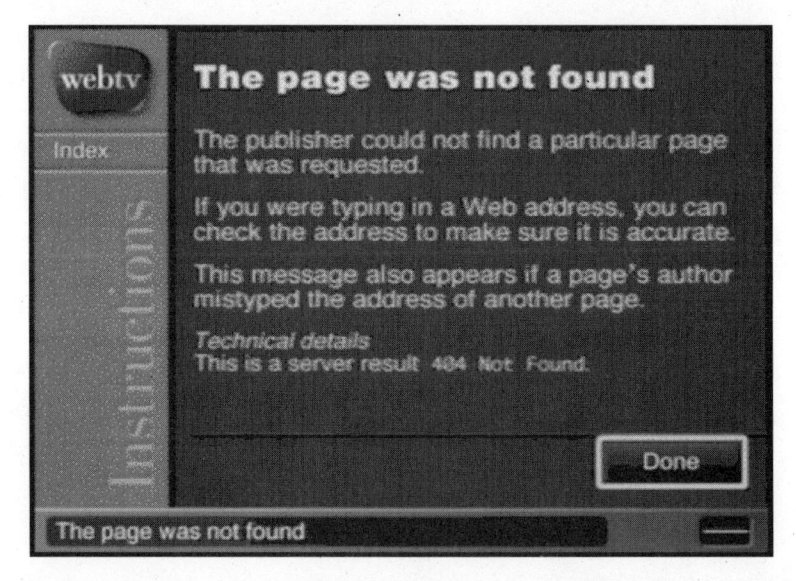

Figure 13-2.   The explanation you receive gives you tips for dealing with the problem.

Red Alert!

Well, not exactly a red alert, but these error messages can be cause for wonder from time to time. As you're bopping along from one Web page to another, you might see a little box pop up with a message containing apparent gibberish. If you think the WebTV Network messages are mysterious, be thankful you're not using a regular computer. There you'll see messages like "403 Forbidden." At least the WebTV Network's "Access is restricted" is a little less intimidating and a little more self-explanatory. The following sections explain most of the messages you'll encounter.

Where, Oh Where...

The "page was not found" notice, shown in Figure 13-2, means that the computer publishing the Web page you are trying to access could not find the page you requested. If you entered a URL manually, the first thing you'll want to do is double-check the address you entered to make sure that it was entered correctly. To do this, follow these steps:

1. Select Options.
2. Select Go To, and then press Go.
3. Select Show Last, and then press Go again.
4. The URL in error appears. Check its spelling while keeping in mind that sometimes the text after the *.com*, *.edu*, or whatever can be case sensitive. That means that something as simple as typing "igloo" instead of "Igloo" could cause the error.
5. If all is well with the URL, the problem could have occurred because the Webmaster mistyped the address in a link to the page. In that instance, you might want to drop a quick note to the Web page's author mentioning the problem.

Anybody Out There?

You'll see the "publisher can't be reached" message if the computer publishing the page you want to view is down for service or is otherwise inaccessible. The best thing to do in this instance is to wait a little while and then try reaching the site again.

Something Suddenly Came Up

If you see the "problem came up while communicating" alert, it means that the connection between the publisher of the page and the WebTV Network was suddenly disconnected. This usually signifies a problem with the publisher's computers or the Internet; therefore, it's likely to take longer to clear up than some of the other alerts.

Technical Difficulties—Please Stand By

The "WebTV technical problem" message means that for some reason the WebTV Network was unable to provide the page you requested. While this error message might eventually go away on its own, you should write the folks at *wecare@webtv.net* if the error message persists. Be sure to include in your note the complete URL of the page you're having trouble with.

Keep Out!

Corporations or government agencies might place some restricted information on the Internet for their employees to access. Should you stumble onto such a site, you'll see an "access restricted" message. (If you were using a computer, you might simply see "403 Forbidden.") Generally, these errors won't go away if you attempt to access the site again, so your time is best spent elsewhere.

I Think I Can, I Think I Can

If you see a message saying, "Most Web addresses begin http://—WebTV cannot visit the address chosen" (see Figure 13-3), it means that you've specified a URL prefix unknown to the WebTV Network. Retrying will not rectify this situation, so you'll have to move on.

TECHNOBABBLE   URL prefix—Prefixes like *http*, *ftp*, *mailto*, and so on are known as URL prefixes. They tell the computer or WebTV Internet terminal what type of information you're trying to retrieve.

13: Traffic Jams and Other Roadblocks

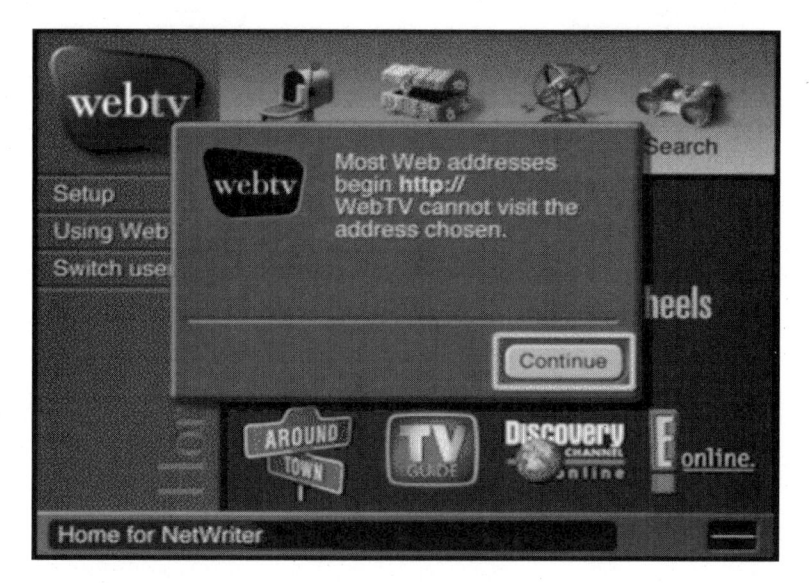

Figure 13-3. *If you see this message, you've specified a URL prefix unknown to the WebTV Network.*

Nobody's Home

Getting a "publisher is unknown" notice (see Figure 13-4 on the following page) usually happens when you mistype a Web page's URL. It means that the publisher you requested does not exist. In rare instances, this message will appear if an Internet site has not renewed its domain registration. The best fix here is to try accessing the page again after confirming its spelling or, if you followed a link, report the problem to the site's Webmaster. In many cases, the Webmaster's address might appear on screen when you encounter a problem. If it doesn't, however, you can usually reach the Webmaster by sending an e-mail message addressed to *webmaster@*, followed by the domain of the site you tried to reach. For example, if you had trouble accessing one of NASCAR Online's features, you might try sending a note to *webmaster@nascar.com*.

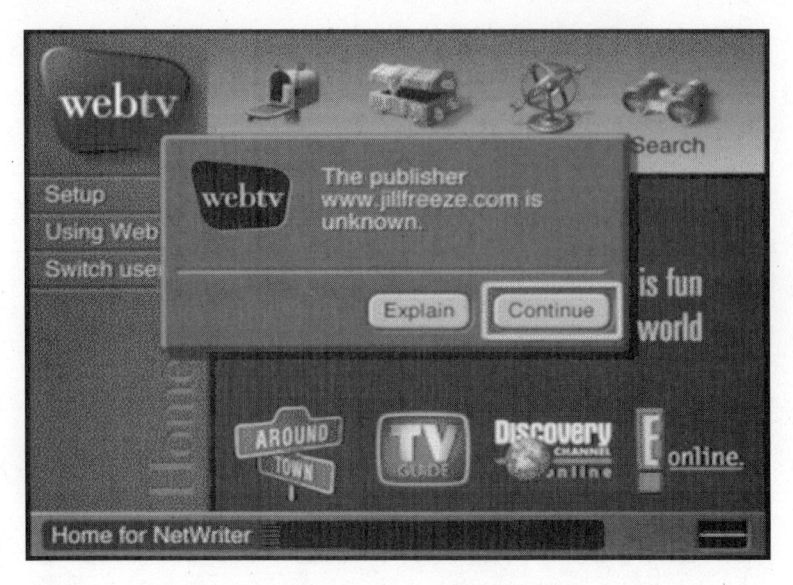

Figure 13-4. *If you mistype a URL or if the address is not registered, you will see this notice. (I'm glad to see no one has taken my domain name!)*

Busy, Busy, Busy

If you most often surf the Internet after getting the kids to school in the middle of the morning or after an early dinner, you might encounter a "publisher is too busy" alert. This means that too many people are trying to contact the publisher at the same time. The good news is that this error is likely to disappear after a retry or two.

Odd Messages

Undoubtedly one of the weirder alert notices, the "publisher responded in an odd way" message means that while your WebTV Internet terminal was trying to communicate with the publisher's computer, that computer responded in a, well, odd way. Most frequently, phone line noise is the culprit, but it can also happen if a Web page contains some sort of mistake. It's worth attempting to access the page again, however, since this error has been known to go away on its own.

More Technical Difficulties?

You've seen the WebTV Network technical problem message; well, here's the publisher technical problem alert. The "publisher technical problem" message (see Figure 13-5) says that the publisher's computer experienced a technical problem while trying to deliver the page to you. While this error is not likely to go away on its own, you might want to try accessing the page again for the heck of it. If the error message persists, you might want to try sending an e-mail note to the site's Webmaster.

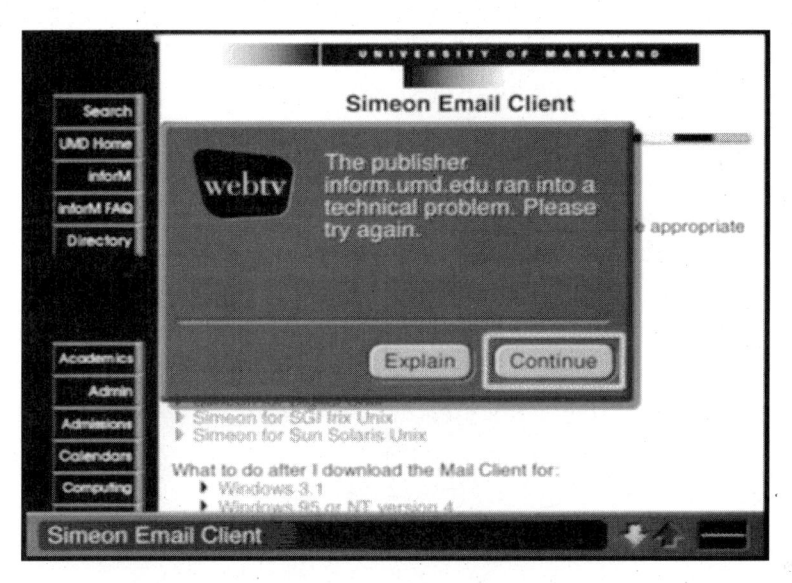

Figure 13-5. *This message will be displayed if the publisher's computer encounters a technical difficulty while transferring a page.*

The Case of the Missing Host

Each URL has a host name. In the case of *www.justpc.com/books*, the host name is *www.justpc.com*. If any part of the host name is missing, you will see the "missing host name" alert notice. Check the URL you entered, and then complete the host name if necessary. If it turns out you didn't remember the complete host name or perhaps wrote it down incorrectly, you might want to try using a search engine to find the site based on any information you remember. (For more information on how to do this, see Chapter 21, "Become a Virtual Bloodhound.")

Forbidden Territory

The "publisher refuses access" message might mean you have attempted to retrieve a page unavailable to you. For instance, many sites require you to register before you can get to the meat of their offerings. There isn't usually a fee, but your registration information does give the site administrators a good idea of who they're serving, which might, in turn, be leveraged to lure advertisers to subsidize their work.

This is one of those error messages that won't disappear unless you become a registered user of the site.

What Do I Do with This?

The "address missing first part" notice is very similar to the bad address error described in the "I Think I Can, I Think I Can" section, but in this case, the *http*, the *mailto*, or other URL prefix is simply missing. Use the steps presented earlier to double-check the address if you entered it manually.

Virtual Gridlock During Rush Hour

If you think the freeway is crowded when you come home from work, you ain't seen nothin' yet! Wait until you try to access the Internet during peak surfing hours. Pages that snap immediately into view on a Sunday morning can load at a snail's pace during the early evening hours. And try as they might, ISPs can't solve the problem quickly enough by simply installing a few more phone lines.

What's a person to do? Try connecting to the Internet during less busy hours, like before 9 a.m. or after 11 p.m. These times enable you to connect before the business day kicks into gear or after eager young surfers have gone to bed.

As long as we rely solely on phone lines for transmitting data, we'll always be somewhat limited in capacity. It's like hosting the Olympics in a rural town that has only gravel two-lane highways—the infrastructure simply cannot accommodate the demand. The good news is that all kinds of alternatives (like cable modems) are in the early stages of development, so things are definitely looking up. In the meantime, take advantage of those relatively quiet times to maximize your surfing pleasure.

The WebTV Network, Unplugged

If you get the "phone line seems to be in use" message (see Figure 13-6), it can mean one of two things: someone else in the house is using your phone, or the phone cord is not plugged into your Internet terminal. If no one is using the phone, check the cord's connection to your Internet terminal. Obviously, if the cord isn't plugged in, you need to do so in order to connect. If it appears to be plugged in, check to make sure that the cord is securely in place. The ends of the cord are fragile and can sometimes break, especially if you repeatedly plug it into and unplug it from your Internet terminal. Fortunately, a replacement can be as close as your nearest dollar store, discount department store, or electronics store.

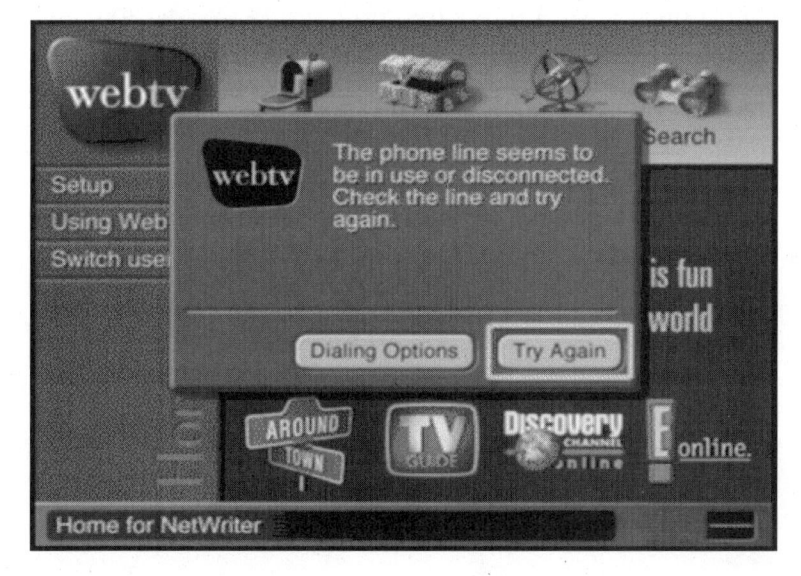

Figure 13-6. *This error is one of the easiest to resolve since it usually entails getting someone off the phone or plugging in the phone cord.*

Don't Try This at Home

Your WebTV Internet terminal has a lot of features, but there are some things it still can't do, at least at this point. After all, the more functions a gizmo can perform, the trickier it becomes to operate and the more there is that can go wrong. Think of an audio CD changer. It's easy to control a single CD, but once you start using a changer, it sometimes seems impossible to program without an engineering degree: CDs fall out of place, eliminating them from the play list; the unit gets jammed...you get the picture. Anyway, because your Internet terminal isn't quite a computer, there are some limitations to what you can do.

You can't download games or other applications because there's nowhere to store them in your WebTV Internet terminal. "But my WebTV Plus Internet terminal has a hard drive," you say? Well, that's true, but that hard drive is dedicated to storing frequently used Web pages, which means faster Web page loading and more full-motion video.

You might come across some glitzy Java Web pages in your Net travels. Unfortunately, your Internet terminal can't deal with them at this point. But the good news is that the WebTV Internet terminal is easy to upgrade, so it's possible that you could see these features within a few short months.

> **TECHNOBABBLE Java**—No, it's not that thick, tarry beverage you consume during late-night surfing sessions. In this case, Java is actually a programming language that adds advanced functions and animation to Web pages.

If you run across a file type that your Internet terminal can't handle, drop a note to *wecare@webtv.net* to let them know what it is and to ask them if there are any plans to support such a file type in the future. The more people who inquire about such features, the more likely it is that WebTV Networks will incorporate them into a future upgrade.

Chapter 14

Push Your WebTV Internet Terminal to the Limit

All the chapters in this book look at things you can do with your Internet terminal no matter what flavor of the WebTV Internet terminal (Classic or Plus) you've chosen to purchase. This particular chapter, however, takes a look at printing from your WebTV Internet terminal and enhancing your television-viewing experience—both of which require some additional investment beyond the basic WebTV Classic setup.

Even if you aren't currently equipped to print or to interact with your TV via the WebTV Network, you might find that reading this chapter will be helpful in determining whether it's worth it to buy a printer adapter or to make the upgrade to WebTV Plus.

A Printout's Worth a Thousand Words

Imagine printing the color picture of your new grandchild that your daughter posted on her Web site, making a hard copy of that yummy pork lo mein recipe you found on a discussion group, or printing an invaluable resource for your dissertation. There are thousands of compelling reasons why the ability to print from the WebTV Internet terminal was a much anticipated new feature.

In Chapter 3, "Before You Buy a WebTV Internet Terminal," I showed you all the WebTV Network–supported printers and parts you'd need, whether you have WebTV Classic or WebTV Plus. In this section, I'll show you how to set your printing options and get the highest quality output.

Get Set Up to Do the Job

The first thing you'll need to do is define which printer you're using. To do this, follow these steps:

1. Starting from the WebTV Network home page, select Using WebTV and then press Go.
2. Select Settings, and then press Go.
3. Select Printing, and then press Go.
4. Select Printer Setup, and then press Go. The Printer Setup screen shown in Figure 14-1 appears.
5. Select the gray printer drop-down box, and press Go to see a list of supported printers. This is also a quick and easy way to see what printers are supported by the WebTV Network at any given time because new printers are continually being released. This screen could come in handy should you decide to purchase a new printer down the road.

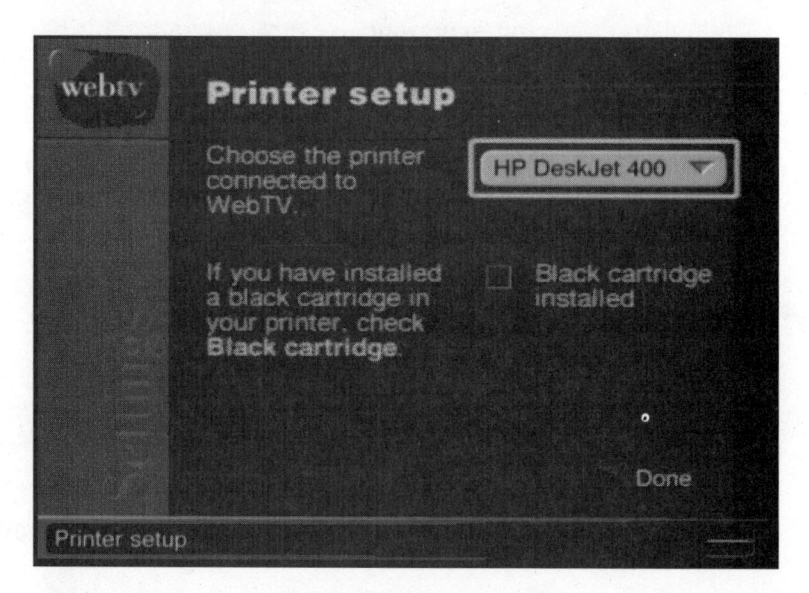

Figure 14-1. *The Printer Setup screen will guide you through the process of hooking up your printer.*

6. Use the arrows to scroll down the list until the appropriate printer is highlighted.

7. Press Go to confirm the selection.

8. If you've installed a black cartridge in your printer rather than a color cartridge, be sure to place a checkmark in the box next to "Black cartridge installed."

9. Select Done, and then press Go to complete the setup.

You Gotta Have Options!

You'll want to be familiar with some of the printing options. You can access them by executing steps 1 and 2 from the previous list, or by pressing the Options button, selecting Print, and then selecting Printing Options. The Printing Options screen in Figure 14-2 shows you the three options currently available.

To put an option into effect, simply place a checkmark in the box next to the appropriate option. Although you can easily tweak these settings at any time, you'll find that you'll rarely change them after the initial setup. But hey, it's nice to know you have options.

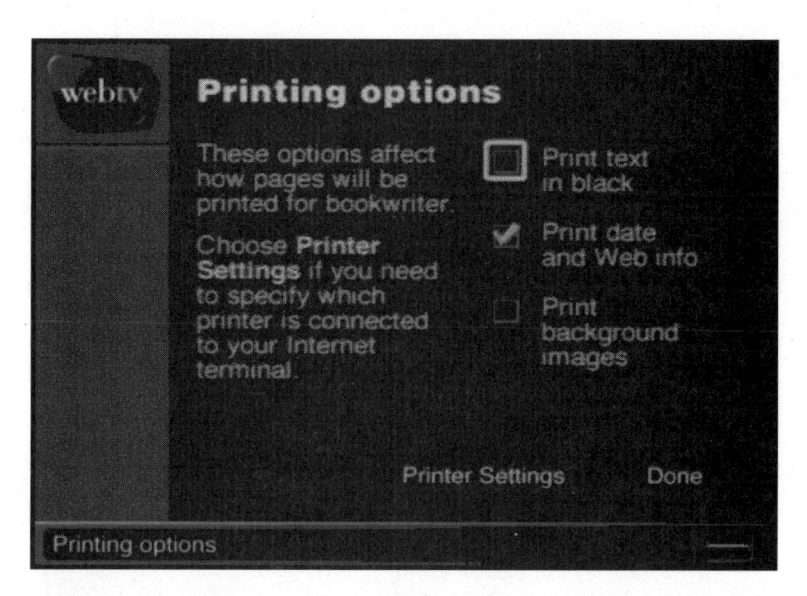

Figure 14-2. *The Printing Options screen gives you full control of your output.*

So what exactly do all these options mean? Let's take a closer look.

- **Print Text In Black.** As you know from Net surfing, most Web pages do not consist of standard black text on a crisp white background. The pages you use to navigate through the WebTV Network are a prime example. Checking the Print Text In Black option enables you to generate standard printer output from even the most colorful of Web pages. Selecting this option conserves toner, too. Imagine how quickly the printouts of some of the WebTV Network's yellow-on-black pages would eat up your printer cartridge.

- **Print Date And Web Info.** Placing a checkmark in this box instructs your Internet terminal to include the date and URL of the Web site you're printing as a small header on the page. This is especially useful when referring to Web information for research. This option allows you to quickly go back to the source to verify that the information is still accurate at a later date. I can't tell you how many unidentifiable printouts I have scattered throughout my house. This is one of those small details that could end up saving your sanity at some frantic point.

- **Print Background Images.** This option is another toner-saving tactic. While background images can be pleasing to the eye, they can really muddle a printer's output. In most cases, you'll want to keep this option disabled to conserve printer supplies and to maintain the legibility of your printout.

Once you've made your selections, select Done and then press Go to lock in your choices.

Ready, Set, Print!

With your WebTV Internet terminal, you have the ability to print either the entire Web page or just the part seen on your TV screen.

To print the entire Web page, press Options, select Print, and then press Go to call up the Print panel shown in Figure 14-3. Confirm that Print is selected, and then press Go. Within a few moments, you'll see the printout you requested.

14: Push Your WebTV Internet Terminal to the Limit

Figure 14-3. *The Print panel lets you print the entire Web page, print the part of the Web page displayed on your TV screen, or set new print options.*

> **TIP** Wireless keyboard owners can press cmd+P as a printing command shortcut.

If you want to print only the part of the page showing on your television screen, press Options, select Print, press Go, and then select Print Screen from the Print panel. Press Go to send your output to the printer.

What you see is not always what you'll get. Take Web page text for instance. Many Web pages use unusual fonts in all kinds of sizes. Because your printer uses fonts that are smaller than those displayed with your Internet terminal, the Web page will be reformatted using these smaller fonts.

Interestingly, there are fewer differences in what you see versus what you get if you opt to print the screen rather than the whole Web page. This is because the print screen command doesn't reformat the text on the screen before sending your output to the printer.

153

WebTV Plus—The Ultimate TV Experience

Have you ever watched TV and wondered if there was a Web site with additional information about your favorite show? Have you ever caught a glimpse of a commercial and wished you could get more details about the product? Have you ever wanted to check to see if tonight's episode of *Party of Five* is a rerun? WebTV Plus can help you do all that and more.

In the sections that follow, I'll show you how to set up your WebTV Plus options and extend your television viewing experience in ways never before possible.

Get Your Options Straight

When a WebTV Plus user turns on the Internet terminal, the first thing that appears is the TV Home screen shown in Figure 14-4.

Figure 14-4. *TV Home is the WebTV Plus owner's launchpad to state-of-the-art TV surfing.*

To get the most out of the WebTV Network's newest functions, you'll want to make sure that your options are set correctly, or that they at least reflect your television viewing preferences. To begin setting the options, make sure that the TV Home screen is displayed on your TV. Select the Settings button and then press Go to see the options displayed in Figure 14-5.

154

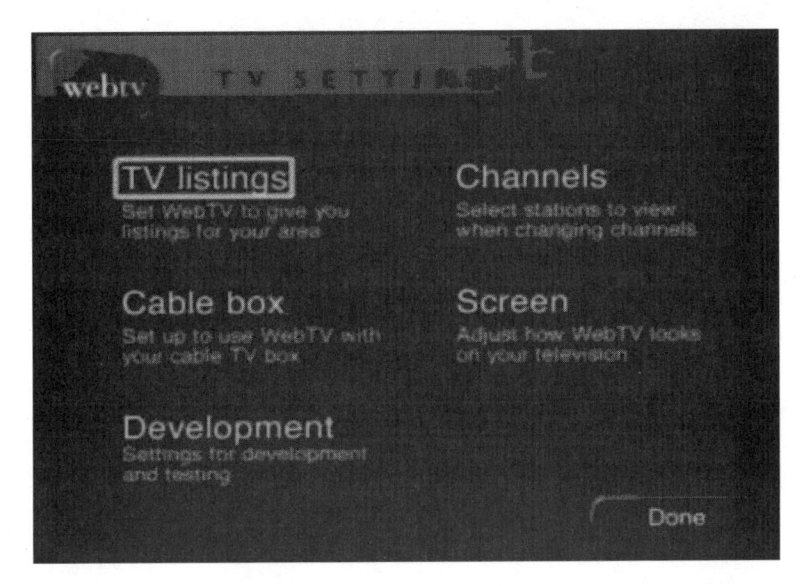

Figure 14-5. *Work your way through each of the items shown to get your TV and Internet terminal optimized for using WebTV Plus.*

Tweak the TV Listings

Select the TV Listings option from the TV Settings page to retrieve the correct TV programming information for your area. You'll set three options on the TV Listings option screen shown in Figure 14-6.

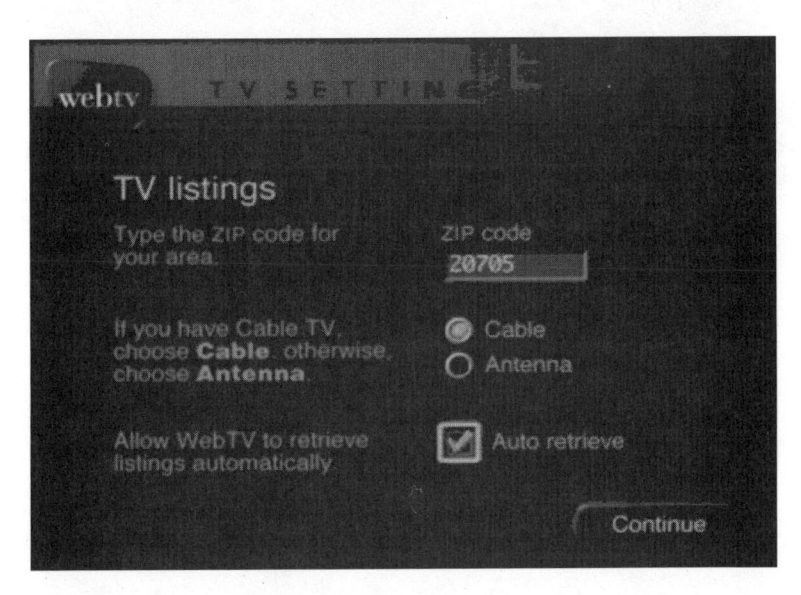

Figure 14-6. *Use this screen to set your WebTV Plus to your preferred TV viewing options.*

The first item you'll see is a text box into which you'll enter your ZIP code. The WebTV Network will pull the ZIP code over from your billing information, so all you'll most likely need to do is verify that what's shown is correct.

The second option entails specifying whether your TV receives its signal from a cable or an antenna. Select the appropriate choice, and then press Go.

Finally, you can tell your Internet terminal to connect and get local listings each day so that TV surfing is always just a click away. If a checkmark is placed in this box, your Internet terminal will fetch local listings each day at the time specified on your "Get Listings" page. While this is a great idea if you always want the current information available instantly, it might not be desirable if you have to switch the phone jack from the Internet terminal to a telephone. (But that's where the line splitter that was included with your Internet terminal comes in handy.)

When you've set these options, you can select Update to download the latest programming information. You might also want to make a mental note of when WebTV Networks says it will perform your daily download. (See Figure 14-7.)

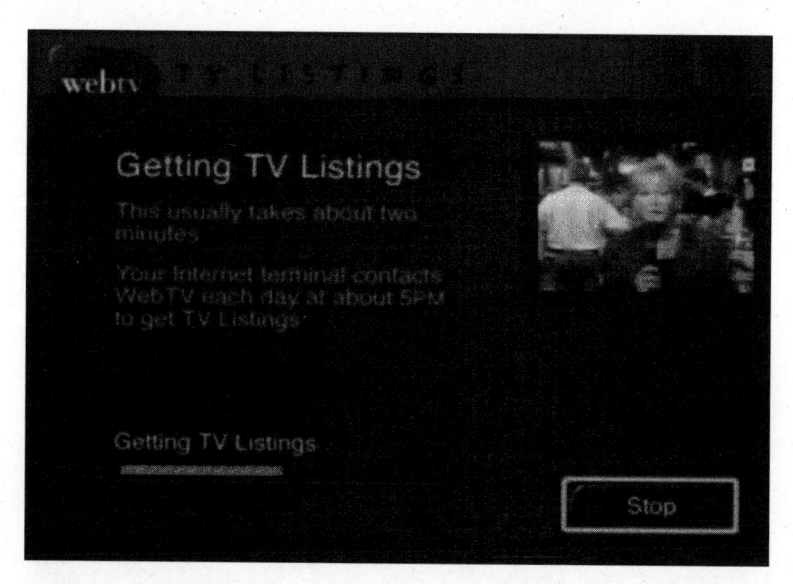

Figure 14-7. *While downloading the current television listings, you can see when your Internet terminal plans to fetch them each day.*

Connect with Your Cable Box

Those of you who use a cable box will want to set these options to make sure that your Internet terminal can communicate with your cable box. From the TV Settings page shown in Figure 14-5 on page 155, select the Cable Box option to be guided through a series of screens that you'll need to program your Internet terminal.

The first screen merely verifies that you use a cable box. Place a checkmark in the Cable Box box, select Continue, and then press Go.

In the second screen, you'll specify the manufacturer of your cable box. To do this, select the Manufacturer drop-down list box (see Figure 14-8), press Go, and use the arrow keys to make your selection. When you've highlighted the manufacturer name, press Go. Select Continue and press Go to move to the next screen, where you'll specify the model name of your cable box. Use the same method you used to select the manufacturer of your cable box. Select Continue, and press Go.

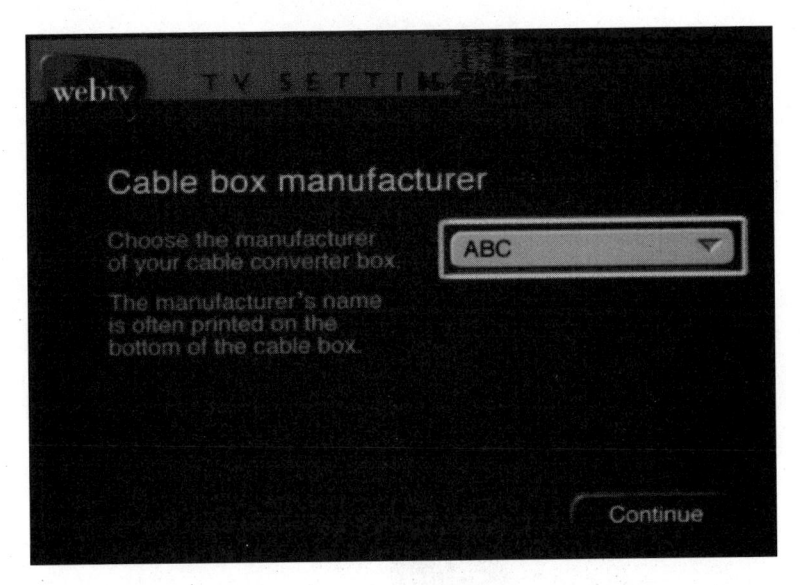

Figure 14-8. *WebTV Networks makes it easy to select the manufacturer of your cable box—simply choose from the list provided.*

WebTV Basics

Next comes your cable box configuration. The WebTV Internet terminal uses an IR Shooter to select channels on your cable box. (Consult your Internet terminal owner's manual for more information on how this IR Shooter should be used in your personal electronics configuration, or refer back to Chapter 4, "Anatomy of a WebTV Internet Terminal," for more information.) Because WebTV Plus works so closely with your cable box, you must tell the WebTV Plus Internet terminal how your cable box broadcasts its signal—on channel 3, on channel 4, or using Video Out. Most cable buyers broadcast from channel 3, the channel to which you tune your TV to use the cable box successfully. Select Continue to move on.

The screen shown in Figure 14-9 is used to test your cable box settings. Simply select each channel to make sure your channels change correctly. If they do, select Done. If they don't, consider going back to adjust your cable box settings and confirm the necessity and installation of the IR Shooter.

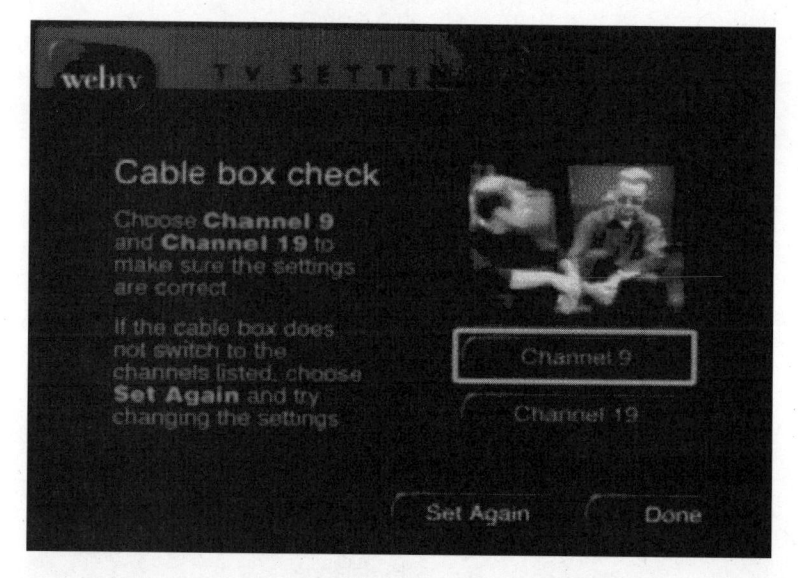

Figure 14-9. *Use this screen to test whether your cable box is working correctly with the Internet terminal.*

Customize Your Channel Surfing

We all have channels we almost never watch. Don't you wish you could just skip over them while channel surfing? With WebTV Plus, you can do just that. From the TV Settings screen, select the Channels option. You'll see a screen like the one shown in Figure 14-10.

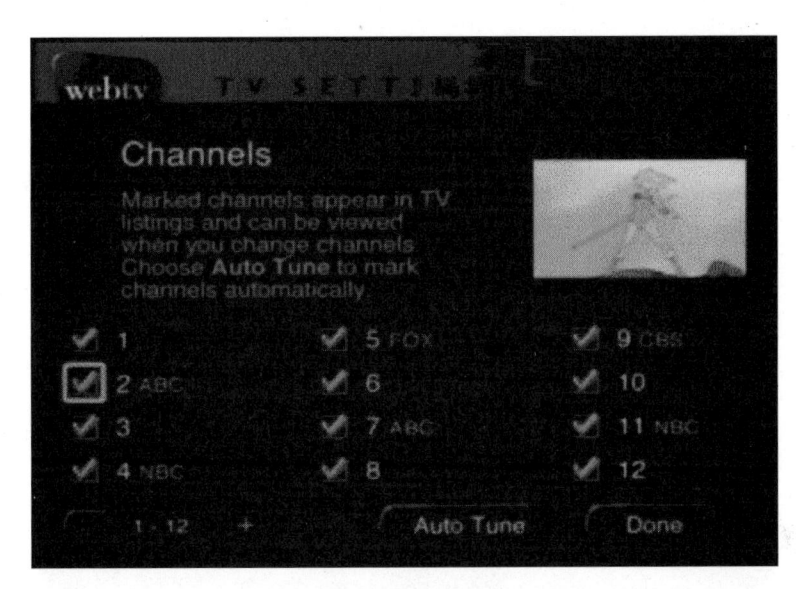

Figure 14-10. *Use this screen to pick and choose the channels you'll watch most often.*

You can choose your channels in one of three ways: by default, which leaves all channels on your list; by manually selecting and deselecting the channels you want to view; or by pressing Auto Tune, which tells the WebTV Network to search for channels broadcasting TV signals and then to remove the unavailable channels from the list.

If you're manually choosing channels, use the plus and minus signs at the bottom left of the screen to display additional ranges of channels. Select Done to begin your custom channel surfing.

Adjust the Picture

The Screen option on the TV Settings page enables you to fine-tune the WebTV Network image on your television set. This series of screens is identical to the screens found on the WebTV Network's home page, which was described in detail in Chapter 7, "It's a Setup."

TV Home—Your Home Base for WebTV Plus Channel Surfing

As mentioned earlier, the TV Home screen shown in Figure 14-4 is what you'll see when you power up your WebTV Plus Internet terminal. Because these TV-related features work primarily with your cable box or local TV channels, the Internet terminal doesn't need to link up to the Internet in order to use these features. You will, however, need to dial in to the Internet if you see the Retrieve TV Listings button underneath the TV picture. (Note that this button will appear only if you have not enabled the automatic program listing fetching option.) Just select this button, press Go, and your Internet terminal does the rest.

Some other elements of TV Home you'll want to be familiar with include the following:

- **WebTV Plus Logo.** Select this icon to be transported to the WebTV Network home page.

- **Web Home.** This button on the left side of the screen takes you to the WebTV Network home page, which is the same on both the WebTV Classic and the WebTV Plus. This Web Home page still acts as your launchpad to the Internet.

> **TIP** Press the View button twice to toggle between TV Home and Web Home.

- **Settings.** This button is used to set up and customize your TV viewing preferences.

- **TV Listings.** Press this button to retrieve or view television listings. (See Figure 14-11 and Figure 14-12, respectively.)

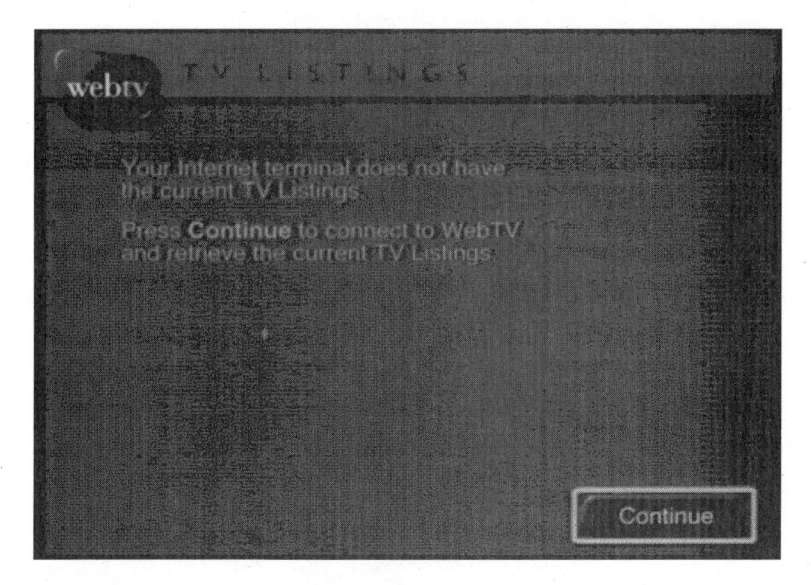

14: Push Your WebTV Internet Terminal to the Limit

Figure 14-11. *If you press the TV Listings button and see this screen, you'll need to download current listings for your Internet terminal.*

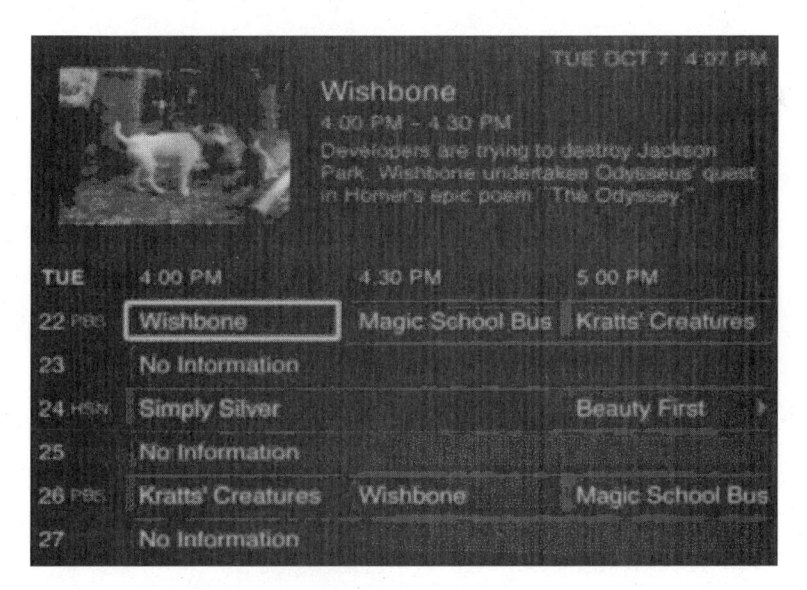

Figure 14-12. *If current listings are available on your Internet terminal, you'll see this television programming grid.*

161

- **Picture Screen.** Select this button and press Go to view the program in full-screen view. To return to TV Home, press the Back button. To move to the WebTV Network home page, press View.

- **Retrieve TV Listings Button/Program Information.** This button performs the same function as the TV Listings button. It will appear below the television picture if no local information is available. If local television listings have been downloaded, you will see program information for the current TV show, including the show's name and air time. If you see a blue "i" icon next to the program information, you can select the icon and press Go to be transported to a Web site related to the program. This is known as a TV Crossover Link.

- **Channel Number.** Select this option and use the arrows to move up and down the channels on your view list, or press Go to see the program.

- **A/B Switch.** Those residing in locations with A-side and B-side cable can use these buttons to choose the desired option. (This applies only to communities that have two coaxial cables for their cable system. You can tell that A-side and B-side cable is relatively uncommon by the lack of universal remote controls that have A and B buttons.)

- **Favorite Channels.** You can use this button to select up to eight of your favorite television channels to store at the bottom of the screen. This allows you to quickly jump from one favorite channel to another without having to scroll through the entire list of channels in sequence.

Move Through Proper Channels

To change channels while using your WebTV Plus, you can use one of the following methods:

- Select the channel number on the TV Home page, and then use the arrows to move up and down through the numbers.

- While in full-screen TV viewing mode, use the arrows to move up and down your viewing list.

- Pull up the TV listing grid (described in the following section), select a show you want to watch, and then press Go to jump to that channel.

- Select any of the favorite channels presented at the bottom of your screen, and then press Go to move to that channel.

Save a Favorite Channel

To save a favorite channel to your list, view that channel and then press the Options button. Select Save Channel, and then press Go. The number of the station will appear at the bottom of your TV Home screen. If the channel was previously saved as a favorite, you will have the option to remove it from your list.

NOTE You can save up to eight channels as favorites. Five of them will appear at the bottom of the screen at one time. You can view the remaining three channels by using your arrows to scroll left or right through the list after you've highlighted one of the channels.

Browse the TV Listings

If you haven't set up your Internet terminal to automatically download each day's TV listings, you can retrieve them by selecting the Retrieve TV Listings button on the TV Home page, and then pressing Go, or you can select the TV Listings button and then press Go. Just select Continue and press Go to perform the download.

Once the current listings are available on your Internet terminal, you can view them by selecting the TV Listings button from the TV Home page. A large television programming grid will appear. Television shows that have already started are displayed on a green background, while all others are displayed on a dark blue background.

The TV grid page also includes program information and a small screen preview of the selected program. Use the arrows to highlight the program you're interested in. When the program is highlighted on the grid, you can view the program description and the small screen preview to decide whether you want to watch the show. Press Go for the full-screen view of the program.

If you're watching a program and it looks vaguely familiar, you can press the Options button, select Program Info, and then press Go to see an information screen like the one shown in Figure 14-13 on the following page. The information presented might help you determine whether the show's a rerun so that you can use your valuable television viewing time on other programs of interest. Or maybe you don't like the program at all. Press the Options button, select TV Listings, and then press Go. You'll have instant access to the TV grid for choosing another show.

Figure 14-13. *The Program Information screen can help you decide whether you want to continue watching a show.*

Another element that might appear on the Program Information screen is the Information icon. Select this TV Crossover Link to instruct your Internet terminal to connect you to a Web site related to the current show. For example, one night I was watching the movie *Beaches*. The additional information icon took me to a comprehensive Web site with all kinds of information about the movie, from cast lists on down. It was a great way to enhance my television viewing experience, and I can't think of a better way to spend my commercial breaks!

Do Two Things at Once: WebPIP

Suppose you find some great stuff on the Web site related to the show you're watching and want to continue browsing, but you'd like to keep watching the show, too. Consider using the WebPIP feature. Even if your TV doesn't

14: Push Your WebTV Internet Terminal to the Limit

have picture-in-picture capability, the WebTV Plus Internet terminal will do it for you. While surfing the Net, press the View button once to see a small TV picture at the bottom right-hand corner of the screen. (See Figure 14-14.)

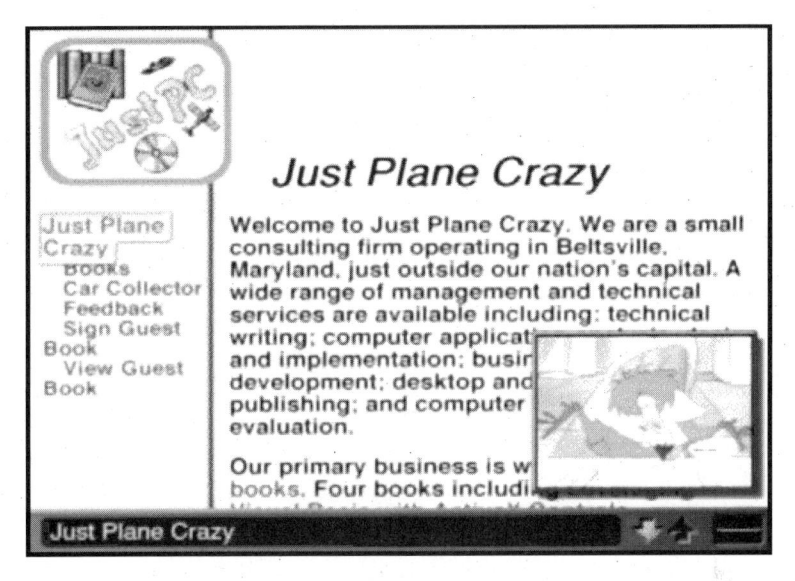

Figure 14-14. *WebTV Plus' WebPIP capability allows you to do two things at once.*

Of course, WebPIP works with any Web site—it needn't be one you were referred to via a TV Crossover Link. So go ahead and research your trip to Walt Disney World while taking in your favorite TV sitcom. Time is scarce enough as it is, so you might as well do two things at once!

PART 3

Internet Culture

Chapter

15 Netiquette, the Rules of the Road — 169

16 BTW, About Those Abbreviations and Emoticons :-) — 185

17 Safety in Numbers (and in User Names) — 193

18 All That Glitters Is Not Gold — 203

Chapter 15

Netiquette, the Rules of the Road

Now that you're an expert on how the WebTV Network and the Internet work, it's time to examine the subtleties of life online. Venturing out on the information superhighway without knowing the rules of the road is like driving a Porsche on the crowded streets of New York City without knowing the meaning of street signs and traffic signals.

I'm not trying to scare you; it's pretty hard to get into trouble simply surfing the Web. It's not like the Internet police will pop out of your TV and handcuff you if you inadvertently violate one of these rules. But if you plan on participating in some of the discussion groups or you intend to make a few new e-pals, knowing these rules of the road will give you everything you need to establish a peaceful online presence. It'll also keep you from looking like a bumbling newbie, and that can be useful, too!

Even though this chapter is titled "Netiquette, the Rules of the Road," what are presented here are not iron-clad rules, but guidelines to something referred to as netiquette.

What Is Netiquette, Anyway?

Back when the Internet was in its infancy, all of its users shared a common background. They had to be computer scientists or researchers to gain access to the Internet. As the Internet grew, a common language and culture evolved. Netiquette—short for network etiquette—is the result of that growth.

Think of netiquette as the Internet equivalent to a regional culture and language. Let's take the United States as an example. My mainstay, Diet Coke, is called "pop" in South Dakota, where I grew up. In Massachusetts, where I went to college, "tonic" was often used to refer to the same beverage. Here in Maryland, "soda" is the preferred term. Internet language, including the emoticons and abbreviations we'll learn about in the next chapter, makes up a part of the Internet's culture. Together they form netiquette—the regional dialect for the Internet, if you will.

Trust me, I didn't come up with these guidelines. In 1995, the Responsible Use of the Network (RUN) Working Group of the Internet Engineering Task Force (IETF) drafted a document (known as RFC 1855) highlighting netiquette guidelines for a variety of users and environments. This document was written as a way to integrate the exploding number of inexperienced users as quickly as possible into the online culture.

For this chapter, I pulled out the items most relevant to the average user, translated them into plain English, and added easy-to-understand examples so that what you read here will be both useful and entertaining. For easy reference, I created "top 10" lists for each of the two major categories—e-mail and newsgroups.

> **NOTE** If you're a glutton for punishment—a person who always wants to learn more and more about a subject—you can find the whole collection of RFCs on the Web at *www.internic.net/ds/rfc-index.html*. You'll learn more than you ever wanted to know about how the Internet works and why things are done the way they are. But be forewarned—the reading isn't as entertaining as this chapter. In fact, it could be argued that the RFCs make a wonderful, drug-free alternative to sleeping pills.

Top 10 E-Mail Rules of the Road

E-mail is great for its immediacy, but like a letter written on paper, it can have its disadvantages. For example, unless you describe your emotions specifically, there's a lot of room for misinterpretation. In addition to pointing out some of these subtleties, the following guidelines illustrate some of the most common mistakes made by people new to the Internet.

> **NOTE** Many of the common mistakes outlined in this chapter also apply to discussion groups, but I've chosen not to repeat them to save space and to keep you from getting bored.

Rule 1. No Peeking!

Be careful what you write; it may come back to haunt you! The Internet is not a perfect place. As in the real world, it's possible that someone might try to sneak a peek at your correspondence. While the likelihood of that happening is pretty small, it's better to be safe than sorry. Use the following rule of thumb: if you'd feel uncomfortable putting a message's contents on a postcard and dropping it into a mailbox, you probably shouldn't e-mail it either.

Rule 2. Knock, Knock

Be sure to verify e-mail addresses before sending a long or personal message for the first time. Let's say you're trying to track down an old classmate by the name of Elise Sudbeck. On an e-mail name search site, you find an *esudbeck@webtv.net*, which you're pretty sure is her, but you can't be certain. Drop *esudbeck* a note mentioning your alma mater and your desire to get back in touch, and then wait for a response before getting personal. It's sort of the Internet equivalent to asking, "Who's there?" before answering your door late at night. Double-check who's at the other end before making yourself vulnerable.

Rule 3. I'm Sorry, I Thought…

Many e-mail addresses are made up of a person's first initial followed by their surname (or as much of it as will fit into the allotted space). Take my e-mail address, for example. I use *jfreeze@justpc.com* for personal e-mail.

My last name is short enough to fit in my ISP's eight-character limit as is. If my name were Donna Stephenson, however, I might have a little trouble—*dstephen* might cause some confusion for people trying to find me since it could just as easily stand for Dwight Stephens. This might force me to consider other alternatives such as *donnas* or even my job title *adviser@umass.edu*.

The point to remember is that there's no sure way to predict someone's e-mail address since Internet service providers can impose arbitrary and unpredictable naming requirements.

> **TECHNOBABBLE   USERID** (pronounced "user-I-D")—The technical term for the part of your e-mail address that comes before the @ sign.

Rule 4.   DON'T SHOUT!

One of the most common mistakes people new to the Internet make is to type their entire message in uppercase letters. My friend Tracy ventured out to a newsgroup to start a dialogue on TV violence. Her toddler managed to mess up her keyboard so that her message appeared in all uppercase letters. For nearly a week, her inbox was flooded with reprimands from self-appointed Internet police. I don't think she's resurfaced since. Because emotion and voice inflection are not always identifiable by words alone, capitalization has emerged as the notation of choice for shouting. Likewise, asterisks (*) are used around a word or phrase to denote emphasis, just as boldface or underlining is used in printed text. I can't *believe* anyone would write an entire message in capital letters. WHAT ARE THESE PEOPLE THINKING?!

Rule 5.   :-)

If you don't know what this symbol means, don't worry. You'll learn much more about smileys and other emoticons in the next chapter. For now, it serves as a gentle reminder to use emoticons to clarify potentially confusing statements. But use them sparingly to avoid diluting their effect. Smileys are like exclamation points: if you overuse them, you'll find yourself soon resorting to double smileys to communicate a higher level of emotion.

Rule 6.   Read Before You Reply

This rule is probably more relevant for workplace use than for leisure use of the Internet, but it's a good one to practice just the same. Before responding to any e-mail, check the other messages in your inbox. You might find that a person who asked for help or advice in one message has solved his or her problem before you even got online, and he or she might have sent a second note saying so. Checking multiple messages from the same person before responding to any of them could save you a lot of time.

It's also a good idea to scan the header of the message before responding to make sure you were the primary recipient of the e-mail. You might have been copied on a note directed to someone else. Figure 15-1 illustrates a normal header.

In this case, *goose@justpc.com* is the primary recipient; *bookwriter@weekly.webtv.net* is the sender; and *wfreeze@accmail.umd.edu* also receives a copy.

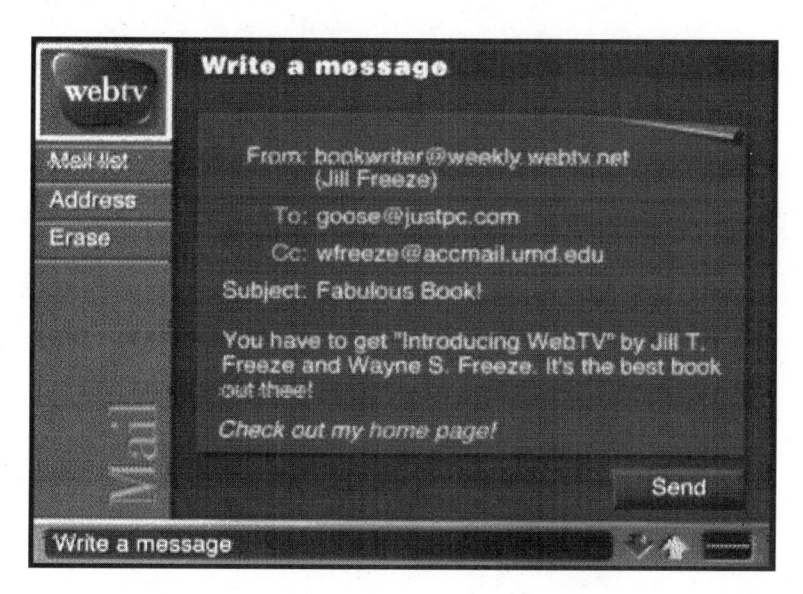

Figure 15-1.   *This screen shows a normal e-mail message header.*

Rule 7. Sign on the Dotted Line

Remember those e-mail headers I told you to check so diligently before responding to a message? Well, some e-mail programs and newsreaders strip them out, showing no visible return address. While most modern applications keep this information visible, you might want to create a signature file that is automatically appended to your messages. (To learn how to do this with your WebTV Internet terminal, see Chapter 8, "E-Mail 101.") This further identifies you as the author of the message or post, which can prove helpful if the information is unavailable in the header.

A word about signatures: think of them as a business card. Include only pertinent information (real name, e-mail address, and so on), and try not to exceed four lines. Longer, more elaborate signatures take additional time to download.

Instead of using a signature like the one in Figure 15-2, consider using a signature like the one in Figure 15-3.

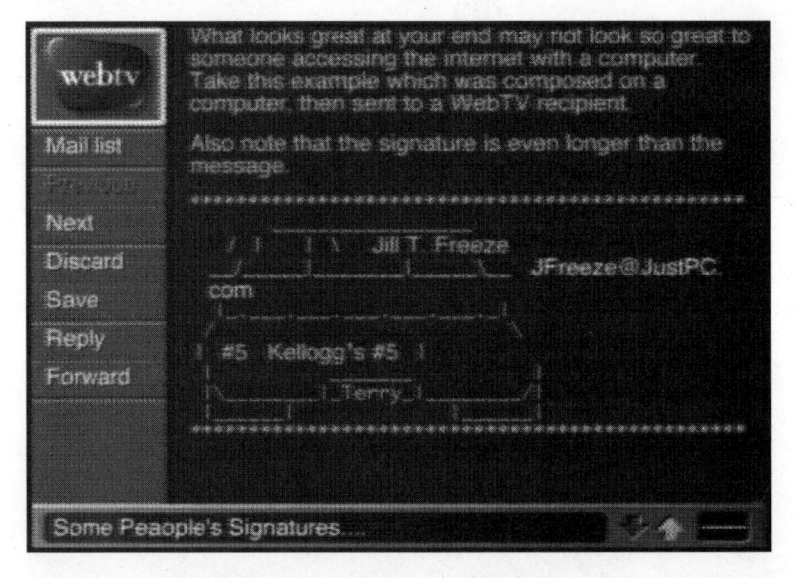

Figure 15-2. *This screen illustrates a longer-than-necessary signature for e-mail. In many cases, a more elaborate signature might get garbled by some newsreaders.*

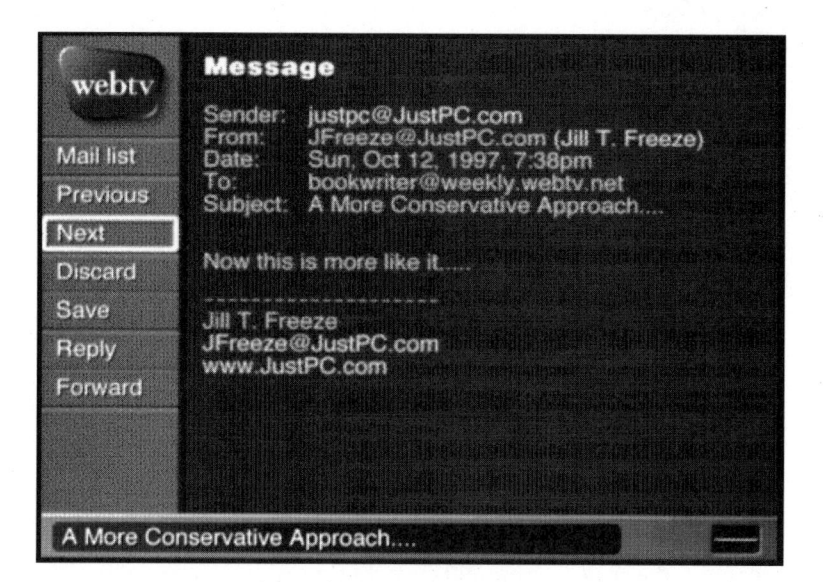

Figure 15-3. *Here's a signature of appropriate length.*

Rule 8. Around the World in 80 Milliseconds

Well, an e-mail message might not circle the globe that fast, but it can be pretty darn quick. Sometimes it's hard to grasp the true scope of the Internet. It's easy to forget that the person you're e-mailing is just as likely to be across the world as across town. Time zone and culture might differ from where you are. There are a few things we can do to make everyone feel comfortable no matter where they live.

- Be patient when waiting for a response to a note. The message you sent this morning might get to its destination within minutes, but its recipient in a far-away land might just be crawling into bed. Give it time (24 to 48 hours, depending on the urgency of the message) before resending it or, worse yet, responding in anger.

- Use caution when including colorful expressions or slang in your e-mail—they might be taken literally by someone who does not speak English as his or her primary language. English is full of lively idiomatic expressions, but idiom often doesn't translate well.

- Humor, especially sarcasm, is another aspect of English that might not translate well. Save the humor until you know the recipient well. But if you can't resist cracking a funny, consider using emoticons or other tell-tale notation such as <grin>, <g>, or *ROTFL* (if you're one to laugh at your own jokes).

Rule 9. I Don't Get It…

My husband will be the first to tell you that I get worked up over the stupidest things sometimes, but one of my pet peeves is e-mail messages without subject lines. When I scan my incoming e-mail while I'm writing, I want to see meaningful subject lines. I want to know whether I should drop everything and attend to the matter, or whether I can deal with it at a more convenient time. Odds are, if the subject is blank, I'll ignore it for a while.

I've even been known to get a little devious with my own subject lines. When I was trying to get in touch with one of my WebTV Network contacts, I knew I had to be creative to catch her attention amidst the fray. Since she's a fellow chocoholic, I simply put "Chocolate!" in the subject line. It worked, too—I heard from her just a few minutes later.

Let's get this straight—I'm not recommending that you use misleading subject lines. After all, that would defeat the purpose. I'm merely pointing out that, as is the case with many things, there's more than one way to get somebody's attention.

Rule 10. Don't Believe Everything You Read

You might not realize this, but in many e-mail programs a user can forge e-mail addresses. Want proof? Look at Figure 15-4.

15: Netiquette, the Rules of the Road

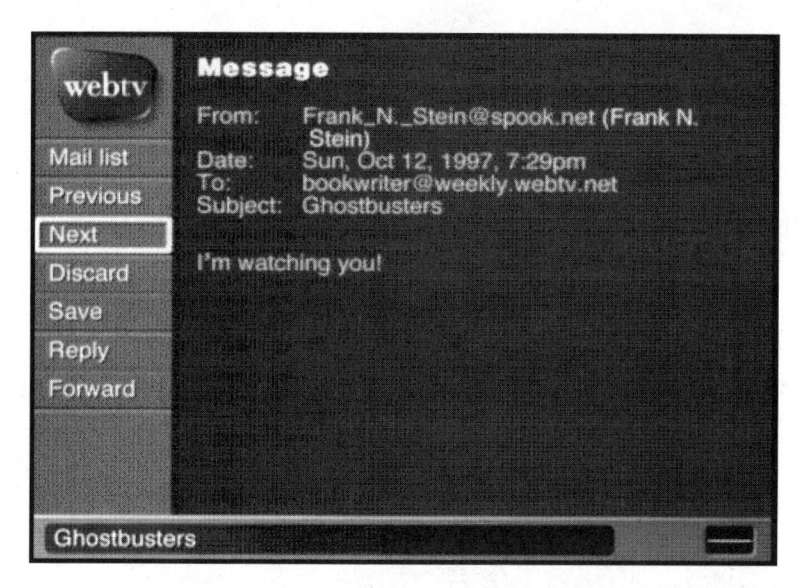

Figure 15-4. *An altered e-mail address indicates that the user has forged the name.*

Often a spoof or a forgery is blatant, as in *seeu@home.soon*. Obviously, someone's attempting to be cute. But there's a darker side to this, too. Businesses mass-mailing unsolicited garbage (usually something utterly distasteful like "Babes Here: Get 'Em While They're Hot") will frequently alter their return e-mail address to avoid an onslaught of angry return messages.

If you can pull it off, impersonating another user (at least on the surface) should be a breeze. I'm surprised soap opera writers haven't latched on to this. Imagine what trouble the odd man out of a steamy love triangle could cause for his competition by merely impersonating him!

The moral of the story is that if you ever get a piece of e-mail that seems highly out of character for the sender, consider doing the following before responding emotionally:

- Select Reply to see if the address matches the one you see displayed in your inbox.

- Send an e-mail note back asking for confirmation of the message.
- Phone the sender to verify whether he or she sent this particular message.

Top 10 Discussion Group Rules of the Road

Discussion groups are wonderful forums. Within them you can exchange thoughts and information with countless people from around the world, pool the wisdom of experts in a variety of fields, and gain the respect of others based on your thoughts and intellect without regard to your appearance, race, sex, or other irrelevant factors. But making the most of the discussion groups involves some giving as well. The following 10 pointers address issues of concern to people new to discussion groups.

Rule 1. Know the Territory

Before posting to a discussion group or mailing list, read the group for a month or two to get a feel for its style. This is perhaps the best way to learn the preferred format of subject lines, topics that are actually discussed in the group, and participants' reactions to humor. Another thing you should do before posting is track down the FAQs (frequently asked questions) for the group to make sure your question isn't already answered there. Some group participants periodically post the FAQs, while other FAQs are published on a Web site. The bigger, more organized groups have both.

TIP To find an index of FAQ Web sites, press GoTo, and then type the following: *ps.superb.net/FAQ/*.

Rule 2. Turn the Other Cheek

If you plan to get involved in some of the discussion groups, you should be prepared to be flamed. There are millions of people in this world, many of whom will disagree with your opinions or comments no matter what they might be. A few people might show their disagreement by sending you volumes of statistics on why you're wrong. An even smaller group might send you notes saying something like, "Look, you dweeb, you're way off base here. What a lunatic! Your e-mail account should be revoked!" These are known as flames. It's wise to ignore these crackpots since letting them know you're riled up could be just the positive reinforcement they need to continue being obnoxious. And it goes without saying that you will never flame anyone, right?

Rule 3. It's a Small World

Remember that a vast majority of discussion groups are read by thousands of people worldwide, and that one of those people might be your current or future boss. For example, if you aspire to be the manager of the Barbie doll section of your local FAO Schwarz, you probably don't want to post a note on *rec.collecting.dolls* griping about the store's high prices. Many discussion groups are archived for future reference, so even though your words may have disappeared from the news server that you use to access discussion groups, they might still be accessible by other methods for quite some time.

> **TIP** Use the Deja News search engine to see what your friends are saying online or to search for all articles mentioning a particular subject. You can use this search engine by pressing GoTo, and typing the following: *www.dejanews.com*.

Rule 4. KISS

KISS—the acronym for Keep It Simple, Stupid—applies to the Internet as well as it applies to anything you do. Unlike TV, snail mail, or radio, where the cost of sending a message falls exclusively to the sender, the cost of e-mail or a discussion group message is absorbed by both the sender and the recipient(s). This cost takes the form of increased time online to download and read the message. In some ways, sending e-mail or posting to a discussion group is like mailing a letter with postage due—the contents had better be worth the cost. While the cost might not seem like much in the scheme of things, it's hard to swallow when that message is unsolicited junk mail.

You might not be able to do much about the people who litter your inbox or post off-topic ads to your favorite discussion group (although I have been known to press Reply and bounce the message back, just to be annoying), but there are ways you can cut costs and conserve resources when e-mailing friends and associates or using discussion groups:

- When responding to a message, delete any unnecessary text. Keep only enough to give the reader proper context for your comments.

- If you decide to go into business on the Internet, don't send large amounts of unsolicited information to people via e-mail or discussion groups. If you must employ direct e-mail and groups as sales tools, send a brief message describing your offerings and then ask interested parties to hit Reply to request further details. Also include wording in the subject line of your message that makes it clear the message is commercial.

CAUTION Before posting any kind of advertising to a discussion group, make sure it's allowed. Trying to advertise in a group that strictly forbids advertising could hurt your business far more than it helps.

- Avoid posting simple "me, too" follow-ups. It takes up valuable bandwidth and frankly, unless you're a recognized expert on the topic at hand, people couldn't care less whether you agree. If you have additional information to pass along, naturally it's OK to do so.

TECHNOBABBLE Bandwidth—A measurement of how much data can be sent over a network (that is, your WebTV terminal) in a specific amount of time.

Rule 5. Get to the Point

When posting an article or comment, cut to the chase. Don't ramble, get on your soap box, or wander off the topic. And whatever you do, don't waste precious time and resources simply to point out people's typos or spelling errors. This, more than anything else, will mark you as an immature newbie, which in turn can ruin your reputation and credibility in the group. But people mellow pretty quickly with an apology and a few intellectual insights. After all, everybody gets carried away from time to time.

Rule 6.   The Line Dance

Okay, I admit it; I watch a couple of soap operas on occasion. One newsgroup, *rec.arts.tv.soaps.cbs*, discusses my favorite soap, *As the World Turns*, among others. Because the number of shows covered and the volume of posts is so high, a few subject-line conventions have emerged. Messages concerning my favorite show begin with *ATWT*, followed by a colon, a space, and then the specific subject matter. A sample subject line might read *ATWT: Lily's New Haircut*. Each show has its own subject line prefix and, in cases where all the shows are involved (such as posts about Daytime Emmy Award nominees), the word *ALL* becomes the prefix. Other groups use a *Q:* to denote a question, *FS:* to mark items for sale, and so on. Reading the newsgroup and its FAQ before jumping in will help you look like an experienced netizen (Internet citizen).

Rule 7.   Don't Be a Spoil Sport!

Although this point could have been discussed in the preceding section, it's important enough to give it its own space: when posting a message to a discussion group that discusses television shows, sporting events, and so on, be careful not to spoil the outcome of the show or event for others. Nothing's worse than scanning the NASCAR newsgroup before watching your videotape of the race only to see some bozo post in huge letters *TERRY LABONTE CLINCHES THE CHAMPIONSHIP TODAY!!!* The race is ruined for you, and you can be sure the person who posted the message will get a fair amount of angry e-mail. If you want to talk about the end of the most recent blockbuster movie or discuss a controversial call by a referee, place the word *SPOILER* in uppercase in the subject line. Insert a few blank lines at the beginning of your message for good measure. That way no one can blame you for spoiling their fun, and you can still talk about anything you want.

Rule 8. Before Hitting Reply…

Discussion groups can pose some interesting challenges when it comes to getting information to the right person. If you want to share your wisdom with the originator of a message by e-mail, there are some things you need to check before sending your message:

- If the header is intact, as illustrated in Figure 15-5, read the article carefully to confirm that the reply-to address matches that of the original author. I can't tell you how many times I've gotten e-mail intended for the originator of a message and because I no longer had access to the original post without a lot of work, I was forced to send the note back to the kind soul telling them that they sent their message to the wrong person. Do yourself (and others) a favor: if you are originating a message, include a signature with your name and e-mail address to simplify responding.

- If you're posting a follow-up to the group, make sure the original author's e-mail address is easy to find so that others can respond directly via e-mail if they want.

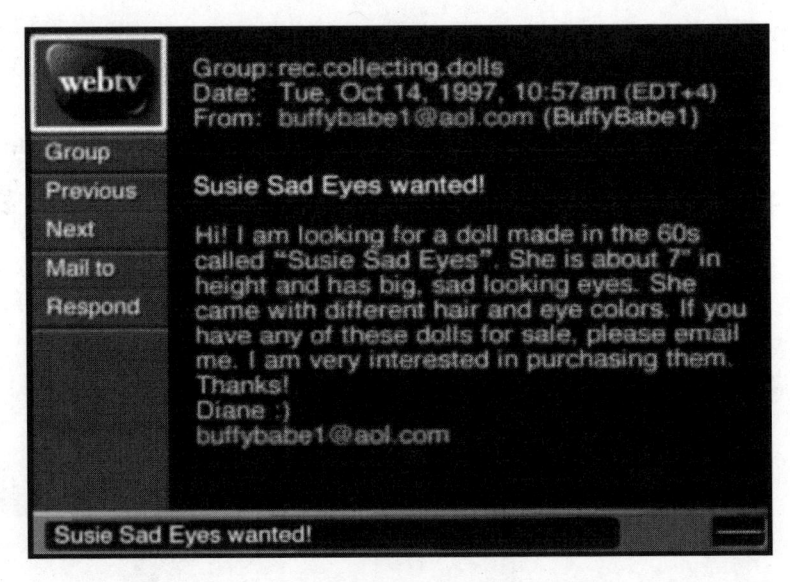

Figure 15-5. *An intact header helps you identify who originated the message.*

- Follow-ups to follow-ups complicate matters even more. In the interest of saving bandwidth, vital header information is often inadvertently edited out. In this case, it's usually best to simply post your contribution rather than risk having it not get to the source. And if you're contributing to a thread that's been around for a while, do your best to keep header information intact. Do, however, try to remove irrelevant message text.

Rule 9.   Use the Discussion Groups to Your Ad-Vantage

Everything has its place on the Internet, ads included. If you even think about posting ads on some groups, however, you'll practically get run off the Internet with e-mail messages and flames. Other groups, like *ba.forsale*, not only welcome ads but see them as the sole purpose of the group. Interestingly, if you post to an inappropriate group, it doesn't seem to matter whether you're launching a business or merely parting with an old collectible gathering dust—the outcome is the same: you will get flamed.

To locate groups that welcome ads, search the various group hierarchies for words such as *marketplace* or *for sale*. Just because a group doesn't include one of these extensions in its name doesn't mean it snubs ads, however. Take *rec.toys.cars*, for example. Collectors from around the world discuss everything from the paint quality of the latest Matchbox car releases to the newest Hot Wheels variations. But ads from fellow collectors also make up a key part of this group's culture. The best way to determine whether ads are accepted in a group is to read the FAQs. If they prove to be elusive, hang around for a while; in a week or two the answer will be obvious.

> **CAUTION** Beware of scalpers! Scalpers are people who frequent toy stores, snatch up all the good stuff (for example, limited edition Hot Wheels, Star Wars figures, Beanie Babies, and so on), and then try to sell it on the Internet for outrageous prices. If you participate in a discussion group regularly, you'll most likely make some new friends who can eventually help you build your collection at cost or for trade.

Rule 10. Give Thanks

If, after reading the FAQs and monitoring a discussion group for a while, you'd still like to post a question to get reactions or input from the rest of the participants, consider doing the following:

- Thank everyone in advance for their help and comments.
- Offer to post a summary of all the recommendations if there's sufficient interest in the subject.
- If you can't generate enough interest to justify posting a formal summary, offer to e-mail a summary to those expressing an interest in your findings.

Generally, the Internet is a cooperative place, and showing appreciation for the time people give you can only help in the long run.

Chapter

16

BTW, About Those Abbreviations and Emoticons :-)

In the last chapter, I talked about conserving resources and what you can do to lighten the load. But careful editing and avoiding unnecessary posting isn't enough. Bandwidth-saving techniques often involve abbreviating words and phrases. In this chapter, I'll cover the most common abbreviations, as well as some of the emoticons and expressions used to convey emotion. To give you an idea of just how much you'll learn, try to decipher the message in Figure 16-1 on the following page.

Internet Culture

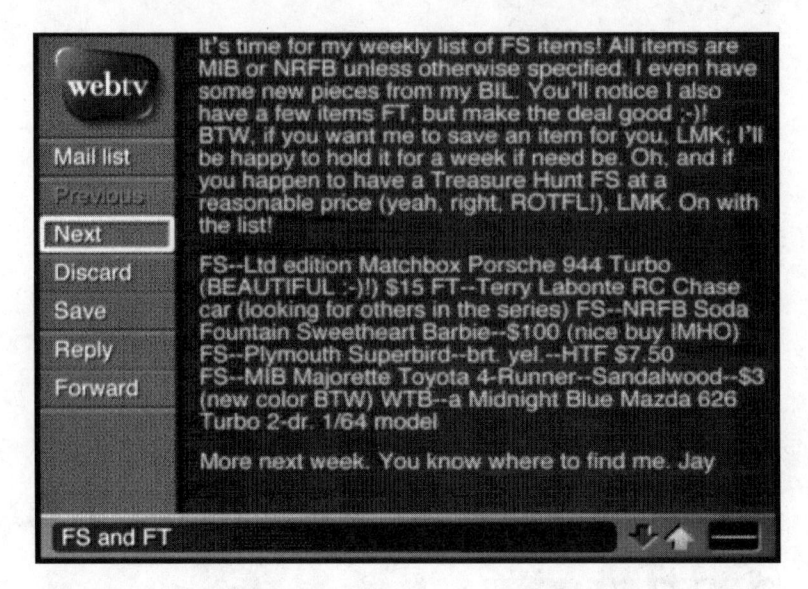

Figure 16-1. *Messages sent via the Internet can sometimes look like they're written in technical jargon.*

OK, are you ready for the translation? Here are the first few sentences:

"It's time for my weekly list of *for sale* items! All items are *mint in box* or *never removed from box* unless otherwise specified. I even have some new pieces from my *brother-in-law*...."

Alphabet Soup

Stumped by the title of this chapter? BTW translates to "by the way," and :-) represents a smile. (If you hold this book in front of you and rotate it clockwise or merely tilt your head to the left, you'll notice that the colon, dash, and close parenthesis form a smiley face symbol.) As you saw in Figure 16-1, translating e-mail and discussion group messages can be a little tricky for the untrained eye. Odds are that if you watch your favorite group for a few days, you'll see a message from a frustrated newbie pleading: "Can somebody please tell me what ROTFL means?" Well, here it is—a guide to many of the quirky abbreviations you'll find lurking in e-mail messages or news articles. You won't find them *all* (things change so quickly on the Internet), but certainly there are more than enough to get you rolling.

16: BTW, About Those Abbreviations and Emoticons :-)

At this point you might be thinking, "Hey, this stuff should be in an appendix, not in the middle of a book." I disagree, and here's why: when was the last time you completely read the glossary of a book? I thought so! These goodies are too much fun and too important to be missed. When you're familiar with the common abbreviations listed in Table 16-1, the example in Figure 16-1 won't even faze you.

Table 16-1. Common abbreviations and their definitions

Abbreviation	Definition	Abbreviation	Definition
ADN	Any Day Now	IMO	In My Opinion
AFAIK	As Far As I Know	INPO	In No Particular Order
B4N	Bye For Now	IOW	In Other Words
BTA	But Then Again	JIC	Just In Case
BTW	By The Way	LMK	Let Me Know
CU	See You	LOL	Laughing Out Loud
CUL	See You Later	OTOH	On The Other Hand
EOT	End Of Thread	POV	Point Of View
FWIW	For What It's Worth	PTB	Powers That Be
FYI	For Your Information	RE	Regarding
G	Grin	ROTFL	Rolling On The Floor Laughing
GMTA	Great Minds Think Alike	RTFM	Read The __ Manual
IAC	In Any Case	TAFN	That's All For Now
IAE	In Any Event	TIA	Thanks In Advance
IC	I See	TPTB	The Powers That Be
IMHO	In My Humble Opinion	TTYL	Talk To You Later
IMNSHO	In My Not So Humble Opinion	YMMV	Your Mileage May Vary

Internet Culture

As you can see, most of these abbreviations are derived from common expressions. Few need further definition. However, one in particular—YMMV—always seems to baffle newbies when they first hear it. YMMV, which stands for "Your Mileage May Vary," simply means, "this was my experience, but yours may be different."

These aren't all the abbreviations you'll see. If you frequent any of the discussion groups that deal in items for sale, you might see some of the abbreviations listed in Table 16-2.

Table 16-2. **Some specialized abbreviations and their definitions**

Abbreviation	Definition
FS	For Sale
FT	For Trade
HTF	Hard To Find
MIB	Mint In Box
MIP	Mint In Package
NRFB	Never Removed From Box
WTB	Want To Buy
WTD	Want To Deal
WTT	Want To Trade

Furthermore, many narrowly focused groups contain abbreviated names of commonly discussed people or topics as shorthand, such as a television show's key characters (DD for Daisy Duke from "The Dukes of Hazzard"), star race car drivers (DE for Dale Earnhardt), or members of the family (MIL for mother-in-law). Rarely does this evolving shorthand need to be explained since the group's readership will normally catch on quickly, given the context of its use. Unfortunately, the only way to learn these secrets is to read a particular group for a while. It's a given that each discussion group will have its own abbreviations—that's simply part of the culture.

I Second That Emotion!

If you thought punctuation was great for expressing emotion in writing (exclamation points to convey excitement; an ellipsis to express a voice trailing off in an unfinished sentence), you'll really be impressed by the use of punctuation on the Internet, such as the smiley face in this chapter's title. Punctuation used in this manner creates an emoticon (a word derived from emotion and icon). Table 16-3 shows some emoticons.

Table 16-3. **Some common emoticons and what they mean**

This…	Means this…
:-) or :)	I'm smiling or happy about the preceding thought/comment.
:-(or :(	I'm frowning or unhappy about the preceding thought/comment.
;-) or ;)	I'm winking at you.
<:-)	Dumb question.
:-*	A kiss.

Those are just some of the basic emoticons. The Internet is flooded with creative variations of the smiley. And, while I'd like to give credit where credit is due, it's next to impossible to trace how most of these evolved. Table 16-4 lists a few of the more elaborate ones I've found over time:

Table 16-4. **A sample of some unusual emoticons**

This…	Means this…
&:-)	From a person with curly hair.
:-(=)	From a person with big teeth.
C=:-)	From a chef.
:-)}</////>	From a guy wearing a tie. (Tie design may vary.)
@->->---	A rose.

Internet Culture

These emoticons are most frequently placed at the end of a sentence to clarify the emotion or intention behind the message. See the message in Figure 16-2 for examples of how these emoticons might be used.

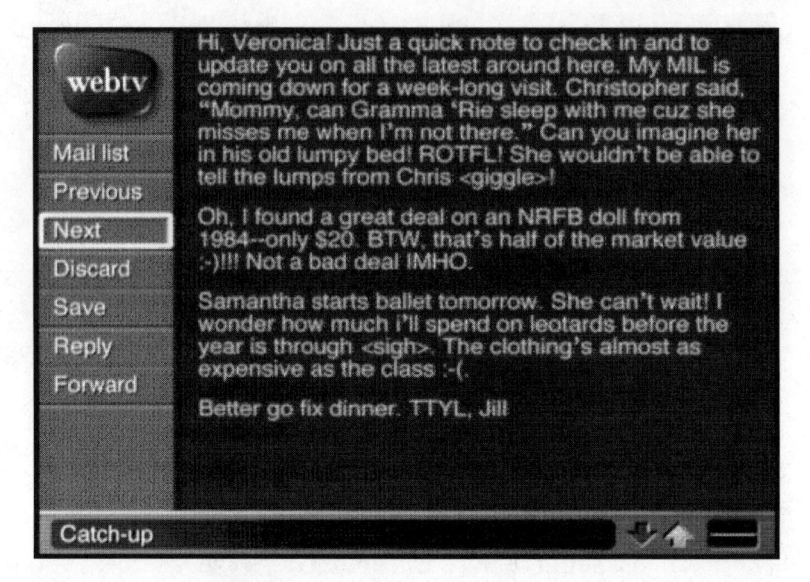

Figure 16-2. *When used correctly and sparingly, emoticons can go a long way toward clarifying the intent of a message.*

> **NOTE** Obviously, emoticons are not a substitute for judicious word choice. A scathing or snide remark could still hurt no matter how many smileys follow it.

If you'd like to learn more about emoticons and their meanings, use the skills you'll learn in Chapter 21, "Become a Virtual Bloodhound," to track down the latest information on the Web, or read the *alt.culture.emoticons* discussion group.

Express Yourself

If abbreviations and emoticons aren't enough, you can express yourself on the Net in yet another way. You'll see expressions as words or phrases embedded between a < and a > (<grin>, for example). These expressions are capable of communicating subtle differences in emotion that are hard to capture with an emoticon. Take a basic smiley emoticon, which communicates contentment. Changing that :-) to a <grin> adds a playful dimension to the message. Table 16-5 contains some of the more frequently used expressions.

Table 16-5. Common expressions and what they mean

This…	Means this…
<grin> or <g>	Grin.
<big grin> or <G>	Big grin.
<blush>	I'm embarrassed by the comment.
<snicker>	Playfully making fun of someone.
<giggle>	Being silly.
<getting on/off my soapbox>	About to begin/end a speech about a subject you feel very strongly about.
<raising eyebrows>	Disbelief over a matter.

It's easy to see how all these elements have come together to form a rich culture that for the most part doesn't discriminate, mainly because it is so diverse. The Internet is a great place to be yourself because you'll always find someone else who shares your beliefs and values, and you won't be judged by your wardrobe or waistline.

Some people believe the anonymity of the Internet makes it a cold place; it's just the opposite, in my opinion. For all you know, *simba@webtv.net* (not a real e-mail address, that I know of) could be a 10-year old fan of Disney's Lion King, or it could be a famous novelist hiding behind a pen name. You never know until that person decides to reveal a clue to his or her identity.

Chapter 17

Safety in Numbers (and in User Names)

In some ways, venturing onto the information superhighway is like making your first visit to a big city—you'll want to conduct yourself so that you have a safe and fun time. That's not to say the Internet is a hotbed of crime, but you'll want to take some basic precautions to ensure your safety and privacy.

This chapter will look at the importance of using a user name, and will show you how to complete online shopping transactions while keeping your credit card information secure.

Protect Your Privacy

When you set up your WebTV Network account, you'll be asked to select a name to use as your e-mail address. In corporate America, e-mail addresses often take the form of a person's first initial followed by their surname. For example, I use *jfreeze@justpc.com* for my e-mail address. It gives clients the sense of dealing with a real person as opposed to some faceless entity at the other end of the modem.

Internet Culture

But occasionally you'd just as soon be faceless at the other end of the modem. While the ability to find you gives potential customers or clients a sense of legitimacy and stability, it's not necessarily a desirable thing if you plan on frequenting chatrooms or discussion groups.

Experienced Internet users who want to locate you could use a number of methods to do so: they could try to go to a Web site based on your domain name (*justpc.com* in my example) to see if such a Web site exists and use it to search for clues to your location; they could plug your name into any number of search engines to draw clues from news articles you may have posted; they could search a host of online phone books and pair the entries with clues found elsewhere…the list goes on and on. But when you get right down to it, the potential bad guys on the Internet don't have any more clues available to them than they do in the real world.

The media alone could scare you away by portraying the Internet as the equivalent of wandering the streets of Washington, D.C., alone in the middle of the night. But before you unplug your WebTV Internet terminal and put it up for sale at a church flea market, rest assured that you can do plenty to have a positive and safe experience on the Internet.

I'm not a pessimist by any means. In fact, it is my belief that crime resulting from using the Internet is far less common than the media makes it out to be. It's a rare incident that couldn't have been avoided by using a little common sense and a few tips from someone who's been surfing the information superhighway since it was a dirt road.

Be Anyone You Want to Be

The best place to start is to select a user name for yourself. Pick something fun that expresses your personality or a passion of yours. If you're a basketball fan, choose something like *celticfan*. Other ideas might include *umassalum*, *catlover*, *fluteplayer*, or *NTRPRZ* for a *Star Trek* fan. Use some creativity to come up with alternatives in case your selection is already taken.

If you've already selected your WebTV Network subscriber name and are listed as an additional user on the account, you can change your user name by adding a new user in the WebTV Users Setup screen (provided you haven't already defined your maximum number of additional users) and then deleting the old user name. This method allows you to confirm that your new user name is available before giving up your old one.

> **TIP** To reach the WebTV Users Setup screen, start with the WebTV Network's home page, and then select Setup. Press Go, and then choose WebTV Users. Press Go again to see a listing of all defined users on your account. Select Add User, press Go, and fill out the necessary information to establish your additional user name. Once it's been successfully added, press Remove User, check the box next to the user name to delete, select Remove, and then press Go. When you're finished removing users, select Done, and then press Go.

If the user name you want to change is that of the subscriber, you might need to contact WebTV Networks' customer support at 1-800-GO-WEBTV to make the necessary change. It might be easiest just to add a user since you have to select which user name you want to use each time you connect to the WebTV Network.

> **TIP** When choosing a password for any online account, be creative in your choice. Using obvious things such as birth years or birthdays can leave your accounts vulnerable to security violations.

Respect the Rights of Others

If you've chosen a user name to maintain your privacy, chances are others have done the same. As you make more friends online, you'll start to correspond with each other using your real names in e-mail messages.

When encountering these friends in online chatrooms, discussion groups, and other public forums, be careful not to reveal their real names. Including their real names in a news article or in the context of a multiperson chat is a direct violation of their privacy. If you include a name by accident, simply apologize and try to be more careful in the future.

The Nuisance of Virtual Junk Mail

Have you ever wondered how you get on all those mailing lists resulting in trash bags full of junk mail each week? While I don't have all the answers to that question, I can tell you how virtual junk mail (known as *spam*) finds its way into your inbox.

Every time you connect to the WebTV Network, you might inadvertently advertise your e-mail address by doing any of the following:

- Posting an article or a response to a discussion group
- Entering a bulletin board or a chatroom
- Signing a guest book on a Web page
- Registering in online membership directories or address books
- Requesting information via e-mail from an online source
- Providing your e-mail address on a survey or Web site registration (although the more reputable companies say they won't share your information with anyone)
- Participating in a mailing list that puts all the e-mail addresses in the header rather than camouflaging the lists under one name

Obviously, it's not practical to avoid doing any of these things since they are the very activities that make the Internet fun. So what can you do?

Complain Effectively

Complaining effectively might not be as easy as it sounds, but a well-placed, well-documented complaint can do wonders to stop spam from an offending company or individual.

When you receive a piece of junk mail, look at the header information as described in Chapter 15, "Netiquette, the Rules of the Road." If the domain name appears to be valid, forward a copy of the spam to the postmaster of the domain (leaving all message headers intact) along with a note explaining that you want the unsolicited e-mail to stop. Address the note to *postmaster@* followed by the domain name used on the spam's header (*postmaster@justpc.com* in my example). Most ISPs have stringent policies against spamming, so the guilty party could lose account privileges or at least be warned that the account might be closed should the user spam again.

NOTE Some spammers will try to cover their behinds by putting an address in the message with instructions on how you can be removed from the mailing list. While you might want to try the method they suggest, be warned that it doesn't always work. The fact remains that if you did not request the information and do not wish to receive it, it is still spam and should be treated as such.

Some of the larger ISPs such as America Online and Netcom are so serious about misuse of the Internet that they've created special addresses for reporting such matters (*abuse@aol.com* and *abuse@netcom.com*, respectively).

Let the WebTV Network Help

WebTV Networks has already banned hundreds of domains known for their spamming from sending e-mail to WebTV Network members. While new domains are frequently added to the banned list, some are bound to sneak through, requiring you to deal with them as you see fit.

Eliminate Junk E-Mail Once and for All

Before you run for the remote at the prospect of eliminating junk e-mail for good, bear in mind that your effort might require some additional work and the memory of an elephant.

With that said, here are some ways to put the spammers to rest:

1. Create a new user name for yourself as described at the beginning of this chapter.

2. Give the new e-mail address to friends and family only. That ensures your new account will be spam-free. Don't use this account to surf.

3. Switch to the old user name (select Switch User, press Go, select the desired screen name on the WebTV Network's home page and press Go) to surf the net, post discussion group articles, and sign guest books to your heart's content. All spam will be sent to the old account, and only the good stuff will appear in your new inbox.

4. Here's where the memory of an elephant comes in. Because you can store up to 150 messages per user name, you'll want to convert using your old user name periodically and look for any important messages that might not have been rerouted to your new name. Of course, you also have the WebTV Internet terminal's message light and the appearance of a letter in the mailbox icon to remind you to check your e-mail, in case your memory fails you.

These steps might seem like a lot of work to eliminate a few pieces of junk e-mail, but as you become more involved in the Internet, the pieces will add up quickly. For instance, I've been maintaining a low profile for the past few months while I write a couple of books, yet I still get between two and ten pieces of electronic junk mail each day. Imagine how quickly you can reach the 150-message limit at that rate.

No matter which method you choose to get rid of spam—even if you simply delete it as it comes in—you're now armed with some of the best strategies for reducing it, or even eliminating it completely.

Shop on the Information Superhighway

Imagine shopping for the holidays without having to battle over a parking space, or without having to jump out of the path of runaway baby strollers loaded with packages. (Where are the babies, anyway?) It's a dream come true, right?

With your newfound link to the Internet, you can enjoy the holidays this winter without all the blood pressure–raising agony. Bake a batch of fresh sugar cookies while your friends brave the preholiday shopping crowds at the local mall.

Later in this chapter, I'll introduce you to a few of my favorite shopping Web sites, but for now we need to deal with the issue of secure transactions on the Internet and safe shopping techniques in general.

Buying from a Buddy—Is It Safe?

After you've spent some time in your hobby discussion group of choice, you might be tempted to expand your collection (or that of a loved one) with purchases from some of the other group participants. Unfortunately, this can have mixed results. As you saw in Chapter 15, scalpers often feed off these groups, making it seemingly impossible to acquire that limited edition Christmas ornament without paying hefty secondary market prices.

But there are a number of kind souls who will help a fellow collector without price-gouging. I met quite a few of these while frequenting *rec.toys.cars*. If you decide to make a purchase from someone you met on a discussion group, follow these tips to improve the odds of having a positive Internet purchasing experience:

17: Safety in Numbers (and in User Names)

- Read the discussion group for a while and watch for any "bad dealer" posts. If you don't see anything about the person you plan to buy from and if the amount of the purchase is fairly significant, you might consider posting a message asking for anyone else's experience with that person. Be sure to request that responses be e-mailed directly to you so as not to inadvertently start a flame war if experiences are mixed.

- Read the discussion group's FAQs to see whether anyone maintains a safe dealer list. Many group veterans will maintain such lists for their fellow collectors. If the FAQs and a few weeks of browsing the group don't direct you to such a list, ask if there is anywhere you can go for your answers.

- Check to see whether the person you're dealing with has a Web page dedicated to her business. If so, she may be more legitimate than her counterpart who is merely posting a few things for sale here and there. This isn't always a sure thing, however.

- Find out whether the person or business accepts credit cards. If they do, you can usually interpret this as a sign of permanence and legitimacy. (But use extreme caution just the same.)

- If the person surfaces only to sell things instead of participating regularly in group discussions, he may not necessarily share your love of the hobby; he might just be a scalper in disguise.

TIP Save some time by going to *www.dejanews.com* and searching on the person's e-mail address to see the discussion group articles he or she has posted over the last month.

- Know what you're buying. If you aren't buying something MIB (mint in box) or MIP (mint in package), get to know your hobby's grading standards. Many hobbies have specific books that collectors have come to accept as the standard for grading. Consult the FAQs for further details.

Is My Credit Card Number Safe on the Net?

This is where the "Safety in Numbers" part of the chapter title comes in. As to whether your credit card number is safe on the Internet, the answer is, "It depends."

WebTV Networks uses something called SSL (Secure Socket Layers) to encrypt your entire business transaction, including your credit card number. This encryption protects your personal information from being viewed by unauthorized parties.

> **TECHNOBABBLE** Encryption—(pronounced "en-crip-shun") means information is scrambled using a code so that others can't read it unless they also have the code.

While SSL is supported by a number of large Internet storefronts, many still do not have the resources to implement such technology. In these instances, you'll want to find alternative methods for shopping with them.

How can you tell whether a site supports SSL? Most commercial Web sites make a big deal out of it by mentioning that fact in key locations on Web pages. Many commercial Web browsers display a small icon indicating whether you're in a secure environment, and some even flash a message saying you're about to access a secure site. My only complaint with WebTV Networks in this instance is that they don't have an onscreen security indicator; you have to base your judgment on whether a site is secure by what you read alone. Call me paranoid, but I like the extra reassurance.

Just because a Web site doesn't support SSL doesn't mean you have to shop elsewhere. Consider any of the following options:

- Jot down the company's phone number, and then call and place the order the old-fashioned way. Not only do you still avoid the Christmas crowds, but you save paper and postage as well. If they have a toll-free number, even better.

- If you're not a phone person and aren't in a hurry, you can send the order via snail mail. This can save you money in the long run if the company's number is a toll call for you.

- Some merchants will take your order online and then hold it for processing until you phone in your credit card number.

- Finally, some merchants allow you to set up an account with them so that all you have to do when visiting their site is enter a userID and password and make your selections. Your credit card information and shipping address remain on file with the merchant so you don't have to rekey and submit them each time you order something.

Shopping online provides other benefits as well. In many instances, you don't have to pay sales tax on the items ordered. While you will be charged postage and handling, you often don't have to spend much to save money overall. Even with the flat-rate shipping fee charged by some merchants, you might still come out ahead, and you don't have to break your back lugging the stuff through a mall packed with full-contact shoppers!

Smart Shopping

In the future, another safe shopping feature will become available. You will be able to use the WebTV Internet terminal's smart card slot to run your credit card number through the machine, just as many merchants do. Naturally, transmitting your credit card information will be done securely so you can shop with confidence. Keep an eye on the "Club WebTV News" for updates, because online publications can be made available quickly to reflect recent changes and enhancements to your WebTV Networks subscription.

Shop till Your Modem Drops!

With all this talk about safe shopping, what kind of person would I be if I didn't give you some good shopping sites to browse? Here are some of my favorites:

- **The Internet Mall.** With more than 27,000 stores, you'll find something for everyone on your holiday gift-giving list. You'll be glad you can shop while sitting down. Stop by *www.internet-mall.com*.

- **Amazon.com.** It's hard to beat this site when it comes to shopping for books. You can set up an account for speedy repeat ordering, and the site will provide recommendations of other books you might like based on past buying patterns. You can browse author interviews, sample chapters of books, scan the bestseller lists, and even write your own book review. Surf to *www.amazon.com* to check it out.

- **QVC.** Get the vast inventory of the QVC television shopping network at your fingertips any time of day. Learn about the hosts and print out your favorite recipes from one of the cooking shows. My favorite features are the high quality photos of most of the items and the site's easy-to-use search engine. They can be found at *www.qvc.com*.

- **Circuit City.** More than just sales promotions, Circuit City Online also provides buyer's guides for camcorders, TVs, VCRs, and other hard-to-purchase items. Visit them at *www.circuitcity.com*.

These are just a few you might want to check out. To find others of interest, read Chapter 21, "Become a Virtual Bloodhound," to see how you can quickly find what you're looking for.

Chapter 18

All That Glitters Is Not Gold

Remember the days when students had to schlep off to the library to do research for their term papers? I was one of those students. I pawed through dusty card catalogs; I scanned library shelves for hours trying desperately to find a book that had obviously been misshelved; and I spent hours taking copious notes from reference books that couldn't be checked out. (But no, I didn't have to walk to school in six feet of snow, never missing a day.)

In all seriousness, gathering data from the Internet using the WebTV Network has simplified the lives of many students. Rather than running out to the library at odd times of the day, students can now use the family TV to do research for their papers from the safety and comfort of their own homes.

But using the WebTV Network as a research tool is not for students only. In fact, sometimes we're all in need of education, no matter how old we are or how many years we've spent in the classroom. Consider the following situations:

- You want to invest in a camcorder, but the salespeople at the local electronics stores aren't sure about the specifications of each unit and how they differ. Where do you get the information you need? The Internet, of course. Browse manufacturers' Web sites to investigate the product specifications and suggested retail price, and then venture out to the discussion groups to get the opinions of people who've been using the equipment you want to buy.

- You have been transferred to a new area but have no clue how to begin house hunting or searching for the best school for your children. You can browse the region's Chamber of Commerce Web page to give you some solid facts about the area before you move to the new location and investigate firsthand.

- Your granddaughter found a box turtle in the woods out back, and you don't know what to feed it. Or maybe she wants to keep it, but you have no idea what kind of home little Tessie turtle needs. You can find all the answers online and can even find forums in which to ask your questions.

- Nobody likes to dwell on unpleasant things, but they can happen. And again, the Internet can help you along the way. Whether you or a loved one has been diagnosed with a condition you'd like to learn more about, or whether you'd like to become involved in an online support group to help you cope with the situation, the information is available from the privacy of your home with the WebTV Internet terminal. It's no substitute for sound medical advice (in fact, advice you find on the Internet should never take the place of a visit to the doctor), but it can help you ask the right questions, make an informed decision, and get the emotional support you need.

These are just a few situations in which the Internet and your WebTV Internet terminal can help you search for the information you need. The possibilities are virtually endless. But we've all heard the old cliché, "Free advice is worth what you pay for it." If that were truly the case, however, nobody would believe a thing they see on the Internet. So what makes the Internet different? How can we be sure that the information we're seeing and basing our decisions on is accurate?

The issue of determining information integrity has grabbed the attention of many prominent scholars because online content is being cited more often as a source in research papers. In this chapter, I'll give you some ways to evaluate the information you find online for its validity, whether you're conducting research for your dissertation or trying to make an informed decision regarding the purchase of a major appliance.

The Importance of Evaluating Online Information

Many people view the Internet as one big encyclopedia full of knowledge, but they lose sight of the fact that real encyclopedias have entries written by noted experts. Furthermore, these entries pass through the hands of droves of editors before publication. While you have experts on the Internet as well, you also have a high proportion of people who think—or pretend—that they're experts. This requires the information-gatherer to sort the diamonds from the rocks.

Fortunately, researchers and librarians have come up with some criteria to help us evaluate the information we find on the Web. These criteria include a Web site's scope of information; the authority and bias of the data contained on the site; the accuracy of the information; the timeliness of a site's content; the permanence of the Web site; any value-added features included on the site; and the presentation of the information.

I'll explore each of these criteria in detail and then take a look at how to evaluate different types of Web sites (for example, sales and marketing Web sites, advocacy Web sites, and personal Web pages) using these criteria.

Scope Out the Information

The depth and breadth of the information found at a given site depends on the intended purpose and audience of that Web site. For example, many government sites archive their data for future use, whereas a personal Web page might report on the latest *Star Wars* action figures found in the stores and then delete that information when it's no longer of value.

To evaluate the scope of a site, look for the following:

- **Stated purpose of the site.** Many Web sites have a stated purpose for their existence. For advocacy or nonprofit organizations, the Web site's purpose might mirror its organizational mission statement or act as an extension of part of its mission. Even personal Web pages may have a stated purpose. Use these statements of purpose for clues to the site's comprehensiveness and potential biases.

- **What they say is covered.** Often a Webmaster will sacrifice overall subject comprehensiveness in order to specialize in a specific area. For example, a gardening club might strive to produce the most comprehensive site on roses rather than publish dribs and drabs on a variety of plants and flowers. If a site chooses to specialize, it's likely that the site not only will attempt to cover the topic in depth but also will provide links to a number of additional reliable sources specializing in the same topic. These focused sites are often some of the best places to glean a wealth of information about a given topic.

TECHNOBABBLE Webmaster—the person who is responsible for coordinating a Web site's content, design, and function.

- **Site comprehensiveness.** You can determine a site's breadth and depth of information by scanning its list of topics, site map, or internal links. The volume of information can also provide some clues to the site's comprehensiveness.

It's easy to see how the items in this list work together to give you a good feel for the scope of a Web site's content. You need to know a lot more than the scope of a site's content in order to evaluate the site effectively, however.

Determine the Authority and Bias of a Site

One of the best ways to assess the biases of a Web site's content is to look at what's presented and ask, "What does the Web site's owner have to gain from presenting the material as he does?"

Obviously, if a company's Web site says its Zoom910 model camcorder is the best thing around, you'll weigh the statement a lot differently than if a noted and trusted consumer advocacy group's Web site states the same thing. The company has something to gain by touting its product, whereas a consumer advocacy group with no biases merely wants to do right by the consumer.

You should look for some of these criteria when attempting to evaluate the authority and bias of a Web site:

- **Who provided the information and why?** If a commercial entity (usually sporting a URL ending in *.com*) produces or even sponsors the Web site, the information is almost guaranteed to be biased in some respect. No profitable company is likely to highlight its shortcomings or product weaknesses for all to see unless they're legally obligated to do so (as in the case of tobacco products and the mandatory Surgeon General's warning). Web sites maintained by advocacy groups or nonprofit organizations (often with *.org* extensions) can also be biased, however, since they exist to right a perceived wrong. As such, they're likely to exaggerate the facts to make a case for their existence. For these reasons, it's important to weigh what is said and put the content into perspective given the potential biases.

- **Is a specific point of view being pushed?** Objective sites will communicate the facts without inflicting a point of view on the reader. When evaluating a site for the integrity of its information, you should also be wary of overly dramatic use of language, which could signal an exaggeration of the facts.

- **Do you see a stamp of approval?** Web sites that are truly exceptional in content tend to draw a lot of attention. A statement of support from noted experts and organizations in a given field increases the odds of the information being reasonably accurate. These stamps of approval can be in the form of reciprocal links, awards given to the site, and posted quotes or comments from field experts.

> **TECHNOBABBLE Reciprocal Link**—Two Web sites provide links to each other, thus forming a reciprocal link.

Once you know where the site's information comes from and you have recognized any potential biases, you're ready to start examining the accuracy of the information itself.

The Pursuit of Accuracy

Unless you know the names of all the field's experts, you might have a tough time evaluating whether what you're seeing on the Web site is legitimate or is simply a product of a wannabe expert.

To assist you in this quest for accurate information, look for the following in the Web sites you visit:

- **Cited sources.** If a Web page cites the sources of its information and the sources appear to be legitimate, chances are the information is accurate. You could double-check them to be certain, but that would defeat the purpose of providing easily accessible information on the Web.

- **Author credentials.** A Web page's author or compiler will sometimes include a link to his or her credentials. You can check this information and decide for yourself whether the person is an expert or even a reliable source.

- **A recognized source of value.** If you're visiting the American Association of Retired Persons (AARP) home page, for example, you'll probably respect any sources this reputable organization links you to. Seeing the site in question referenced by a variety of prominent and reliable sources gives the site, and the information contained therein, more credibility.

Day-Old Data

The information may have been accurate when it was posted, but is it still accurate? One of the problems that has plagued print media since its beginning is its long turnaround time. The content of printed materials (with the exception of newspapers, of course) often becomes stale before it ever reaches the hands of its desired audience. It's a sad fact of this industry, but it's one of the things that makes the Internet so intriguing. Information can be updated within minutes to reflect pivotal news events, changes in the law, or other pertinent information that can change at a moment's notice.

However, just because you can quickly update Web content doesn't mean it gets updated frequently in reality. A leading toy manufacturer finally made its online presence known. But, like the Web sites of many other large corporations, the information quickly became stale and worthless and was seldom updated. Web pages created by the collectors of this manufacturer's products, however, soon became the freshest, most reliable source of information. It makes you wonder why the corporation even bothered expending the effort (not to mention the money) to get online in the first place.

How do you avoid the pitfalls of day-old data? You can assess the freshness of a site's information by looking for the following:

- **"Expiration" date.** Many Web pages have a "revised on" date reference somewhere on the page. Depending on the type of content the page provides, the information could be considered old after as little as an hour. Many news pages are updated as frequently as every 15 minutes, whereas some other pages undergo a scheduled weekly update, which is more than enough. This is one of those instances where your judgment comes into play. Figure 18-1 shows an example of a Web page's revision date.

Figure 18-1.   *Use the WebTV Internet terminal's Info display to assess the timeliness of a Web page's content.*

- **Revision policy.** In addition to a revision or modification date, many Web sites also display a policy for updates. Statements such as "This page is updated every 15 minutes" are common. Unfortunately, in many cases you must keep revisiting the page to see if the information has been updated.
- **Hibernating hyperlinks.** Stumbling onto nonexistent pages when trying to follow a Web page's links might also be an indicator of a poorly maintained and potentially out-of-date Web page.

Using out-of-date information can have undesirable results in many circumstances. If the data appears to be old, you might want to consider looking elsewhere before relying too heavily on such questionable information.

Here Today, Gone Tomorrow

Whether a site is permanent or transitory can tell you a great deal about the information it provides. Finely crafted Web sites produced by college students can disappear after the students graduate. Sites that move from ISP to ISP can be fronts for shady activity. It's wise to know what you're dealing with, so consider checking for the following:

- **Now you see it, now you don't.** Whether due to a system upgrade or a new organizational affiliation, Web sites occasionally need to be moved. Look for notices about impending change of location for the Web site. Most reputable Web sites will plan a change of location and will prepare users well in advance by placing a notice prominently on the home page. Sites that suddenly change location without notice should raise a red flag in your mind.
- **The Web page owner's relationship to the host site.** If the Web page belongs to the government or a major corporation, chances are good that its location is relatively stable. If, however, the page is maintained by a student using a university Internet account, count on it moving or even disappearing altogether within a few years, or maybe even months.

- **Transitory information.** Occasionally a Web page's information may be of temporary value. Consider a politician's election page or a page dedicated to the aftermath of a tragedy like an earthquake or plane crash. Once these pages have served their purpose, they most likely will not continue to be updated and will often disappear after a certain amount of time. If you need information from a transitory page, it's best to get it when you see it.

Time is always of the essence, especially on the Internet, where the number of Web sites grows by some staggering number each month. Unless you see signs that a Web site archives its data for future access, it's best to get the information while you can.

Value-Added Site Features

Some Web sites include value-added features such as search engines, sections moderated by an expert, navigational help, and the like. Because of the time and effort that went into designing and creating them, these sites are likely to be around much longer than their typical counterparts.

Beauty Is in the Eye of the Beholder

We've all seen flashy Web pages with little content to back up the special effects, but some presentation and design elements do in fact contribute to the professionalism and legitimacy of a Web site. These include intuitive site organization targeted to the specific audience, appropriate use of graphics and other multimedia features, and navigational links back to the home page or the site map. Use of these elements implies a planned, stable Web site that you can revisit with confidence.

Question Your Sources

Given all these factors, how can you possibly evaluate a site's worthiness as a resource? Just use the questions below as a guide. The more questions you answer "yes" to, the higher the quality of the source.

1. Is it clear who is sponsoring the Web site?

2. Can you verify the legitimacy of the company, organization, or individual (with a phone number or street address, not just an e-mail address)?

> **CAUTION** Because it can be hard to verify the legitimacy of an individual, it's wise to use extreme caution when relying on a personal Web page as a source of information. For best results, try to find the source of the claim or statistic to verify the information.

3. Is the page relatively free of typos and grammatical errors? While these may not seem like important considerations, they communicate a lack of quality control, which means other information might go unverified.
4. Are the sources of factual information cited so that you can double-check the page's claim with the original source?
5. Is the information advertising-free? If not, is all advertising on the page clearly set apart from informational content?
6. Is a date posted on the page indicating when the content was last updated?
7. Has the page been completed as opposed to being under constant construction?
8. Are the biases of the company, organization, or individual clear?
9. Can you determine when the Web page first appeared on the Internet?

Web pages are not substitutes for sound research, but they can be a vital source of timely information and links to more obscure resources. By using the preceding questions as a guide, you should have a better feel for which Web sites are potential gold mines of information.

PART 4

The Fun Part

Chapter

19 Over a Dozen Creative Uses
for Your WebTV Internet Terminal   215

20 Over a Dozen Ways to
Save Time and Money Surfing the Net   227

21 Become a Virtual Bloodhound   239

22 Web Sites of Interest to Young and Old 251

Chapter 19

Over a Dozen Creative Uses for Your WebTV Internet Terminal

I challenge you to walk into a bookstore someday and count the number of "cool sites on the Internet" books. They're everywhere, but what's really worth noting is that in a majority of cases they do little more than present a list of sites, with one-paragraph descriptions and URLs for the sites—information you can get from any old search engine. (See Chapter 21, "Become a Virtual Bloodhound," to learn how you can find the information you want on the Internet.) Granted, these books have presumably weeded out some useless sites, but still, not a whole lot of value has been added.

This chapter, however, takes a look at how you can actually use some of the many resources on the Internet to enhance your lifestyle and productivity.

Make a New Friend

It's easy to make new friends on the Internet (although you should be familiar with the contents of Chapter 17, "Safety in Numbers [and in User Names]," first). You can make friends by reading your favorite discussion group and then contacting someone with similar values or interests;

you could meet them in a chatroom; or you could discover them while participating in a mailing list. But no matter where you meet them, you now have e-mail at your disposal, so getting to know one another and keeping in touch will be easy and affordable.

Pick the Best College

Whether you're a junior in high school or a senior citizen wanting to pursue a longtime passion, you might want to find a college offering classes in a specific area of interest. It's a big decision, so why not use the Internet to narrow down your choices?

Perhaps the best place to start is ".edu: U.S. News Colleges and Career Center" at *www.usnews.com/usnews/edu/home.htm*. By searching on your intended major, you can get a list of appropriate colleges along with the location, size, and admissions criteria of each school. You can even apply online. Once you've searched on your college criteria, you get a list of colleges meeting exactly those requirements. From that list, you can select the desired college and then press Go to learn more about the institution you selected. From this "At a Glance" page, you can view vital statistics about the college's enrollment numbers, religious affiliation, admission selection requirements and deadlines, key telephone numbers, tuition and room and board costs, and more.

You can use the buttons at the top of this page to jump to the school's Web site or to create a map and set of directions to get to the college from your home. The buttons will also allow you to see a photo gallery of your chosen school, get details about its academic programs and campus life, and see how it rates against other colleges in its league.

Can't afford to attend the school of your choice? Browse the countless financial aid options while cruising through .edu, and learn how to fill out some of the more common financial aid forms. You'll probably need to take one of the standardized scholastic acceptance tests before you apply, so you'll appreciate the calendar of test dates that .edu makes available.

Want to know if the major you're considering will earn you enough money after graduation to pay the bills? You can read articles detailing the career outlooks for specific fields. You can also access a variety of articles of special interest to college students, such as campus political activism, studying abroad, and juggling school demands with a part-time job.

All this information is fine and dandy for someone entering college for the first time, you say, but what if you're interested in attending graduate school? The .edu site has graduate school rankings, financial advice, and career counseling links to help you plan your educational path.

U.S. News & World Reports has put together a gold mine of college information in their .edu pages. If you connect to this site, be prepared to spend some serious time here. It's the closest you'll ever come to one-stop college information, so have fun browsing and bask in how much money you'll save on all those select-a-college books!

Have fun searching for the perfect college, and revel in how much money you saved by not buying all those select-a-college books!

Put Those Leftovers to Good Use

It's the Sunday after Thanksgiving, and you're fresh out of creative ideas for turkey leftovers. In fact, your family might start taking hostages if you produce another turkey sandwich! What do you do?

Use your WebTV Internet terminal to surf over to the Epicurious Eating Recipe File at: *www.epicurious.com/e_eating/e02_recipes/recipes.html*. You can search well over 6,000 recipes from the likes of *Bon Appetit, Gourmet,* and *House and Garden,* or even recipes from new cookbooks. Your search is based on key ingredients or the type of dish you specify. (In case you're curious, I found over 125 recipes for turkey, ranging from turkey lasagna to turkey quesadillas.) Or, if you prefer, you can just browse through the database for inspiration. This site may very well be responsible for restoring family peace at the end of November!

Pick the Perfect Pooch

Say *that* quickly three times in a row.... Seriously, have you contemplated getting a dog but weren't sure which breed would be best for your family and the size of your home or property? The Waltham Pet Foods Company has created "Select-a-Dog" (*www.waltham.com*) to help you make the best decision possible.

The questionnaire asks you a series of questions, ranging from how much money you want to spend feeding the dog each week to the ages of children that would be living with the dog. The site analyzes your responses and then returns the best breed of dog, based on the answers you provided. You see a color picture of the dog and a description of the breed's traits. In most cases, "Select-a-Dog" provides you with more than one breed that closely matches your criteria. Simply select the breed's name, and press Go to see similar information on the other breeds you chose.

Chart a Path

Have a baby shower coming up? Need to host a silver wedding anniversary party? Wouldn't it be nice to include a professional-looking map with step-by-step directions (see Figure 19-1 in the invitations so that your guests know how to get there? We've all received those illegible scrawlings that do more harm than good, but now you can be the envy of all your friends by including a map that actually helps your guests get to their destination.

Figure 19-1 *Help your guests get to the party on time by including step-by-step directions and a map in your invitations.*

All you need is a printer hooked up to your WebTV Internet terminal. Go to one of the following addresses:

- MapQuest at *www.mapquest.com*
- Zip2 at *www.zip2.com*
- CyberRouter at *route30.delorme.com*

Become a Virtual Volunteer

More than a million nonprofit organizations in the United States alone rely on the support of volunteers to fulfill their mission. Whether you're a retired corporate executive who'd like to act as an advisor to such an organization or a homemaker who wants to help further the work of a favorite cause, distance need not exclude you. A lot of advice can be exchanged via e-mail, and in many cases, an organization can use people in different locales to spearhead regional fund-raising efforts.

You can link up with organizations needing your help by browsing their Web sites or by sending them e-mail expressing an interest in their efforts. More recently, however, a number of online volunteer clearinghouses have emerged. As nonprofits rely increasingly on the Internet to recruit volunteers, you'll see even more of these sites crop up.

The best way to find organizations needing help in your area is to press the Search button and then type in the word "volunteer," followed by the name of your city, state, or preferred cause. A sample entry might be "volunteer maryland animals" or "volunteer orlando." The search engine will return a list of Web sites that will point you in the direction of a host of opportunities unique to your location and special interest. Simply select the site you wish to visit, and then press Go to see if there's a good match between what you can offer and what the organization needs most.

Expand Your Collection, or Learn More About It

Maybe you've collected Barbie dolls for years and finally have more time (and let's be honest, more money as well) to devote to building your collection. The Internet is a great place to learn more about your collection,

The Fun Part

whether it's miniature die-cast cars, postage stamps, or Christmas ornaments. You can get the lowdown on the value of some of your pieces, learn interesting tidbits about factory errors that resulted in extremely limited (and valuable) runs, or even get a sneak peek at what's coming down the road so that you can plan and budget your purchases.

Many manufacturers of collectibles have set up Web sites. Some of the more prominent ones include:

- Matchbox Toys at *www.matchboxtoys.com*
- Hot Wheels at *www.hotwheels.com*
- Barbie Collectibles at *www.barbie.com*
- Enesco (Precious Moments, Cherished Teddies, and other products) at *www.enesco.com*
- Coin Universe at *www.coin-universe.com*
- Hallmark Cards at *www.hallmark.com*
- Lladró figurines at *www.lladro.es*
- LGB trains at *www.lgb.com*
- Fleer or Skybox trading cards at *www.skybox.com*

While manufacturers provide a reliable source of information about upcoming products, keep in mind that they're going to be biased. The more objective and critical reactions of die-hard collectors and the related gossip may be more your cup of tea. To find sites like these, press Search, type in your preferred collectible, and then press Go to see a list of related sites. It may take some time to weed out the good from the bad, but once you do, you'll be amazed at the way these sites and the people who frequent them enrich your collecting experience.

> **TECHNOBABBLE** **Rings**—Many sites dedicated to collectibles have formed "rings" to link similar sites. For instance, by pressing the Barbie ring icon on a selected Web page, you are automatically transported to the next Barbie site in the ring. This is a terrific way to immerse yourself in data about your favorite collectible.

Of course, you can also purchase items for your collection from a variety of online storefronts or from a fellow collector in a discussion group. Just reread Chapter 17 before doing so.

Plan Your Dream House

We've all dreamed of living in a spacious home complete with a decadent master bath, a room for each kid, a sunny breakfast nook, and a kitchen to die for. Why not give in to your fantasies if only for a few moments? Visit Builder Online at *www.builderonline.com* to search a sizable database of online house plans. You can choose the style of the house, its size, and the number of bedrooms and baths, and you can even specify the desired number of stories in the house. Figure 19-2 shows an example.

Figure 19-2. *Choose which part of the house you want to view by selecting the name of the desired area and then pressing Go.*

While the site is commercial in nature (they want you to buy those plans you fell in love with), it's still a fun place to browse. Just be ready to drool...

Choose Your Junk Mail

It may seem like you have no control over the junk mail that gets stuffed in your mailbox, but now you can at least control the catalogs you receive. Visit any of the following sites to add your name to or remove it from a catalog mailing list. But be sure to read their policies carefully about whether they will share or withhold your name from other interested parties. You don't want to be surprised at receiving catalogs you never intended to order.

- Catalog Site at *www.catalogsite.com*
- Catalog World at *www.catalogworld.com*

Learn More About a Medical Condition

The world of medicine can really baffle a person. What's worse is that medical professionals will sometimes dump a diagnosis on you and then rush you out of the office before you can even catch your breath to ask a simple question. While no printed fact sheet can (or should) replace the wisdom of a professional, it can answer a few of your questions and make you an educated patient. Browse these Web sites for an overview of hundreds of medical conditions:

- HealthGate Free Medline at *www.healthgate.com* is a potentially bountiful resource if you know how to spell the condition you wish to research.

- Healthfinder at *www.healthfinder.gov* is a great resource if you're looking up one of the conditions it has listed. This site has a large number to choose from, but neither of the conditions I wanted more information about was available.

- Thrive at *www.thriveonline.com* provides lots of information, although some of it is older than that found on other sites. On the other hand, I did find what I needed here, so with a little patience and digging, this may be a good bet for you, too.

- Mental Health Net at *www.cmhc.com* is a tremendous resource and reading area on mental health issues ranging from depression to anxiety.

- Prevention's Healthy Ideas at *www.healthyideas.com* offers ideas for a more natural approach to health care.

Web sites dedicated to educating consumers about the medicines they take are also available. Because not all physicians thoroughly explain potential side effects of these medications, it might often be up to you to learn more details. Check some of these sites for more information:

- To get the latest information on drugs recently approved by the FDA, visit *www.fda.gov/cder/da/da.htm*. You might even be more up-to-date than your doctor by browsing this site.

- Visit HealthTouch at *www.healthtouch.com/level1/p_dri.htm* to search on the name of your medication, but be sure to have the correct spelling. You can learn all about the medicine you're taking from this site, including what it does, what the potential side effects are, and so on.

- RxList at *www.rxlist.com* provides more information (it even includes some clinical studies) than HealthTouch, but there is a downside—RxList is a little harder to navigate and it has a smaller number of medications listed. It does list the 200 most commonly used drugs, however, which means your odds of finding the information you need are still pretty good.

Hundreds, if not thousands, of Web sites are dedicated to specific medical conditions, which you can find using a search engine as described in Chapter 21. You might also find a number of special support groups (either a discussion group or mailing list, or sometimes both) on the Internet. Read Chapter 11, "A Nose for News (or Gossip)," for more information on how to find a specific discussion group, or visit *www.liszt.com* to search for a mailing list.

Have a Good Laugh

As you've read this book, you've probably noticed my love of humor. It creeps in at some of the strangest times, I know, but it's my favorite coping strategy. If you want a good laugh or need to come up with a funny icebreaker for a speech you have to give, consider tapping into the vast resources of the Internet. Humor sites range from politically incorrect jokes to Microsoft jokes to profession-specific jokes.

Visit a few of these sites, but don't do it in the middle of the night—you might wake the kids when you start laughing!

- LaughWEB, a must-see for those wanting a good laugh on just about any topic imaginable, can be found at *www.intermarket.net/laughweb*. Jokes are divided into categories and are rated on their funniness, so you can be guaranteed a good laugh. But be forewarned—some of the material could be considered offensive. Then again, just about any joke could be offensive, depending on how you look at it...

- Wanna make fun of your own name or the names of others? Check out the Internet Anagram Server at *www.wordsmith.org/anagram*. I'm sorry to say that my name is so boring, no anagrams were found. But I take great comfort in knowing I'm married to "a sneeze we fry" (Wayne S. Freeze to the anagram-impaired). At least *his* name is interesting.

Plan Your Vacation

Grandkids out of school for the day and clamoring for someplace fun to go? Have a week's vacation you need to use before the end of the year or you'll lose it? Surf the Net for great ideas, whether you're planning your trip a year ahead of time or an hour ahead of time. (You'll find even more money-saving travel tips in the next chapter.)

Consult the following Web sites to locate special events of interest:

- Festivals.com at *www.festivals.com* lets you search a database of over 20,000 festivals, fairs, and special events worldwide. You can conduct your search based on the location, the dates, or the type of event, so finding something fun to do just got a whole lot easier.

- If you're craving cotton candy and carnival rides, surf over to FairsNet at *www.fairsnet.org* for the most complete listing of fairs out there. This site even includes links to fair home pages (where available) so that you can get the latest information about your special event.

- If music is your passion, visit Festival Finder at *www.festivalfinder.com* to locate information on over 1,300 music festivals in North America.

These sites can help you choose a travel destination:

- Travel.org: The Directory of Travel at *www.travel.org* is your one-stop shop containing destination links worldwide.

- Another terrific resource is CityNet at *www.city.net*, which includes not only destination links but also links to movie theater information, local newspapers, and so on.

Extend Your TV Viewing Experience

We all have a favorite TV show that we just can't seem to get enough of, whether it's a daily soap opera or a weekly science fiction thriller. Luckily, the television networks and some very dedicated fans have produced a phenomenal number of Web pages and newsgroups enabling us to get our fix of the show between airings.

If you want more information about a TV show, perhaps the place to start is the Web site for the network that broadcasts the show. To do so, press GoTo and enter *www.* followed by the network name (ABC, NBC, CBS, or FOX) and then *.com*. PBS is the exception—its URL ends with *.org*. Press Go to proceed to the site. Because these sites are so large and well traveled, navigating through them to find your favorite show should be pretty easy.

But the best stuff, in my opinion, is the information gathered by the fans. Some of the better fan sites will provide you with obscure facts about your favorite actors, color photos, biographies, and even links to online interviews and question-and-answer sessions. You can also learn how to join a fan club or how to write to your favorite star.

To find information about your favorite show, check out these sites:

- Ultimate TV at *www.ultimatetv.com* for a searchable megadirectory of resources (including Web pages, discussion groups, and episode lists) dedicated to TV shows.
- Sony Online at *www.sony.com* for information on a whole host of popular contemporary shows.

Chapter 20

Over a Dozen Ways to Save Time and Money Surfing the Net

OK, raise your hand if this is the first chapter in the book you turned to. Go on, admit it. It's a rare person who can turn their back on the concept of saving time and money.

In fact, you can never have enough time and money, which is why this chapter goes to great lengths to show you just how much of both you can save surfing the Net. You might think $20 a month for Internet access is a sizable chunk of money, but after I show you just how much money you can save using your WebTV Internet terminal, you might even want to buy two WebTV Internet terminals to double your savings. (Not really, but the savings will impress you anyway.)

Hang Up the Phone and Grab the Remote

How much did you spend on long distance calls last month? I'm not trying to be nosy, but it really is relevant to the point I'm trying to make. Did you know that for the monthly cost of your Internet access, you'd be lucky if you could get three hours per month of long distance time? And that's if you could secure a dime-a-minute rate any time of day. Seriously, that's a measly

45 minutes a week you could spend chatting with your grandchild about his school science project; that you could spend getting caught up on the events in your daughter's pregnancy; that you could spend cultivating a new friendship....

I don't know about you, but I think this is one of those instances where quantity counts. I like being able to connect any time of day to share a funny story with a friend. There's something comforting about knowing that you can ask someone a question without having to bug them on the telephone. They can go about their business and give you their undivided attention when it's convenient, which is nice for both parties.

But say none of the people you call regularly have Internet access. You can point out to them that if they spend as much money calling you as you do them, it might be worth getting them to link up, too. (In case you're wondering, neither WebTV Networks nor Microsoft Press told me to make this point. It was my own idea entirely. Of course, I would be most grateful if you'd recommend this book to your friends as well <wink, wink, nudge, nudge>.)

SOS (Save Our Stamps)

Some of us just aren't phone people. We'd rather write a 20-page letter than spend five minutes on the phone. Besides, long distance phone rates are expensive. If you think sending a letter is cheaper than using the telephone, just think of all the postage you can save by connecting to the Internet (plus you don't risk paper cuts on your tongue from licking envelopes). E-mail can be an extremely cost-effective alternative for staying in touch, and compared to the time delay of letter writing, the quick turnaround of e-mail is really significant. For example, if you live in Maryland and send a letter to your parents in rural South Dakota via the U.S. Postal Service, it takes four to five days for the letter to get there. Assume that your parents answer the letter and place their reply in the mail the same day. Another four to five days must pass for the letter to get back to you, and that's not factoring in weekends. Suddenly, close to two weeks have passed before you receive the answer to a question or a reaction to your big news. If you're anything like me, you've forgotten what you wrote to them in the first place by the time you get a response!

End the waiting and use e-mail. You'll love the quick response time, and what will really blow you away is the first time you're connected at the same time as your recipient. You'll find yourselves firing e-mail back and forth quicker than fourth graders pass notes in the classroom.

Magazine Mania

I have a confession to make. As I stand in long grocery store lines, I've been known to grab my favorite magazine, flip through it, skim the best parts, and then put it back. In fact, I rarely buy the magazines displayed at the counter because I usually have ample time to read the parts I would have read had I bought the magazine in the first place. So why throw my money away, right?

Now before you accuse me of stealing, I must say I've given up my old habit in favor of an even better approach—browsing online versions of magazines. I don't get everything I'd get in the printed edition, but the online versions are still an invaluable entertainment and research resource. Check out the magazine list at *www.newslink.org/mag.html* (see Figure 20-1), sponsored by the *American Journalism Review,* to see if your favorite is online, and then simply follow the link to see what it has to offer.

Figure 20-1.   *See the likes of* Motor Trend *magazine on your TV screen.*

The Fun Part

How can magazine publishers afford to do this if it lets people avoid buying the paper versions? Simple—the publishers sell online advertising as well, so the more people that visit their Web site, the more they can charge for online advertising. And in many cases, the pared-down online version doesn't dissuade their regular subscribers from renewing anyway.

If you're frugal like me or want to sample a magazine before buying a copy or subscribing to it, this link will definitely save you money in the long run by helping you make informed magazine purchases.

No News Is Good News (or Is It?)

Think of all the things we could do if we eliminated that hour (or more) we spend watching the news every day on television. We could finally get ourselves on a good exercise regimen; we could plant a colorful bed of flowers and tend to them each day; we could read that new Stephen King novel we've been dying to get our hands on; we could prepare a healthy meal instead of settling for fast food again.

Chances are there's something you'd rather spend that extra hour doing. But you can't live in a vacuum—you need to know what's going on in the world. So how do you find the news you need, and leave all the useless fluff behind?

Well, if you haven't already guessed where I'm going with this, it's time to recaffeinate yourself. Seriously, you'd be surprised at just how much time a good Internet news site can save. We all have different needs when it comes to the kind of news we like to track and what locales we want to know more about. Only you can determine which site will ultimately become your favorite. You've gotta start somewhere, however, so here are a few places you'll want to check out:

- You've probably already seen this site in your travels around the WebTV Network's pages, but it's worth mentioning again. USA Today at *www.usatoday.com* gives you access to a host of national and local news.

- Another valuable tool is Reuters Online at *www.reuters.com*. This searchable newswire service gives you up-to-the-minute news on specified subjects, or you can scan its headlines for the biggest news.

- You can never go wrong with CNN (*www.cnn.com*) as a reliable, frequently updated news source.

Finally, for concentrated local coverage, visit *www.newslink.org/news.html* (the *American Journalism Review*'s list of newspapers online) or check your favorite television network's home page for links to a local affiliate. Most networks' news centers maintain home pages dedicated to hometown issues or at the very least provide storm tracking for hurricanes and blizzards.

Avoid Club Confusion

If you've ever belonged to a video or music club, you know what a pain it can be to remember to return those dated postcards. How many videos have you ended up keeping even though you didn't like them because returning them was such a hassle?

Now with your WebTV Internet terminal, you can join the clubs knowing that you can quickly and conveniently say no to the merchandise you don't want. So if you've hesitated joining thus far, take another look. Belonging to a club can be a convenient, economical way to get the newest releases first. Browse the Columbia House Record, Video, and CD Club at *www.columbiahouse.com* to locate videos, computer games, and audio CDs and cassettes.

Finance Your Dream Home

Remember those decadent house plans you found in the previous chapter? Well, the money to pay for the house is going to have to come from somewhere. Surf over to Homes and Land Electronic Magazine at *www.homes.com* to check out their nifty mortgage calculator. You can figure out how much your mortgage payment would be based on how big your down payment is and the interest rate you secure. You can also discover whether it's more economical for you to buy or rent, as well as perform other interesting calculations.

The Fun Part

By running some sample analyses, you can see just how much house you can afford given your income. All you have to do is enter some basic numbers and let the mortgage calculator do the rest. Just be sure to read the instructions carefully to avoid getting unpredictable results. For instance, the way you determine the interest rate can be confusing, so be sure to read all the details.

Get Carded

Is anyone else in shock over the price of greeting cards? I mean, what used to be a relatively minor expense in relation to a gift has now turned into a big deal. The average greeting card costs well over $1.50. I used to send Christmas cards to more than 70 people until I saw I was spending in excess of $125 on purchasing and mailing these cards alone. That's a considerable chunk of anyone's holiday gift-giving budget. Last year I started slicing people from my Christmas card list right and left just to bring the cost down. But I felt like such a Scrooge....

This year I plan to try something a little different. Rather than crossing people off my list altogether, I may opt to send a virtual greeting card—it's free, and it tells people I'm thinking of them. While I wouldn't advise doing this for your spouse's birthday, it's a great no-cost way to bring a smile to someone's face on a rough day.

> **CAUTION** Since the artwork available at these Web sites changes regularly, we cannot guarantee that the content will be appropriate for all ages. To make sure young surfers access an appropriate site, consider browsing pages such as *www.barbie.com*, *rw.warnerbros.com/ns1_indx.html*, or *www.lionking.org/postcard*.

Watch for special banner ads from sites offering this service around holidays like Valentine's Day, Mother's Day, and so on. Or visit any of these sites for a "just because" occasion:

- At the E-Cards Web site at *e-cards.com*, you can send a free electronic postcard to anyone with an e-mail account and Web access. During times when the site has an advertising sponsor, money will be contributed to the World Wildlife Fund for each card sent. Best of all, none of this costs you a penny. Figure 20-2 shows a sample virtual card from this site.

20: Over a Dozen Ways to Save Time and Money Surfing the Net

Figure 20-2. *Virtual greeting cards offer a cost-effective, personalized option for people who want to brighten a friend's day on impulse. And, in the case of E-Cards, you can even help save endangered species!*

- If you want a banquet of choices, consider this list of the best 100 virtual greeting card sites: *www.cyberpanda.com/postcard*. If you look carefully, you'll notice that you can also send virtual flower bouquets.

- Can't find anything you like at the site above? Try *www.pnx.com/kbs/greet.htm*. But keep in mind that some of these sites may contain artwork or photography that is not appropriate for young Internet surfers.

Listen Up!

Are you tired of trying to figure out who in the world sings that song you've been hearing on the radio 20 times a day? Try Billboard Online at *www.billboard.com*. Here you'll find the weekly ratings of songs in various genres, along with audio tracks of many of the top-rated artists and songs. While it'll take some time to download the audio track (don't worry, we're talking a few minutes, not hours), your mind will rest when you finally know who sings the song.

When you find a link to an audio track, select it and press Go. Choose only Real Audio or WAV tracks, however, since your WebTV Internet terminal cannot play MPEG audio yet. If you have a choice, select Real Audio 3.0 tracks, because this will give you the quickest results.

> **TECHNOBABBLE** **Real Audio**—a technology used for playing sound tracks on computers or computer-like devices.

Now for the obligatory tie-in to the chapter's theme—Billboard Online gives you the opportunity to sample snippets of today's hottest music, which, in turn, helps you choose the CDs you want to buy before shelling out the money. Because each album has three or more tracks available for your listening pleasure, you stand an even better chance of spending your music bucks wisely. And no more fighting over those headphones in music stores!

Get There Inexpensively

You'd be surprised at how much you can save by being your own travel agent. You can shop for airfares or select an economical hotel from the comfort of your family room. Travel resource sites are an interesting lot, however. Because some of them are sponsored or underwritten by specific companies, you might not see as broad a selection as you might expect, so read your results carefully.

To locate the best airfare, try these sites:

- Travelocity at *www.travelocity.com* gives you the opportunity to search for airfares based on price or time of departure. You can also take advantage of last-minute travel bargains or select a hotel. Some services do require you to sign up for an account, but the accounts are free.

- One of my favorite airfare sites is Flifo at *www.flifo.com*. From here you can search for a flight based on a variety of criteria, and you can even check the arrival times of incoming guests.

- Don't like flying? Try Amtrak at *www.amtrak.com* to learn about the schedule and fares for each stop along the Amtrak line.

20: Over a Dozen Ways to Save Time and Money Surfing the Net

Having saved hundreds of dollars on airfare, it's only natural that you'd want to conduct your own search for a place to stay, too. Try some of these resort and hotel sites:

- TravelWeb at *www.travelweb.com* lets you search for hotels based on a number of criteria, and then links you to online reservations systems where available. This site also provides photos of the properties and information about their amenities. The problem here is that the hotel selection is limited to certain chains.

- Browse the Hotel and Travel Index Online at *www.traveler.net/htio* to see information, including reviews, on thousands of hotels throughout the world.

- Perhaps the best deals are made by locating the desired hotel's site directly. Take the Holiday Inn Sunspree in Orlando, for instance. By going to *www.kidsuites.com*, you can search the hotel's reservation system to check for availability of a room during the specified dates. Use the tips in Chapter 21, "Become a Virtual Bloodhound," to learn how and where to find the property you're looking for.

Taxing Times

It's April 14th, and you're panicking because you don't have your taxes done. Just as you're about to fill out the last page, you discover you need some obscure tax form from the IRS. It's also 9:00 P.M., so the library is closed and you have to be at work early in the morning for a meeting. What's worse is you went to the library last weekend and spent hours tracking down and photocopying all the forms you thought you needed. Grrr!

If you have the WebTV Internet terminal printer adapter and a compatible printer, you might be in luck. By visiting the IRS's Web site at *www.irs.gov*, you might be able to print the forms and the instructions you need in a snap. Have the form numbers handy, fire up your printer, and you're ready to go!

Read 'Em and Weep (or Buy 'Em)

I've lost track of how many books I've purchased only to find that after reading the first chapter I just can't get into the story. Sometimes the style is too dry; other times the book has no personality. But no matter what the case, books are too expensive to just toss our hard-earned money at them. Sure, you scarf up the latest Tom Clancy, Mary Higgins Clark, or Danielle Steele novel because you know what to expect, but when you try a new author for the first time, it's nice to know what you're getting into without loitering for hours in the bookstore (unless you have the luxury to do so).

The Washington Post's Chapter One feature at *www.washingtonpost.com/wp-srv/style/longterm/books/books.htm* gives you the opportunity to read the first chapters of books before you buy them. You can also browse bestseller lists and read a host of book reviews, which—in theory—should help you find a book you'll enjoy.

Comparison Shop Without Wearing Out Your Shoes

Believe it or not, many of your favorite stores are also online, so it's possible to comparison shop without getting blisters. And just as grocery stores in proximity to one another compete for your business, online merchants do the same.

Take two of the biggest book merchants on the Web, for example: Amazon Books at *www.amazon.com* and Barnes and Noble at *www.barnesandnoble.com*. Amazon has a huge following among netizens because it was one of the first and the biggest bookstores on the Web. With Barnes and Noble on the scene, the two rivals are vying for your business by offering deep discounts on books on the bestseller lists and other price reductions. This high level of competition will continue on the Internet as e-commerce sites keep sprouting up. It pays to shop around, and you're the one who stands to benefit.

For convenient comparison shopping, try either of these Internet malls:

- The Internet Mall at *www.internet-mall.com* is one of the largest with over 4,500 stores. And you thought that 200-store mall in your town was big!

- At RealMalls at *www.realmalls.com*, you can decide whether you want to locate a mall near you or shop online. Or, if you're going on vacation, use RealMalls to scope out all the good shopping in the area you'll be visiting.

Lose Your Package?

Aunt Millie didn't receive that package you sent her for her birthday? Next time, use package tracking to protect your goodies. While that terrycloth robe is replaceable, those special photos of the baby might not be. So the next time you mail a package, write down the tracking number, and surf to one of these sites to monitor its progress:

- UPS at *www.ups.com*
- Federal Express at *www.fedex.com*
- Airborne Express at *www.airborne.com*
- DHL Worldwide Express at *www.dhl.com*

Be Your Own Operator

How many times have you had to dial directory assistance to get the phone number of the florist in your grandmother's town? Save yourself the pricey fees by looking up your own phone numbers at one of the following Web sites:

- Big Book at *www.bigbook.com* gives you access to searchable yellow pages complete with maps, driving directions, and the ability to maintain your own address book based on listings you select. Figure 20-3 on the following page shows an example.

The Fun Part

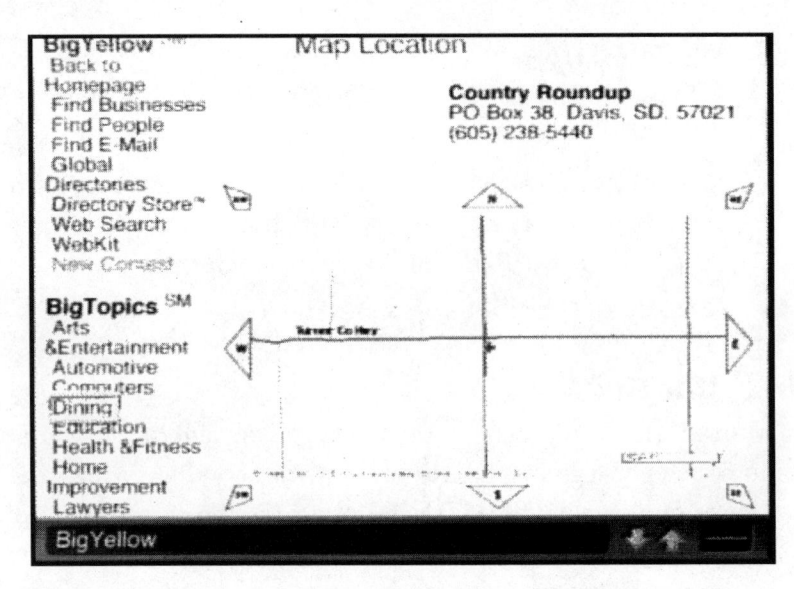

Figure 20-3. *The entry for the Country Roundup, my parent's place in Davis, South Dakota. If you're ever in the neighborhood, stop by and tell Bucky you bought his daughter's book!*

- With the AT&T Toll-Free Internet Directory at *www.tollfree.att.net/dir800*, you can obtain the toll-free number to many of your favorite businesses. Let them pick up the tab for your call.

- Switchboard at *www.switchboard.com* will help you find a variety of businesses in a selected category within the area you specify. You can also obtain personal white page listings from this site.

Chapter 21

Become a Virtual Bloodhound

With millions of Web sites on the Internet, finding the information you want can be overwhelming and downright intimidating. So how can you find the proverbial needle in the haystack? There are essentially three approaches: guessing, browsing, and searching.

The first of the three probably sounds the least promising, but it's actually one of the quickest ways to find what you want.

Say you're planning a trip to Walt Disney World and are wondering if it has a Web site you can browse for current information. If you want to use the guessing approach, enter *www.* followed by what you guess might be right, in this case *disneyworld,* and then *.com.* (The *http://* portion of the address will be provided for you, as shown in Figure 21-1.)

In this case, you'll be connected directly to the Walt Disney World home page without having to browse a long list of sites produced by a search engine. You can try this with any number of companies and organizations. Flip back through Chapters 19 and 20, for instance. You'll notice that many of the Web site URLs mentioned there are what you might have guessed they'd be.

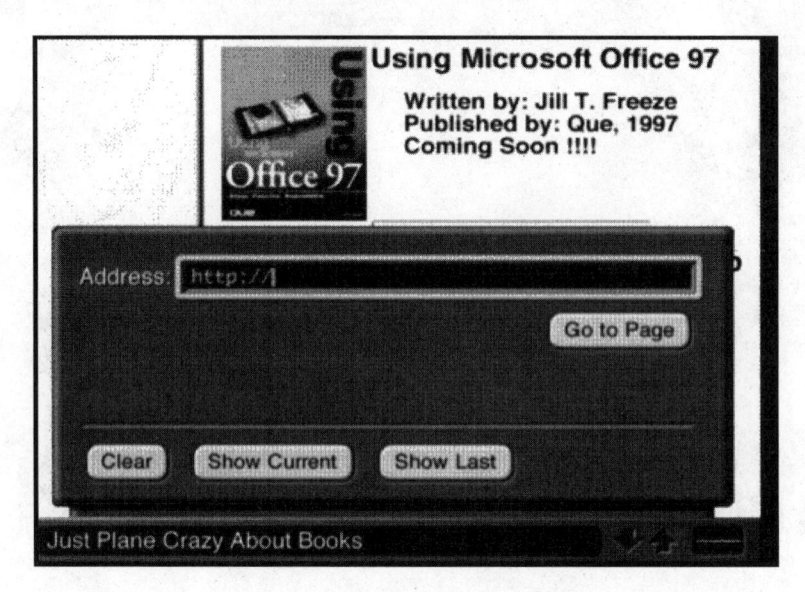

Figure 21-1. *Use this screen to get to the information you want in a snap.*

Still a little hesitant to try your hand at guessing? Check out the following tips, fire up your Internet terminal, and play around a bit. What's gonna happen if you try a wrong address? It's not like walking out of a department store where loud sirens go off when the clerk forgets to remove the magnetic strip from the video you just purchased. No need to be nervous about it. And unlike dialing the wrong number, you don't disturb anyone while you experiment. Read the tips and give it a shot.

- Most URLs have a *www.* at the front of them, so be sure to type that in first. Now type your favorite corporation, institution, or organization name, or even a brand name or product name followed by .com. For example, *www.porsche.com* for the auto manufacturer, *www.kelloggs.com* for the makers of popular breakfast cereals and Pop-Tarts, and *www.dietcoke.com* for the energy that wrote this book. (I mean the soft drink company.) The possibilities are endless.

- If you're really adventurous, you might want to try the name of a favorite object or hobby and see where it lands you. You might be disappointed, though. I tried *www.turtle.com* for my four-year-old son, Christopher, and found an electrical parts supplier. Trying *www.cats.com* for three-year-old Samantha was just as disappointing. (It turned out to be a site for strategic risk management software.) Even so, you stand an equally good chance of stumbling onto a gem, so it's worth a shot.

- Many of the Web sites you will be looking for will have the *.com* extension at the end of their domain name. But there are exceptions to this. If the entity you are seeking is a college or a university, attach the *.edu* extension instead of *.com*, as in *www.umass.edu*. (Go, Minutemen!) Or if the site belongs to an organization like the American Association for Retired Persons (AARP), try the *.org* extension, as in *www.aarp.org*. Many associations dedicated to various medical conditions use the *.org* extension, as do a number of nonprofit cultural and social cause organizations. The *.gov* extension is reserved for government agencies like *www.fda.gov*.

- If the entity is hard to categorize, start with *.com*, and then try the other extensions if you come up dry.

If plugging in random names isn't your cup of tea, consider using a subject index to browse categories of interest.

Systematic Surfing: When You Kinda Know What You Want

If you want to poke around sites devoted to a general topic like aviation, as opposed to a specific topic like P-38 Lightnings, you might want to consider browsing a subject index until something catches your fancy. You already have Explore easily accessible from the WebTV Networks' home page, but there might come a time when you want even more information at your fingertips.

Subject indexes (as shown in Figure 21-2 on the following page) categorize sites based on the topics they present, so you can simply work your way through a given list. However, since subject indexes are most often created by humans (rather than by computers), they tend to be smaller than the lists generated by search engines. But that might not be a bad thing.

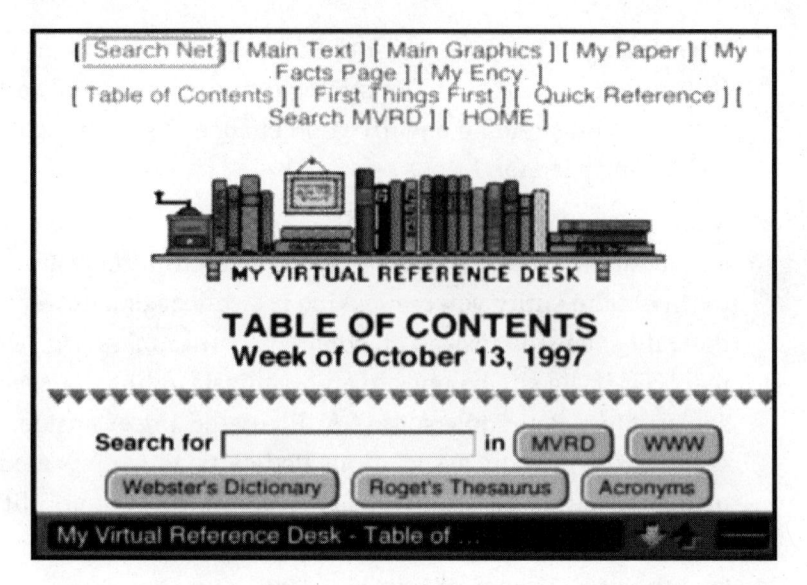

Figure 21-2. *When I need to do a lot of research in a hurry, I often visit My Virtual Reference Desk (www.refdesk.com) to find links to many of the best reference resources on the Net. It's organized by subject, so I can quickly home in on what I need.*

Search engines frequently show Web sites with titles like "Billy-Bob's Cool Fishing Lure Links." While the links might very well be good, they could just as easily lead to other, uh, less-than-professional links. Sites listed in the indexes are oftentimes approved by (or at least have been visited by) the index staff, which filters out some of the useless sites, too.

So where do you find all these neat indexes? Try some of these on for size:

- **Yahoo**. Perhaps the largest subject index on the Web, Yahoo at *www.yahoo.com* is a searchable subject index capable of accessing data from a variety of databases. You can either click your way through a hierarchy of subjects or fill out the text box to search the index.

- **Magellan**. This index reviews and rates a number of sites and makes them available on its Web site, and is located at *www.mckinley.com*. You can perform searches on the reviewed sites only or on the Web in general. Oh, and check out the Search Voyeur where you can see realtime lists of what searches others are performing at the same time. The subjects (and their spellings) could entertain you for a good long while!

- **My Virtual Reference Desk**. This is an outstanding place to start if you need to do some quick research. With hundreds of links to useful resources in a variety of subject areas, you could spend weeks just wandering aimlessly and soaking up knowledge. Visit this site at *www.refdesk.com*.

- **Lycos**. You'll learn more about this powerful search engine in the next section, but if you're in the mood to meander through cyberspace, you might want to browse Lycos at *www.lycos.com*.

Search for Answers

The first time I considered trying a search engine, I had to think twice. Just the term "search engine" sent shivers up my spine. I had creepy visions of huge hunks of dusty machinery lurching into motion in some faraway computer room when I pressed the button to submit a query. Of course, the term "Web crawler," along with the spider logo the Lycos search engine uses, added to the vividness of my mental picture. Then one day I got brave. Or maybe curiosity got the best of me—who knows for sure? But somehow the thought of thousands of Web sites (that's all there were back then) at my fingertips was more than a little intriguing.

Lycos was the first modern-day search engine I tried. And if I remember right, "cats" was the first word I ran a search on. My eyes nearly popped out of my head at how quickly the search engine returned a list of hundreds of sites (and today's search engines have gotten even quicker). All I had to do was select a site and click on its name, and I was immediately transported to the new location.

So how do the search engines work? Indexing some 80-million-plus Web pages seems like a formidable task, but here's an oversimplification of how it works: Each search engine maintains a list of millions of URLs. Search engines get new URLs in one or both of two ways: people provide them or a Web crawler goes from page to page, scouring them for new URLs.

> **TECHNOBABBLE** **Web crawlers**—These are programs that search engines turn loose on the Web to gather URLs. Interestingly, many search engines actually give names to these Web crawlers. For example, Excite, the search engine used by WebTV Networks, named its Web crawler "Architext Spider."

The Fun Part

Because the search engine keeps a list of URLs and what its Web crawlers find, the list becomes out of date as people change their Web pages. When you try to follow a link that is obsolete, you will get a message like the one shown in Figure 21-3.

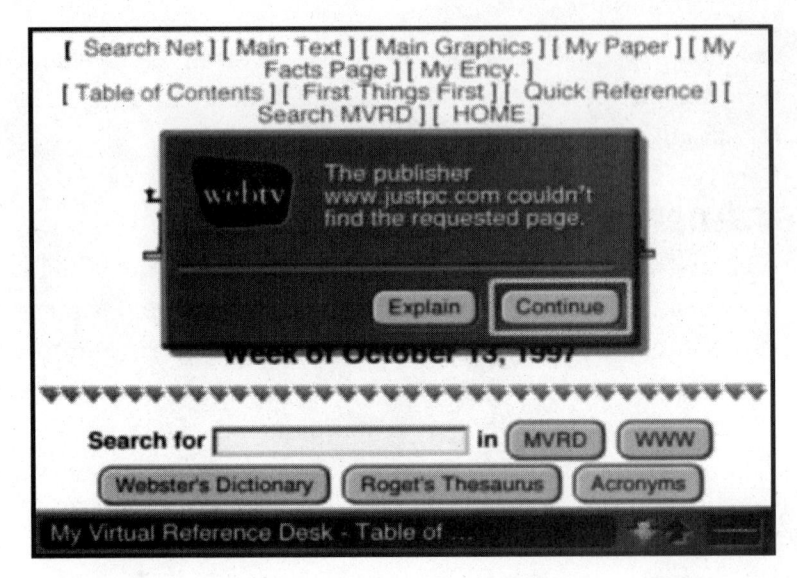

Figure 21-3. *If you follow a link to a URL that no longer exists, you will get a message like the one shown here.*

When the search engine completes a search, it'll return a report of the results. Commonly, search engines will present 10 sites at a time, although some will allow you to tweak the number a bit. These reports usually take one of two forms—Web page title and summary (as shown in Figure 21-4) or Web page title only (as shown in Figure 21-5).

244

21: Become a Virtual Bloodhound

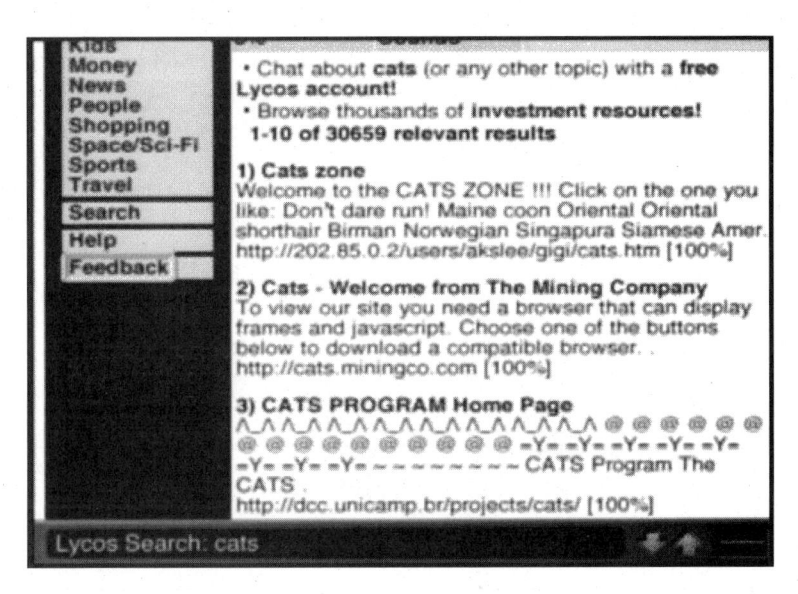

Figure 21-4. *Viewing the Web page title and a summary is one of the best ways to quickly get a feel for what kind of information resides on the page. In many cases, you can determine whether a given Web page is commercial or informational.*

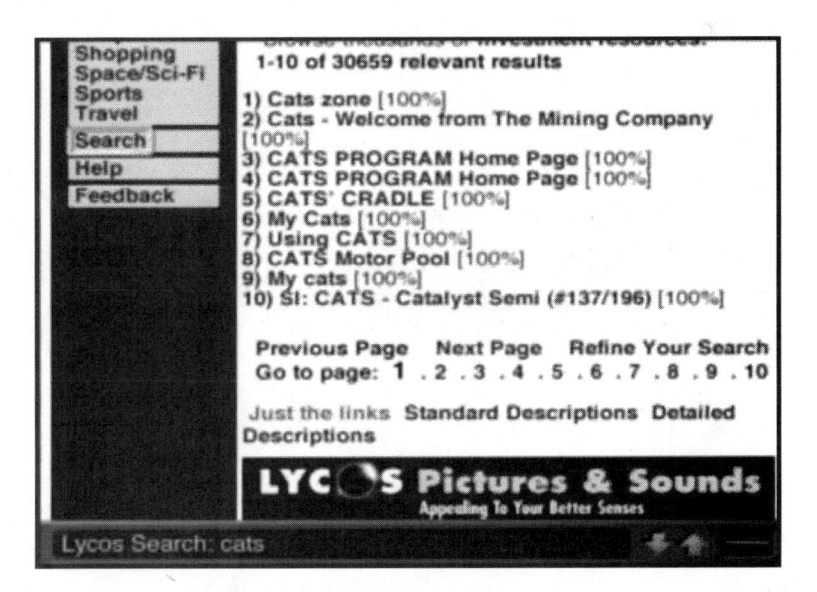

Figure 21-5. *The Web page title report allows you to skim more results at one time by displaying more Web pages on the screen.*

245

The different report formats do much more than reflect personal preferences for viewing data. Each method has its place for homing in on the information you're seeking.

- **Web page title and summary.** Use this report if you aren't quite sure what site you're searching for, since it gives you the URL as well as the page title and a summary. The URL can be extremely useful for determining such things as whether a site is an official corporate Web site or is a loyal fan's tribute to a favorite product, celebrity, or collectible.

- **Hyperlinked Web page title only.** This report enables you to fit more references on your screen, which is useful when you want to see more than the maximum number of listings at once.

And there is always the slim possibility that the search engine won't find anything based on your search criteria. (See Figure 21-6.) If this happens, you may want to consider double-checking the spelling of the word you searched on, or choose a new word or phrase altogether.

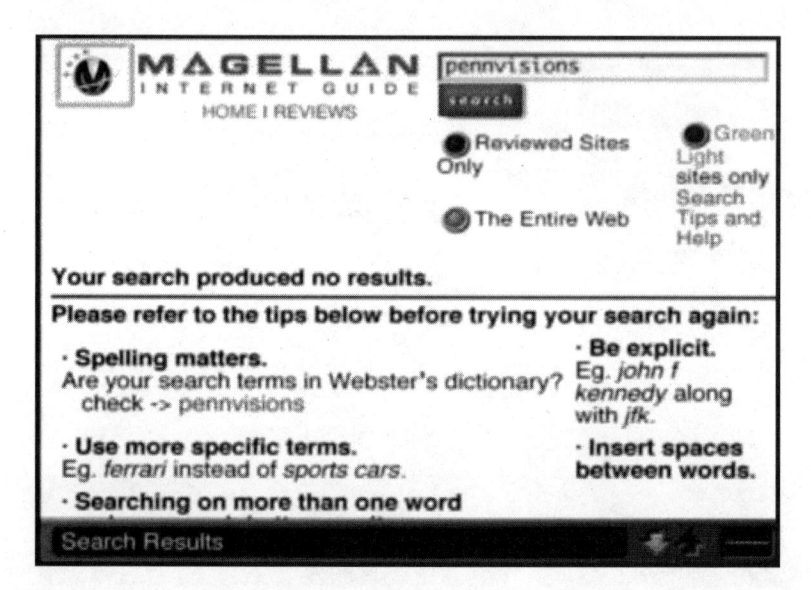

Figure 21-6. *In the rare instances where the search engine comes up dry, you will see a message similar to this one.*

Say Exactly What You Mean

Unlike humans, who can decipher what you mean by the context and voice inflection of what you say, the search engine needs to be told each nuance in order to find exactly what you want.

For example, you can search on "car dealership" and be inundated with thousands of Web pages, or you can use "Maryland car dealerships" to narrow it down a bit. The best results, however, come from something more specific—like "Maryland Toyota dealership"—which should give you a handful of Web pages covering what you want.

A number of search engines also let you search phrases by including the desired words in quotation marks. This means that if you enclose the words "paint store" in quotation marks, you'll get only Web pages that use the words paint and store together, not those that merely use both words in different locations throughout the Web page. For instance, "Wayne's Paint Store" would be retrieved, whereas "Susie orders the paint for the store" would not.

Choose Your Weapon

Not all search engines are created equal. How well they help you can depend on the size of the search engine's URL list, how search results are sorted or prioritized, how the results are displayed, and how new the information in the engine's database is. Here is a list of some of the most popular search engines and their attributes.

- **Excite.** Let's start with the search engine that automatically gets accessed when you press the Search button. Excite's database contains more than 50 million Web page listings. This ranks it among the largest search engines out there. Results are displayed in the following format: the document title, a percentage rating indicating its relevance to your query, the URL, and a summary generated by Excite made up of some of the most prominent sentences on the Web page.

- **Alta Vista.** With more than 31 million Web pages in its database, Alta Vista's biggest strength lies in its real-time indexing of over 14,000 Usenet groups. That's right—if you want to monitor all the discussion groups for a certain person's posts or want to see everything said across all groups on a given topic, this is the best place. It might not be the biggest game in town when it comes to indexing Web pages, but everything has its own set of strengths and weaknesses. Alta Vista is located at *www.altavista.digital.com*.

- **InfoSeek.** Located at *www.infoseek.com*, this search engine's database contains over 50 million Web page listings and is updated regularly and growing rapidly with the help of its constantly roaming Web crawler. While InfoSeek is one of the larger search engines, its search and reporting capabilities are a bit limited. For instance, InfoSeek does not have an advanced query option like many of the search engines have, but it does return search results with a relevancy rank expressed in percentages, which can be extremely useful in screening the results.

- **Lycos.** Boasting more than 70 million Web pages, Lycos at *www.lycos.com* is the granddaddy of them all. Like InfoSeek, Lycos gives each search result a relevancy ranking along with an excerpt from the page so that you can see what you're getting before you follow the link. What's more, Lycos lets you browse the top five percent of the most-visited Web sites on the Internet with ease, so you'll be among the most "with-it" Web surfers out there. And they've gotten rid of that old spider logo and replaced it with a sleeker, more high-tech look. Definitely worth a peek.

Search engines are like clothing—very rarely does one size fit all. You need to play with each one before settling into a favorite, and even then your choice is likely to change as new features are added or as your search needs change.

Check Up on Old Friends (and Enemies)

In past chapters, I've talked about how easy it is to make new friends on the Internet, but what about your old friends? You know, that next door neighbor kid you shot hoops with in sixth grade, or the college roommate you ate gallons of ice cream with on bad test days…. There's a darn good chance you can track them down again with the help of the Internet.

And let's be honest, we all have one of those ex-boyfriends or ex-girlfriends or archrivals we're dying to find out what happened to, and now thanks to the volumes of information online, we may finally be able to get the goods on them. It's really quite easy with a few well-narrowed searches in the right places and a little detective work.

So where do you start? If you have a good idea what city or even what state the person resides in, you can access the All-in-One Search Page at *www.albany.net/allinone/all1user.html#people* to find his or her telephone number and address (assuming it's listed). If the person has a unique name, you might be able to locate him or her without having to specify a city or state at all.

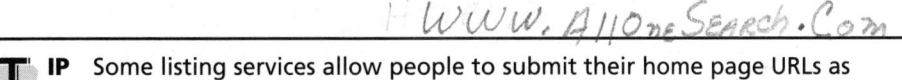

> **TIP** Some listing services allow people to submit their home page URLs as well. This can be a fun way to get up-to-date on that old flame's life!

One of the things that's so great about the All-in-One site is that you can also search for e-mail addresses and perform phone-number-to-address or phone-number-to-name searches. The All-in-One site is literally a one-stop people-finder.

> **TIP** Looking for someone outside the United States? Visit Buttle & Tuttle's Telephone Directories On The Web page at *www.contractjobs.com/tel*.

But say the person's name is Jim Smith. There are probably thousands of Jim Smiths in this world, so how do you narrow it down? Here are a few tips. Some might be common sense, while others might simply require you to know where to look for the information.

The Fun Part

- If you think there's a good possibility that the person you're searching for is active on the Internet, use DejaNews at *www.dejanews.com* (or any of the search engines with discussion group searching capabilities, like AltaVista) to scour the discussion groups for the person's name. To continue with our example, enter Jim Smith and see what groups mention the name or have participants with that name. You'll get a large number of results here, too, but you can at least include or exclude people from your list based on the type of discussion group they participated in.

- Finding "your" Jim Smith might require reading some of the discussion group articles to scan for familiar views or philosophies or ways of saying things. This might seem like a ton of work, and it is, but it's a better use of your time than calling every Jim Smith in Los Angeles. It's cheaper and less time-consuming, too.

- If you find a likely candidate, make note of the e-mail address and drop a quick note asking that person if they know you. But be sure to be polite—some people get extremely cranky when they receive e-mail not applicable to them. Thanking them in advance for any help and apologizing for your intrusion can go a long way toward smoothing ruffled feathers.

- If you think the person is likely to be looking for you, too, try visiting the PeopleFinder at *www.peoplesite.com* to browse the site for the person you're trying to locate or to place your own "searching for" blurb.

You can find someone on the Internet in any number of ways. Don't rule out the possibility that you might just run into them while participating in a discussion group or mailing list dedicated to a common passion of yours.

The world may be a big place, but thanks to the Internet, it gets smaller each day.

Chapter 22

Web Sites of Interest to Young and Old

The WebTV Internet terminal's affordability and ease of use lends itself well to younger and older audiences alike. In fact, I've been told that the WebTV Network's subscriber base is more than 25% senior citizens! Pretty neat, in my opinion. And the WebTV Internet terminal's Kid-Friendly restrictions, when enabled as shown in Chapter 7, "It's a Setup," allow even the youngest Web surfers to experience the treasures of the Internet without the risk of stumbling onto some of the more, uh, shall we say, risqué Web sites.

In this chapter, I'll show you some of the more interesting sites dedicated to youngsters and seniors. And, unlike some other Internet books, I won't show you sites you can easily find yourself by using the Explore option. You spent your hard-earned money on this book, so you deserve more than a rundown of the sites already listed in the index that came with your WebTV Internet terminal.

Kiddie Links

From bestselling children's book authors to kids' favorite TV shows, you'll find all manner of sites devoted to children's interests. From WebTV Network's Explore option, you can jump to the likes of *Sesame Street, Mister Rogers, Nickelodeon,* and so on, but here are a few more you and the younger members of your family might enjoy.

The Very Hungry Web Site

The Official Eric Carle (author of *The Very Hungry Caterpillar*) Web Site at *www.eric-carle.com* updates fans about the bestselling author's soon-to-be-released children's books. (See Figure 22-1.) The Web site also has answers to frequently asked questions about the author and provides teachers with an online forum to exchange ideas for using Eric Carle's works in the classroom. Kids can even sign Eric Carle's guestbook.

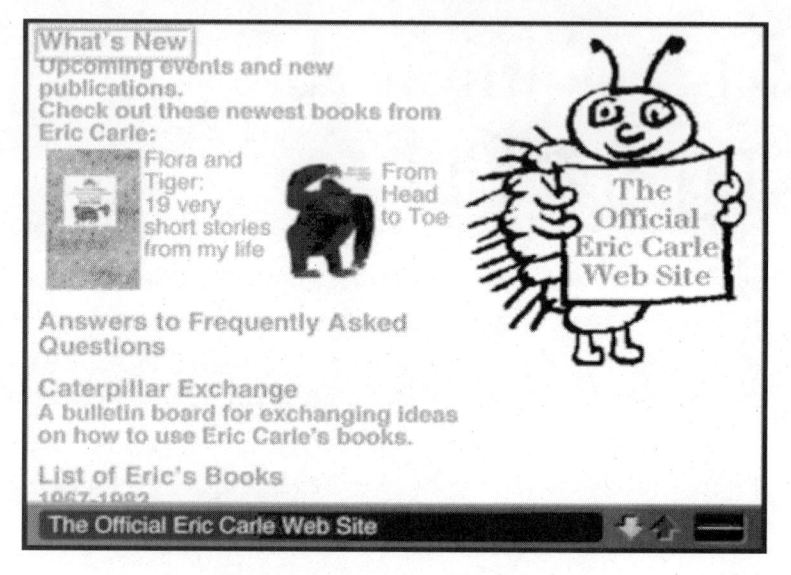

Figure 22-1. *The Official Eric Carle Web Site lets fans and readers of all ages get to know the man behind countless bestselling children's titles.*

Rockin' and Writin'

Raise your hand if you remember "Conjunction Junction" or any of the other SchoolHouse Rock videos that aired on Saturday mornings back in the 70s. It brought tears to my eyes the first time I shared these videos with my kids. There's nothing like hearing your own little ones belt out the words to songs you enjoyed as a child, especially when those songs are educational as well.

Now, thanks to this Unofficial SchoolHouse Rock Web site (see Figure 22-2) at *genxtvland.simplenet.com/SchoolHouseRock/index-h.html*, you can hear these songs, read their lyrics, and learn about how SchoolHouse Rock came into being.

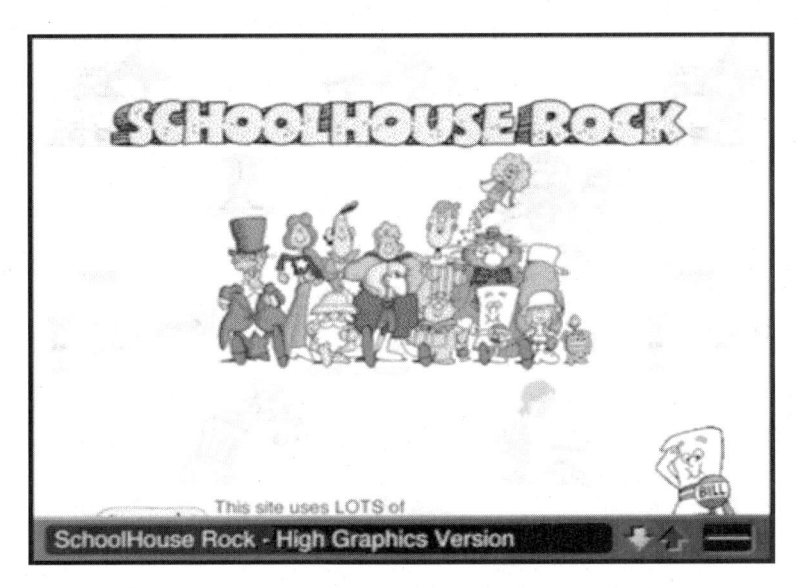

Figure 22-2. *Learning the parts of speech or the multiplication tables has never been so much fun!*

This site has won a lot of awards and is definitely worth the visit if you're a SchoolHouse Rock fan. Even if you're not familiar with the vignettes, it could be worth it to see the nursery school teacher's face when your child starts singing "Interjection, for excitement or emotion..." on the first day of school.

Tamagotchi! (Bless You!)

Tamagotchi might sound like someone sneezing, but the popularity of these virtual pets is nothing to sneeze at. It seems like every child (some of them not so young, either) has some kind of virtual pet on their toy wish list, whether it's a Tamagotchi, a Giga Pet, or a Nano Pet.

Naturally, this wildly popular toy (class of toys is probably more accurate) has spawned a number of related Web sites. Sites produced and endorsed by the manufacturers, featuring virtual pet care tips, growth charts, pictures, and the like, include the following:

- **Tamagotchi.** Bandai America, Inc.'s Tamagotchi Fever! Web page at *www.bandai.com/tamagotchiarea/index.shtml* tells you what a Tamagotchi is, updates you on newly available designs, tells you how to care for your Tamagotchi, and shows you what your Tamagotchi will look like when it grows up.

- **Giga Pets.** The official Giga Pets home page at *www.gigapets.com* shows pictures of all the Giga Pets currently available, presents care tips for a specific Giga Pet (the tips change regularly), and even lets you get in on the action by helping the manufacturers decide which Giga Pet they should produce next.

- **Nano Pets.** You'll find the official word on all Nano products (manufactured by Playmates) at *www.playmatestoys.com/pages/Nano/nano.htm*. You can even submit your own questions about how to care for your new pet or baby.

- **VirtualPets.com.** For a peek at all the virtual goodies on the way, visit *www.virtualpet.com/vp*. VirtualPets doesn't sell the pets, but this site does give you a look at all the products out there. You can even view the frequently asked questions to help you decide which pet is right for you.

If you run one of these toys' names through any of the search engines, you'll find countless Web sites created by virtual pet owners. Many of the sites are little more than diaries documenting the life (and death) of their virtual pets, but with some careful sifting through such pages, you might also uncover some valuable tips. Hey, it's worth a shot if it keeps Cyber Spot from biting the dust!

The Play's the Thing

Normally, I'm not a gambling woman, but I'm betting that if you have a TV (obviously you do, or you wouldn't be reading this book) and are a kid, act like a kid, or have one that visits you occasionally, you either have a gaming system (such as a Sony Playstation, a Nintendo 64, or a Sega Saturn) or you want one desperately. Well, maybe not desperately, but those games have caught your attention from time to time, right? I wanted an Atari something fierce when I was a kid. I never got one, so I've taken the liberty of indulging (some say spoiling) my kids. They have a Saturn, a Genesis, a slew of PC games, and we're contemplating yet another gaming system.

Web sites can be a great source of game reviews, "cheat codes," and gossip regarding upcoming new features. (Now, before you get all worried about this cheat code stuff, let me assure you that cheat codes can save your sanity when your four-year-old decides to play one of these games. You can make him "immortal" so that he can play nonstop without whining, "Daaaddy, I can't get this started again!")

But I digress. My point is that you can find lots of neat tips online to get the most out of your games (or to avoid sinking money into a real dud). Here are some places you'll want to check out:

- **Sega Online.** Visit Sega's home page at *www.sega.com* to see what games are available on each game platform. You can also visit the Sega store or find tips for getting through your favorite games.

- **Sony Playstation.** Surf over to *www.playstation.com* to see what Sony has in store for the Playstation.

- **Nintendo.** At *www.nintendo.com,* you can get the latest scoop (including screen shots) on upcoming games, access tips for many of the games, and you can see which games will be available for your favorite gaming platform.

If you still want more game-related information, there are plenty of additional Web sites and newsgroups you can track down with a simple search—many of them are dedicated to a specific game.

Golden Web Sites

Looking for legal advice? Want to learn more about that new medication the doctor just prescribed? Want to find other seniors to chat with? Plenty of sites of special interest to seniors have been designed to keep you busy and informed.

Get the Best from a Specialist

The SeniorLaw home page at *www.seniorlaw.com* (see Figure 22-3 on the following page) gives you the focused information you need to make educated decisions about your legal affairs. Hundreds of thousands of lawyers practice in the U.S.; with specialties ranging from corporate law to criminal defense, finding an attorney who knows elder law can be a challenge. Not only does this Web site point you to other elder law specialists on the Web, but it publishes important updates on Medicare and Medicaid. It also offers information on estate planning and trusts. Check it out!

Figure 22-3. *This searchable Web site lets you access quickly the information you need.*

Link to the Care You Deserve

SeniorLink at *www.seniorlink.com* claims to be the first national online eldercare resource and referral home page. This page also links you to a host of sites devoted to arthritis, financial planning, and other special concerns of senior citizens. If you want a starting point for finding quality care and services, this is it.

Senior Schmoozing

Remember those cybercommunities I mentioned in Chapter 12? Well, this is the perfect place to begin chatting with other seniors on a variety of topics. Visit the SeniorCom Web site at *www.senior.com* (see Figure 22-4) to sign up for your free chat account. You can also browse articles from the Senior News Network and even do some online shopping.

Stay Informed

You could spend days looking at all the goodies on the SeniorNet page (*www.seniornet.org*). Whether you're into chatting, looking for special senior discounts, or you want to join a book club, you'll enjoy this site shown in Figure 22-5. (Look, they even have a special deal for buying a WebTV Internet terminal, so tell all your friends!) No mere description can do this site justice—you'll have to see for yourself.

Figure 22-4. *Chat to your heart's content in the comfort of your own home.*

Figure 22-5. *Special deals for seniors abound, including this one for purchasing a WebTV Internet terminal.*

Meet Other Caring Grandparents

The Caring Grandparents of America (CGA) has a home page at *www.uconnect.com/cga* where you can share creative grandparenting ideas with others, skim articles related to grandparenting, or discover new projects to engage in with your grandkids.

A Bookstore Especially for Grandparents?

You bet! It's online at *www.cherryvalleybooks.com/grands.cfm*. In addition to books dedicated to grandparenting and grandparents in general, this virtual bookstore carries a lot of general childcare books to help you get ready for that extended visit. Of course, if you're a grandparent, you've already raised your own kids, but hey, things change!

So Many Sites, So Little Time

Obviously, the few sites presented here don't even begin to scratch the surface of what's available online. That's why it's so important to get comfortable with using search engines and to follow interesting links you find. You could spend hours or even days working your way through search engine results to find useful and fun sites. Newspaper or magazine articles or award-winning Web pages listed in Web indexes can jump you to the best of the Web more quickly.

> **TIP** Look at your favorite magazines carefully. Many of them have recently introduced special columns to highlight topical Web sites. Don't underestimate the potential of these leads. I've found some of my favorite sites this way!

Appendix

The WebTV Internet Terminal and WebTV Network Troubleshooting Guide

If something isn't working quite the way you think it should or if you see an alert message pop up on screen, consult this appendix for suggestions on how to deal with the situation. If the problem persists, try calling 1-800-GO-WEBTV for further assistance. Also consult Chapter 13, "Traffic Jams and Other Roadblocks," for information on any of the more common alert messages you might encounter.

Keyboard-Related Issues

My wireless keyboard isn't responding.

Check the angle of the keyboard. Is it pointing directly at the WebTV Internet Terminal? If not, move the keyboard around to see whether the results are better. If you're still having a problem, try pressing Return to execute a command (such as selecting a button or following a link). If nothing seems to happen, the batteries in your keyboard probably need replacing. If, on the other hand, you hear a "plunk" sound and see the yellow highlight around the button or link turn green when you press Return, the keyboard is successfully communicating with the WebTV Internet terminal.

My keyboard seems to be "stuck."

Because the wireless keyboard uses infrared signals to operate, it's possible that if you move the keyboard between the time you press a key and release it, your Internet terminal might not "see" you release the key. If

Appendix

this happens, your keyboard might behave as if one key is stuck. Should this occur, simply place the keyboard back in line with the Internet terminal and press the key once more. That should clear it up.

Remote Control–Related Issues

My remote control seems sluggish.

Are you pointing the remote control in the direction of the Internet terminal? Try pointing it right at the unit to see if anything changes. Still not working? Try pressing Go to execute a command (such as selecting a button or following a link). If the remote still doesn't respond, the batteries in your remote control probably need replacing. If you hear the "plunk" sound and see the yellow highlight around the button or link turn green when you press Go, the remote control is successfully communicating with the WebTV Internet terminal.

Service-Related Issues

I haven't received any e-mail messages in days.

Assuming, of course, that people really are sending you messages, the problem could be that you have too many e-mail messages stored away, and your inbox is overloaded. Normally the WebTV Network will let you know when you're running out of room via an onscreen message, but it's possible you might not have seen it. To rectify the problem, go into the Storage section of your Mail List and delete unwanted messages. Your inbox should be alive again in no time. Send yourself an e-mail to verify that it's working properly again.

I deleted a message that I meant to keep.

If the message was deleted less than a week ago, you're in luck. The WebTV Network holds on to discarded messages for a week before they are permanently removed. To retrieve the message, select Mail from the WebTV Network home page, press Go, choose Storage, press Go, select Discarded, and then press Go. Open the message you want to retrieve, select Save from the menu on the left side of the screen, and then press Go. The message will be saved until you deliberately discard it.

I subscribe to a mailing list and am leaving for vacation. Can I temporarily stop receiving e-mail so that my inbox doesn't overload?

While you can't stop e-mail that has been sent to the primary user, you can do so for any secondary user by following these steps:

1. Connect as the primary user.
2. Select Using WebTV from the WebTV Network home page, and then press Go.
3. Select Your Account, and then press Go.
4. Select the user whose e-mail you'd like to suspend.
5. Select Can Use E-Mail, and then press Go.
6. Place a checkmark in the Block E-Mail checkbox, select Continue, and then press Go to complete the request.

E-mail to that account will be stopped until you enable the account.

How can I save an incomplete e-mail message to finish later so that I don't have to start all over again?

The best way to do this is to go ahead and send the unfinished message to an invalid e-mail address on purpose, such as *wecare@webtv.ne* (notice there is no "t" at the end). The message will be returned to you along with a note from the Postmaster saying that the mail couldn't be delivered. When you open the message, you'll see an Edit Message button. Selecting this button will allow you to return to the original message and make any additions. Just don't forget to change the e-mail address when you've finished writing so that your message gets to its intended recipient.

My Internet terminal is asking me if I've moved to a new number.

If you've unplugged your Internet terminal for any reason, a message will be displayed asking you whether you're connecting from the same number. Select the same number if the unit was merely unplugged or Different if you've moved your Internet terminal to another location. If you've selected Different, the WebTV Network will use a local dial-up number in the new area. If you're using the OpenISP option, logging on might result in toll charges if you dial in to an area that would be a long distance call from your new home.

A certain Web page tells me to select the image of my state, but my Internet terminal will select only the whole United States.

What you're seeing is something called an image map. Web page developers often use images as navigational tools through their site, which not only makes the page aesthetically appealing but saves users the trouble of having to type in text or read through a large list of text links. To use an image map, highlight the entire image and then press Go. An arrow pointer will appear within the image. Use the arrow keys or buttons to position this pointer in the desired location. When you're satisfied with its placement, press Go and continue surfing as usual.

OpenISP-Related Issues

I saw a message saying that my password was wrong when I connected.

The most likely possibility is that the password was entered incorrectly. Try rekeying it first, with the keyboard or remote pointing directly at the Internet terminal. If that doesn't solve the problem, call your ISP to see if there's a special password for PPP access.

Every time I try to connect to the WebTV Network, I get nothing but busy signals.

You can try surfing at a different time of day, or you can try contacting your ISP to see if you can get a backup dial-in number should the primary number be too busy.

Glossary

Need to quickly find the definition of a term? Check below for the answers you want instead of flipping through the whole book.

Around Town   A button that provides instant access to local information (weather, movie listings, and so on). Just select Around Town on your WebTV Network home page to check out what's happening in your neighborhood.

Artemis Research   The name WebTV Networks, Inc., operated under before their product was announced in July 1996.

AT Keyboard   A corded keyboard for the personal computer with function keys across the top. This PC keyboard can be attached to WebTV Classic via a cord as a less expensive alternative to the optional wireless keyboard. An AT keyboard cannot, however, be attached to WebTV Plus.

Chat   Real-time online conversations that can occur in two formats: bulletin board style or IRC (Internet Relay Chat). The quickest way to participate in a chat using the WebTV Network is to select Community on the WebTV Network home page, press Go, select Chat, and then press Go. This will put you onto the launch page of Talk City's chat area.

Chatroom   An area on the Internet in which people discuss a particular topic. This topic is usually what the room is named, but often the discussion will stray, just as a course of human nature. Also, a chatroom can be set up for any specific group, such as your extended family spread across the continent, George Washington University alumni, and so on.

Club WebTV News   The free monthly online newsletter for WebTV Network subscribers. To find it, select Using WebTV, press Go, select "Club WebTV" from the list of options; and then press Go.

Cursor   The blinking bar in a Web page text box, e-mail message page, or anywhere else you might be expected to insert text.

Glossary

Cybercommunity A virtual community or virtual neighborhood formed by folks engaging in conversation through electronic media. A cybercommunity can evolve among regular participants of a discussion group or chatroom—it's sort of a shared attitude, a feeling of camaraderie, and a way of saying things that bonds the people within a cybercommunity together.

Discuss The WebTV Network term for Usenet groups. To access discussion groups using your Internet terminal, select Community, press Go, select Discuss to read and post messages, and then press Go.

Download The act of adding new software to your WebTV Internet terminal. When a new version of WebTV Network software becomes available, you can instruct your Internet terminal to automatically install the latest version of the software.

Drop-Down List Box Gray boxes with downward-pointing arrows. When you encounter these while surfing the Web, select the box and press Go to see a list of allowable choices for the given box.

E-Mail Short for electronic mail, which uses a computer to send messages from one place to another. To read or send e-mail, go to the WebTV Network home page, select Mail, and then press Go. Select from the options presented.

Emoticons A group of punctuation marks that when combined in a certain sequence and viewed from a certain angle take on a new meaning. Take the classic smiley face, which is formed by typing a colon, followed by a minus sign, and then by a close parentheses. :-)

Explore A directory of Web sites, organized by subject, that were chosen by the folks at WebTV Networks.

Favorites A navigational aid to help you move quickly to items of personal interest. The WebTV Network allows you to save links to favorite Web sites and favorite television channels (available with WebTV Plus only).

Flame The act of sending hypercritical or abusive e-mail in reaction to a message e-mailed or posted to a discussion group.

Glossary

Folders A means of organizing your favorite Web sites for quick access.

Form Text boxes on a Web page. You might be asked to type certain information into these text boxes, whether to perform a search on your favorite search engine or to request a catalog from an online merchant.

Go The button located in the middle of the arrow buttons on your remote control. This button must be pressed in order to execute a command. For instance, to follow an Internet link, use the arrows to select the desired link, and then press Go to move to that link.

Goldman, Phil A co-founder of WebTV Networks, Inc.

Gopher One of the first Internet navigational aids, originally developed at the University of Minnesota and named after the school mascot. Gopher is a text-driven, menu-based method that preceded the World Wide Web as we know it today.

Host A computer linked to the Internet that is capable of transmitting and receiving data. In the case of WebTV Networks, the computers that store your e-mail and Favorites lists are the hosts.

HTML The standard language used to publish documents on the Web. (The acronym stands for Hypertext Markup Language.) It is this standard that makes Web documents readable to any Web browser supporting the HTML standard.

Hyperlink A connection in one document that links to another document via word, phrase, or image. If you use your arrows to select one of these words or phrases and then press Go, you will be transported to another Web page.

Icon A graphic used to represent a function or task. For example, on your WebTV Network home page, the mailbox icon is what you select to perform any e-mail–related functions.

Internet A group of linked computer networks.

Internet Explorer A Web browser created by Microsoft.

Internet Relay Chat (IRC) A real-time, Internet-based chat service where the user can find "live" participants from around the world.

Glossary

Internet Service Provider (ISP)   A business providing access to the Internet.

IR Shooter   An infrared device that allows your WebTV Plus remote control to control your cable box. This is especially important if you plan to make use of the TV viewing features offered by WebTV Plus.

Kid-Friendly   The safest, most restricted access available through the WebTV Network. Kid-Friendly enables you to preapprove appropriate sites for your young Internet surfer.

Leak, Bruce   A co-founder of WebTV Networks, Inc.

Link   Many use this term interchangeably with hyperlink.

Menu   A list of items from which you can make a selection. On the WebTV Network home page, you'll see a menu down the left side of the screen that lists TV Home, Using WebTV, and Community.

Modem   The hardware inside your Internet terminal that makes it possible for your Internet terminal to connect to the WebTV Network.

Mosaic   One of the first Web browsers.

Netscape Navigator   A Web browser created by Netscape.

Network   A group of computers linked together.

Options Panel   A panel that slides up from the bottom of the screen when you press Options while using your WebTV Internet terminal.

OpenISP   An option that allows you to use your own ISP with your Internet terminal to gain access to the WebTV Network. This option is most commonly used by people who live in areas without a local dial-up number to the WebTV Network. It is also used by people who already have Internet accounts for their PC, because Open ISP can save them money on their WebTV Network subscription cost.

Password   A secret word that must be typed in before access to your account is granted. This is a great way to protect your privacy and to protect children from seeing adult content on the Internet.

Glossary

Perlman, Steve The man who started it all. It was Steve Perlman, founder of WebTV Networks, Inc., who spent the initial sleepless nights conceptualizing the WebTV Network.

Search Engine A program that locates specified information on the Internet. Excite, Lycos, and Infoseek are a few of the many search engines available.

Shortcuts A key or keystroke combination that provides fast access to a desired item or command. With the WebTV Network, you are able to assign shortcuts to seven of your favorite Web pages using the function keys at the top of the wireless keyboard.

Software The instructions that make your WebTV Internet terminal work. For example, Discuss is the WebTV Network's own newsreader software. The WebTV Network also has its own Web browser and e-mail software built in. And best of all, they're frequently upgraded with minimal hassle free of charge to WebTV Network subscribers.

SurfWatch A program that gives younger surfers less restricted access to the Internet while still screening out the majority of inappropriate content.

TCP/IP The common protocol that helps computers and computer-like devices talk to one another. (The acronym stands for Transmission Control Protocol/Internet Protocol.)

TV Crossover Links An "i" icon that appears while you're watching a TV show with WebTV Plus. This icon leads you to a hyperlink to Internet content related to the show you're viewing.

TV Home The launch pad for additional WebTV Plus features. It's the TV counterpart to the WebTV Network home page you've come to know and love.

Upgrade Since the WebTV Network is a rapidly growing technology, the software inside the Internet terminal is often upgraded to give you access to the latest and greatest features available.

Glossary

VideoFLASH A special WebTV Network technology that allows full motion video to be displayed on your screen without extended download time.

Web See World Wide Web.

WebPIP The WebTV Plus feature that turns any TV into a picture-in-picture capable television, even if your TV doesn't have its own PIP capability. While you can't watch two TV shows at once (yet), you can browse the Internet while taking in your favorite sitcom.

WebTV Classic The first Internet terminal to hit the market offering Internet access in a set-top box. WebTV Classic and WebTV Plus are pretty similar except for the enhanced television viewing features available with WebTV Plus. For many users, WebTV Classic is more than enough to do the job, and you can't beat the price!

WebTV Plus WebTV Plus takes the standard WebTV Internet terminal and adds to it the following TV enhancement capabilities: online TV listings and programming descriptions, WebPIP, and TV Crossover Links.

World Wide Web A global hypertext system that uses the Internet as its means of transportation. On the Web, you select specific words or phrases in order to be transported to another related document.

INDEX

Note: An *italic* page-number reference indicates a figure.

A

abbreviations, 186–88, *187, 188*
A/B switches, 162
access, restricting, 72–73
accounts
  adding users, 71–73
  changing billing information, 73–74
  setting up, 43–51
  switching, 77
accuracy, verifying, 118
AC Input plug, 34
acronyms. *See* abbreviations; smileys
addresses, e-mail
  adding to address book, 88–90
  deciphering, 171–72
  editing entries in address book, 90
  forging, 176–78
  forms of, 193
  looking up in address book, 90
  privacy issues, 193–95
Advanced Research Projects Agency (ARPA), 5, 6
advertising
  posting to discussion groups, 180, 183
  where it's welcome, 183
Airborne Express Web site, 237
airfares, Web resources, 234
All Groups page, 6, 121
All-in-One Search Page, 249
Alta Vista, 248
Amazon.com, 201, 236
American Journalism Review, 230, 231
America Online, 40
Amtrak Web site, 234
Anagram Server, 224
ANT In jack, 33
Architext Spider, 243
ARPANET, 5–6
Artemis Research, 9
articles, discussion group
  posting, 123–24

articles, discussion group, *continued*
  reading, 122–23
  replying to, 124, 182–83
ASCII art, 86
AT&T Toll-Free Internet Directory, 238
ATM cards, 30
AT-style computer keyboards, 24–25, 59–60
audio/video input and output jacks, 33

B

background music
  choosing type, 70–71
  turning on and off, 70
Back key, 114
Bandai America Web site, 253
bandwidth, 180
Barbie Collectibles Web site, 220
Barnes and Noble Web site, 236
bias, looking out for, 206–7
Big Book Web site, 237–38
Billboard Magazine Online, 233–34
billing information
  changing, 73–74
  setting up, 49–50
books
  book merchants online, 236
  Chapter One online feature, 236
browsing
  best times for, 146
  how to navigate Web pages, 113–16
  list of discussion groups, 121
Builder Online, 221

C

cable boxes, 157–58
cables
  keyboard extender, 25
  S-Video, 22, 33
cable television
  getting local listings, 156
  and WebTV Internet terminal, 157–58
cache, Web terminal, 115
call waiting, 32, 74–75

Index

Caring Grandparents of America Web site, 257
Carle, Eric, 252
catalog mailing lists, 222
CC line, 87
CH 3/4 switch, 33
channels, TV
    changing, 162
    customizing surfing list, 159
    storing favorites, 162, 163
Chapter One online feature, 236
chatrooms
    creating, 132–33
    finding, 127, 133–35
    getting started, 127
    going directly to, 132
    how they work, 126–27
    New2WebTV chatroom, 128
    one-on-one talking, 131
    overview, 125
    signing up, 134–35
    tips for participating, 135
    types of, 126–27
cheat codes, 254–55
check, paying by, 50
children
    caution about image files and, 123
    levels of WebTV access for, 72, 73
    Web sites for, 251–55
Circuit City Web site, 202
CityNet, 225
cleaning up e-mail messages, 94, 98–99
Club WebTV News, 10, 77
CNN Web site, 231
Coin Universe Web site, 220
collectibles
    learning about, 219–21
    and shopping online, 198–99
colleges, choosing, 216–17
Columbia House Web site, 231
Command key, 63–64
Community button, 6, 127
CompuServe, 40
computer keyboard, lack of, 14–15, 19, 24
    See also keyboard, AT-style; keyboard, onscreen; keyboard, wireless

Connected indicator, 30
credibility, verifying, 118
credit cards
    and online shopping, 200–201
    smart card slot for, 30
    and WebTV Network sign-up, 45, 47, 49
cursor, defined, 82
Customer Care
    dialing in, 75
    vs. do-it-yourself troubleshooting, 139
cybercommunities, 137. *See also* chatrooms
CyberRouter Web site, 219

D

Deja News, 179, 250
deleting
    e-mail messages, 93, 98–99
    folders, 108–9
    Web pages from Favorites list, 109–10
Department of Defense, 5
DHL Worldwide Express Web site, 237
dialing options, 74–75. *See also* telephone
dialing prefixes, 74
dial tone, 75
dial-up access, 21–22
Directory of Travel, the, 225
discarding. *See* deleting
discussion groups. *See also* articles, discussion group; messages, discussion group
    and advertising, 180, 183
    browsing list, 121
    buying from participants in, 198–99
    defined, 6, 117
    and FAQs, 178
    featured by WebTV, 120
    flames, 178–79
    getting involved, 121–24
    hierarchy, 118–19, 121
    how they work, 118–19
    netiquette, 178–84
    posting *vs.* e-mail, 124
    showing appreciation, 184
    vs. Usenet, 6
drop-down list boxes, 100, 103, *104*
drugs. *See* medical Web sites

Index

E

E-Cards Web site, 232, *233*
education. *See* research, online
EKG monitor icon, 78
electronic mail. *See* e-mail
electronic signatures, 85–87, 174, *174*, 175
e-mail. *See also* messages, e-mail
    creating signature for, 85–87
    defined, 4
    vs. discussion group postings, 124
    junk mail, 195–98
    vs. letter-writing, 228–29
    vs. long distance calls, 227–28
    message indicator light, 30
    message limit, 83–84
    messages that bounce, 97
    netiquette, 171–78
    overview, 81–83
    password-protecting, 65–66
    privacy issues, 193–95
    quick test, 81–83
    restricting access to, 73
    retrieving automatically, 99–100
    retrieving daily, 99–100
    sending test message, 81–83
    setting options for, 84–88
    troubleshooting, 260–61
e-mail addresses
    and address book, 88–90
    choosing, 50, *51*
    deciphering, 171–72
    forging, 176–78
    forms of, 193
    privacy issues, 193–95
e-mail names, 50, *51*, 171–72, 193, 195.
    See also user names
emoticons
    and netiquette, 172–73
    using, 189–90, *189*
Enesco, Inc., Web site, 220
Epicurious Eating Recipe File, 217
Eric Carle Web Site, 252
error messages
    access restricted message, 142

error messages, *continued*
    address missing first part message, 146
    and address problems, 142–44, 146
    bouncing e-mail messages, 97
    host is missing message, 145
    page not found message, 140, 141
    phone seems to be in use message, 147
    problem came up message, 142
    publisher can't be reached message, 141
    publisher is too busy message, 144
    publisher is unknown message, 143–44
    publisher refuses access message, 146
    publisher responded in an odd way
        message, 144
    publisher technical problem, 144–45
    URL problems, 142–44
    WebTV Network technical problem
        message, 142
Excite, 243, 247
expansion slots, 31
Explore icon, 77

F

fairs, Web sites, 225
FAQs, 178
Favorites icon, 77, 106
Favorites list
    adding Web pages to folders in, 105–6
    assigning shortcuts to Web pages in, 112–13
    creating folders in, 107–8
    defined, 105
    deleting folders in, 108–9
    deleting Web pages from folders in, 109–10
    moving Web pages between folders in, 110–12
    organizing Web pages in folders, 107–13
    and predefined folders, 111–12
    viewing list of Web pages in, 106–7
Favs key, 106, 112
FDA Web site, 223
Federal Express Web site, 237
festivals, Web sites, 224–25
flames, 178–79
Fleer trading cards Web site, 220
Flifo Web site, 234

271

Index

folders
    adding Web pages to, 107–8
    creating, 107–8
    deleting, 108–9
    deleting Web pages from, 109–10
    moving Web pages between, 110–12
    naming, 108
    organizing Favorites in, 107–9
    predefined, 111–12
foreign exchanges, 21, 22
forging e-mail addresses, 176–78
forms, Web
    defined, 103
    drop-down list boxes, 103, *104*
    text boxes, 103, *103*
forwarding e-mail messages, 93
friends, finding, 249–50
friendships, online, 136–37, 215–16
function keys
    assigning Web pages to, 112–13
    wireless keyboard, 61

G

gaming systems, 254–55
Giga Pets Web site, 254
Goldman, Paul, 9
Gopher, origin of, 7
Go To panel, 102, *102*
grandparents, Web sites for, 257–58
graphic images
    and discussion groups, 123
    including links in signatures, 86
    sources for, 87
    troubleshooting, 262
    using caution, 123
    viewing *vs.* not viewing, 107
greeting cards, virtual, 232–33

H

Hallmark Cards Web site, 220
Healthfinder Web site, 222
HealthGate Free Medline, 222
HealthTouch Web site, 223

Healthy Ideas Web site, 223
heart monitor icon, 78
hobbies, and shopping online, 198–99
Home key, 76
home page, WebTV Network
    Community button, 6, 127
    elements of, 76–78, *76*
    vs. launch page, 51
    WebTV Plus, 51, 77, 154, *154*, 160–62
home pages, defined, 51
Homes and Land Electronic Magazine Web site, 231–32
Hotel and Travel Index Online, 235
hotel Web sites, 235
Hot Wheels Web site, 220
house plans, 221
HTML
    defined, 87
    including in signatures, 86
http:// prefix, 102, 142
humor
    and netiquette, 176
    Web sites, 224
Hypertext Markup Language. *See* HTML

I

icons, defined, 77
image maps, 262
information superhighway, birth of, 7
InfoSeek, 248
input jacks. *See* audio/video input and output jacks
Insert mode, 60
Internet. *See also* World Wide Web
    defined, 4
    growth of, 4–5, 8
    history of, 5–8
    netiquette, 170–84
    speed problems, 146
    and television, 9, 10
Internet Explorer, need for, 105
Internet Mall, the, 201, 237
Internet name, 50, *51*. *See also* user names
Internet Relay Chat. *See* IRC

Index

Internet service providers
    and local access, 21–22, 38
    and OpenISP, 22, 38–43
    overview, 38
    predetermined by WebTV Networks, 37, 42
    in rural areas, 21, 22, 38
    and setting up OpenISP, 42–43
    shopping for, 40–41
Introducing WebTV screen, 44, *44*
IRC
    defined, 126
    and WebTV Network, 128–35
IR shooter, 32, 158
IRS Web site, 235
ISPs. *See* Internet service providers

J

Java, defined, 148
junk mail. *See also* catalog mailing lists
    keeping e-mail messages simple, 179–80
    stopping flow of, 195–98

K

keyboard, AT-style
    buying for WebTV Classic, 24–25
    connecting to WebTV Internet terminal, 59–60
    shortcut keys, 59, *60*
keyboard, lack of, 14–15, 19, 24
keyboard, onscreen
    how to use, 58–59
    reordering keys of, 66–67
keyboard, wireless, 59, 61–64, 259–60
keyboard adapters, 25
Kid-Friendly access, 72, 73
kids
    caution about image files, 123
    levels of WebTV access, 72, 73
    Web sites for, 251–55

L

language
    abbreviations, 186–88, *187, 188*
    expressions, 191, *191*

language, *continued*
    smileys, 189–90, *189*
LaughWEB site, 224
Leak, Bruce, 8–9
Learn To Choose Items screen, 45, *45*
letterwriting, 228–29
LGB trains Web site, 220
links, Web
    including in signatures, 86
    reciprocal, 207
    rings as, 220
Lladro figurines Web site, 220
local dial-up access, 21–22, 43
local TV listings, 155–56, 160, *161,* 162, *163–64*
login name, ISP, 41. *See also* e-mail names
long distance calls
    and dial-up access to WebTV Network, 21–22
    vs. e-mail, 227–28
Lycos, 243, *245,* 248

M

magazines, online list, 229–30
Magellan, 242, *246*
mail. *See* e-mail
Mail icon, 77
Mail List
    cleaning up messages, 94, 98–99
    options for viewing, 84–85
    reading messages, 92–93
    viewing list, 91–92
Mail Setup screen, 84, *84*
mail signature, 85–87, 174, *174, 175*
malls, shopping, 201, 237
MapQuest Web site, 219
maps, creating, 218–19
Matchbox Toys Web site, 220
medical Web sites, 222–23
Medline, 222
Mental Health Net, 223
messages, discussion group
    including original in replies, 118
    replying to, 124, 182–83
    special language elements, 187–91, *187, 188, 189, 191*

Index

messages, discussion group, *continued*
    spoilers, 181
    and subject lines, 180
messages, e-mail
    CC line, 87
    cleaning up, 94, 98–99
    creating signature for, 85–87
    deleting, 93, 98–99
    deliberate bounces of, 97
    vs. discussion group postings, 124
    forwarding, 93
    full Mail List, 99
    headers for, 173
    limit to number of, 99
    list of possible responses to, 93
    new message indicator, 100
    order of listing, 84–85
    quick test, 81–83
    reading, 91–93, 173
    replying to groups, 87, 88
    replying to individuals, 93, 173
    retrieving automatically, 99–100
    retrieving daily, 99–100
    saving, 83, 93
    saving unfinished messages, 97
    sending, 97
    sending while in chatrooms, 131
    special language elements, 187–91, *187, 188, 189, 191*
    and speed, 175–76
    subject lines of, 176
    undelivered, 97
    viewing after saving, 93–94
    viewing list of, 91–92
    WebTV limit, 83–84
    writing, 95–97
messages, error. *See* error messages
microphone jack, 32–33
Microsoft Corporation, and future of WebTV, 9–10, 12
mortgage calculator Web site, 231–32
mouse *vs.* remote control, 14
moving Web pages between folders, 110–12
MPEG audio tracks, 234

music
    background music, 70–71
    Billboard Magazine Online, 233–34
    mail order clubs, 231
    music festival Web sites, 225
My Virtual Reference Desk, *242,* 243

N

names, finding, 249–50
Nano Pets Web site, 254
navigating Web pages, 113–16
netiquette
    cultural differences, 175–76
    and discussion groups, 178–84
    and e-mail, 171–78
    FAQs, 178
    flames, 178–79
    overview, 170
    shouting, 172
    smileys, 172–73
Netscape Navigator, need for, 105
New2WebTV chatroom, 128
news, online, 118, 231
newsgroups, 117. *See also* discussion groups
news Web sites, 230–31
nicknames, 97
Nintendo Web site, 255

O

Official Eric Carle Web Site, 252
online chats. *See* chatrooms
online research. *See* research, online
online shopping. *See* shopping, online
onscreen keyboard
    how to use, 58–59
    reordering keys of, 66–67
OpenISP
    cost of, 39–40, 43
    defined, 22
    disabling, 43
    setting up, 42–43
    troubleshooting, 262
Options key, 114

output jacks. *See* audio/video input and output jacks

P

package tracking, 237
PAP (Password Authentication Protocol), 41
passwords
 changing, 66
 creating, 65–66
 ISP, 41
 what to use, 135, 195
PCs
 purchase considerations, 15–17
 vs. WebTV Internet terminals, 11–18
people, finding, 249–50
PeopleFinder Web site, 250
Perlman, Steve, 8–9
personal computers
 purchase considerations, 15–17
 vs. WebTV Internet terminals, 11–18
pets
 choosing, 217–18
 virtual, 253–54
Philips Magnavox
 remote control, *56*
 as WebTV Network partner, 9
phone. *See* telephone
phone numbers
 entering in WebTV sign-up process, 47
 finding online, 237–38
picture-in-picture feature, 18, 164–65
picture quality, 11–12, 75–76
pictures. *See* graphic images
posting discussion group articles, 123–24
Power key, 61
PPP (Point-to-Point Protocol), 41
Prevention's Healthy Ideas Web site, 223
printers
 adapters for, 32
 setting up, 150–52
 suitability, 26–27
printing
 screen, 153
 selecting options, 151–52

printing, *continued*
 setting up printer, 150–51
 Web pages, 152–53
protocols
 PAP (Password Authentication Protocol), 41
 PPP (Point-to-Point Protocol), 41
 TCP/IP, 6
pulse dialing, 74

Q

QVC Web site, 202
QWERTY keyboard, 66–67

R

reading
 discussion group articles, 122–23
 e-mail messages, 91–93
Real Audio, 234
RealMalls, 237
Recent key, 115–16
reciprocal links, 207
Reload button, 115
remote control
 list of buttons, 56, *57*
 number pad, 56
 overview, 55–57, *56*
 programming, 34–35
 troubleshooting, 260
 and typing, 58–59
 using for Web surfing, 14–15
 using onscreen keyboard, 58–59
removing. *See* deleting
replying
 to discussion group messages, 124, 182–83
 to e-mail messages, 87, 88, 93
research, online
 accuracy of data, 208
 checklist, 211–12
 determining Web site bias, 206–7
 how to evaluate, 205–11
 overview, 203–5
 permanence of Web sites, 210–11
 timeliness of data, 208–10

Index

restricting user access, 72–73
Reuters Online, 231
RFCs, 170
RFU adapters, 22, 24, 34
rings, for linking Web sites, 220
rural locations, 21–22, 38
RxList Web site, 223

S

saved e-mail messages, 93–94
SchoolHouse Rock, 252–53
screens, moving to next, 44. *See also* television
screen savers, 34–35
scrolling, 78
search engines. *See also* subject indexes
   Deja News, 179
   how they work, 243–46
   most popular, 247–48
   strategies for searching, 247
Search icon, 77
Sega Online, 255
Select-a-Dog site, 217–18
sending e-mail messages, 97
senior citizens
   Web sites for, 255–58, *256, 257*
   and WebTV, 251
SeniorCom Web site, 256, *257*
SeniorLaw Web site, 255, *256*
SeniorLink Web site, 256
SeniorNet, 256, *257*
service agreement, 48, *48*
shopping, online
   for books, 201, 236
   catalog sites, 222
   and collectibles, 198–99
   and comparison shopping, 236–37
   credit card safety, 200–201
   and discussion groups, 198–99
   list of Web sites, 201–2, 237
   malls, 201, 237
   QVC Web site, 202
   safety tips, 198–99

shortcut keys
   for AT-style keyboards connected to WebTV terminals, 59, *60*
   wireless keyboard, 61, *62, 63, 64*
shortcuts to favorite Web pages, 112–13
shouting, 172
signatures
   how to use, 174, *174, 175*
   virtual, 85–87
Signing Up screen, 45, *46*
Skybox trading cards Web site, 220
smart cards, 30
smileys
   and netiquette, 172–73
   using, 189–90, *189*
songs, finding online, 233–34
Sony
   Online Web site, 226
   PlayStation Web site, 255
   remote control, 56
   as WebTV Network partner, 9
   WebTV Plus Internet terminals, 29–35
sound files, including links in signatures, 86
spam, 195–98
spoilers, 181
Storage area, 93, 98, 99
subject indexes, 241–43
subscriber name. *See* e-mail names
surfing, channel, 159. *See also* browsing
SurfWatch, 72
S-Video, 22, *23,* 33
Switchboard Web site, 238
Switch User button, 77

T

Talk City
   creating chatrooms, 132–33
   finding chatrooms, 128–30
   one-on-one talking, 130
   and WebTV Networks, Inc., 127
Tamagotchi Fever! Web site, 253
tax information, 235

TCP/IP, 6
telephone. *See also* Internet service providers
   connecting phone line to WebTV Internet
      terminal, 31–32
   entering phone number in WebTV sign-up
      process, 47
   finding phone numbers online, 237–38
   foreign exchanges, 21, 22
   local dial-up access, 21–22, 43
   long distance calls *vs.* e-mail, 227–28
   troubleshooting connection problems, 147
   WebTV Network dialing options, 74–75
television. *See also* WebTV Internet terminal
   adjusting screen image, 75–76, 160
   cable TV considerations, 157–58
   centering image on screen, 76
   changing onscreen text size, 67–70
   Crossover Link, 164
   customizing channel surfing, 159
   full screen view *vs.* WebTV Network
      view, 162
   and the Internet, 9, 10
   obtaining local program listings, 155–56, 160,
      161, 162, 163–64
   older TV sets, 22, *24*
   picture-in-picture feature, 18, 164–65
   picture quality, 11–12, 75–76
   printing screen, 153
   programming remote control, 34
   scrolling screen, 78
   storing favorite channels, 162
   and WebTV Classic *vs.* WebTV Plus, 18–19
   and WebTV display quality, 11–12
terminal. *See* WebTV Internet terminal
text, onscreen, changing size, 67–70
text boxes, 103, *103*
threads, 122
Thrive Web site, 222
thumb-surfing, 55–57, *56*
timed out, 78
toll-free numbers, finding, 238
touch-tone dialing, 74

Travelocity Web site, 234
TravelWeb, 235
travel Web sites, 224–25, 234–35
troubleshooting
   address problems, 142–44, 146
   e-mail, 260–61
   OpenISP, 262
   phone problems, 147, 261–62
   remote control, 260
   WebTV Network service, 260–62
   wireless keyboards, 259–60
TV. *See* television
TV Home screen, 154, *154,* 160–62. *See also*
      home page, WebTV Network
TV listings, obtaining, 155–56, 160, *161,* 162,
   163–64
TV sets. *See* television
TV shows, Web sites, 225–26
typing, 58–59

U

Ultimate TV Web site, 226
undelivered e-mail messages, 97
Unofficial SchoolHouse Rock Web site, 252–53
unrestricted access, 72
updating WebTV Internet terminals, 13–14, *13,*
   14, 52–53, *52, 53*
uppercase, 172
UPS Web site, 237
URLs
   adding to Favorites list, 105–6
   entering, 102
   prefixes, 102, 142
   troubleshooting, 142–44
USA Today Web site, 230
U.S. Department of Defense, 5
Usenet
   history of, 5–6
   WebTV name for, 6
U.S. News Colleges and Career Center, 216–17
user ID, 172

Index

user names
  alternative, 197–98
  in chatrooms, 130, 135
  choosing e-mail name, 50, *51*, 171–72, 193, 195
  and junk mail, 197–98
  and privacy issue, 135, 193–95, 197
users
  adding, 71–73
  restricting access, 72–73
  switching accounts, 77
User Setup screen, 195
Using WebTV button, 77

V

video clubs, 231
video games, 254–55
virtual pets, 253–54
VirtualPets Web site, 254
virtual signatures
  creating, 85–87
  how to use, 174, *174, 175*
volunteerism, 219

W

Washington Post Web site, 236
WAV audio tracks, 234
Web. *See* World Wide Web
Web browsers, 105
Web crawlers, 243
Web Home. *See* TV Home screen
Webmasters, defined, 206
Web pages. *See also* Web sites
  accessing, 102
  adding to Favorites list, 105–6
  assigning to function keys, 112–13
  changing display of, 107
  deleting from Favorites list, 109–10
  designed by WebTV Network, 12
  information panels of, 114, *114*
  list of recently visited, 115–16
  moving between folders, 110–12

Web pages, *continued*
  navigating, 113–16
  organizing in folders, 107–13
  picture quality, 12–13, 75–76
  printing, 152–53
  reloading, 115
  scrolling, 78
  viewing pictures, 107
WebPIP, 164–65
Web sites. *See also* Web pages
  accuracy of data in, 208
  Amazon.com, 201, 236
  Anagram Server, 224
  Billboard Magazine Online, 233–34
  for books, 236
  Builder Online, 221
  catalog mailing lists, 222
  for collectibles, 219–21
  determining bias of, 206–7
  Epicurious Eating Recipe File, 217
  evaluating information content, 205–11
  FAQs, 178
  finding phone numbers on, 237–38
  forms on, 103–5
  guessing at names of, 239–41
  humor sites, 224
  including links in signature, 86
  Internet Mall, the, 201
  for kids, 251–55
  linking with rings, 220
  magazines online, 229–30
  for maps, 218–19
  medical resources, 222–23
  mortgage calculator, 231–32
  newspapers online, 231
  news sites, 230–31
  online shopping, 201–2, 236–37
  package tracking, 237
  permanence of, 210–11
  research checklist, 211–12
  for saving time and money, 227–38
  Select-a-Dog site, 217–18
  for seniors, 255–58
  subject indexes, 241–43

Index

Web sites, *continued*
    tax information, 235
    and timeliness of data, 208–10
    travel resources, 224–25, 234–35
    TV shows, 225–26
    using search engines to find, 243–48
    U.S. News Colleges and Career Center, 216–17
    virtual greeting cards, 232–33
WebTV Classic, 18–19, 24–25, 59. *See also* WebTV Plus
WebTV Internet terminal
    and cable boxes, 157–58
    Classic *vs.* Plus, 18–19
    entering URLs, 102
    first in stores, 9
    front panel, 29–30
    installation checklist, 26
    installation requirements, 22–25
    keyboard options, 15, 19, 24–25, 58–64
    limitations of, 147–48
    onscreen instructions for use, 77
    vs. PCs, 11–18
    Power key, 61
    prepurchase considerations, 21–27
    printing from, 19, 25–26, 152–53
    pros and cons, 11–13
    purchase considerations, 15–17
    retrieving e-mail automatically from, 99–100
    Sony WebTV Plus features, 29–35
    television prerequisites, 22–25
    thumb-surfing, 55–57
    typical users, 17–18
    updating, 13–14, *13, 14,* 52–53, *52, 53*
    using remote control, 14–15
WebTV Network
    changing passwords, 66
    choosing a name, 50, 194–95
    creating passwords, 65–66
    customizing environment, 65–71
    dialing options, 74–75
    e-mail overview, 81–90
    error messages, 139–48
    featured discussion groups, 120

WebTV Network, *continued*
    getting local TV listings from, 155–56, 160, *161,* 162, 163–64
    home page, 51, 75, 76–78, *76,* 154, *154,* 160–62
    Introducing WebTV screen, 44, *44*
    and IRC chatrooms, 128–35
    launch page, 51
    local dial-up access, 21–22, 43
    message limit, 83–84
    and Microsoft, 9–10, 12
    and online research, 203–12
    and online shopping, 198–202, 236–37
    OpenISP option, 22, 38–43
    phone problems, 147
    retrieving e-mail automatically, 99–100
    signing up, 43–51
    storing messages, 83–84
    suggested uses, 215–26
    troubleshooting, 139–48, 259–62
    updates, 13–14, *13, 14,* 52–53, *52, 53*
    Web site, 21
WebTV Networks, Inc.
    adding users to, 71–73
    changing billing information, 73–74
    cost of access, 39–40, 43
    cost of equipment, 12
    history of, 8–9
    and Microsoft, 9–10, 12
    payment options, 49–50
    predetermined ISP, 37, 42
    restricting user access to, 72–73
    service agreement, 48, *48*
    setting up accounts, 43–51
    subscriber base, 251
    and Talk City, 127
    Web site, 21
WebTV Plus
    features, 29–35
    and keyboard, 59
    picture-in-picture capability, 18, 164–65
    TV Home screen, 51, 77, 154, *154,* 160–62
    vs. WebTV Classic, 18–19
    wireless keyboard, 62, *63, 64*

Whisper feature, 130
Windows CE, 9, 10
wireless keyboard, 59, 61–64, 259–60
World Wide Web. *See also* Web sites
    birth of, 7
    defined, 4
    netiquette, 170–84
    overview, 101–2
    speed problems, 146
writing e-mail messages, 95–97

Y

Yahoo, 242
young people
    caution about image files and, 123
    levels of WebTV access, 72, 73
    Web sites for, 251–55

Z

Zip2 Web site, 219

About the Authors

Jill T. Freeze is a freelance management consultant who has worked with such organizations as the John F. Kennedy Center for the Performing Arts, the National Endowment for the Arts, the Smithsonian, and the White House. She has been following the development of the WebTV Network since its "coming out" party in July of 1996. Her attention was drawn to the WebTV Network technology for several reasons: it was a low-cost way to access the Internet; it provided an easy way for computer-phobic people like her parents to get online; and because Jill's been visually impaired since birth, she welcomed the opportunity to do her surfing on a huge television screen. Her formal education includes a bachelor's degree magna cum laude from the University of Massachusetts at Amherst (in arts administration and writing) and a master's degree from George Washington University (in nonprofit administration). In addition to writing *Using Microsoft Office 97* (Que, 1997), Jill has worked closely with her husband, Wayne, on several advanced computer programming books. With two writers and two toddlers in the same house, Jill finds that humor is her favorite coping strategy.

Wayne S. Freeze is currently a computer and technology consultant to the University of Maryland at College Park. He recently left his position as Technical Support Manager to pursue writing full time. In addition to authoring Car Collector (a software package that allows car collectors to catalog and inventory their collections), he has written several computer books, including *Leveraging Visual Basic with ActiveX Controls* (Prima Publishing, 1996), *Programming ISAPI with Visual Basic 5* (Prima Publishing, 1997), *The Visual Basic 5 Programmer's Reference* (Ventana Press, 1997), and *The SQL Programmer's Reference* (Ventana Press, 1997). Having worked with computers for more than 25 years, Wayne has seen them evolve from room-sized machines to palmtop devices. Wayne's formal education includes degrees in electrical engineering, computer science, and business management.

The manuscript for this book was prepared and submitted to Microsoft Press in electronic form. Text files were prepared using Microsoft Word 97 for Windows 95. Pages were composed by Microsoft Press using Adobe PageMaker 6.51 for Windows, with text in Melior and display type in Frutiger Condensed. Composed pages were delivered to the printer as electronic prepress files.

Cover Designer
Greg Hickman

Cover Illustrator
Michael Victor

Interior Graphic Designer
Kim Eggleston

Interior Graphic Artist
Travis Beaven

Principal Compositors
Jeffrey Brendecke, Steven Hopster

Principal Proofreader/Copy Editor
Patricia Masserman

Indexer
Julie Kawabata

Everything you need to know about the best computer books available anywhere.

mspress.microsoft.com

Microsoft Press

Take the whole family siteseeing!

Want to update your stock portfolio? Explore space? Recognize consumer fraud? Find a better job? Trace your family tree? Research your term paper? Make bagels? Well, go for it! The OFFICIAL MICROSOFT® BOOKSHELF® INTERNET DIRECTORY, 1998 EDITION, gives you reliable, carefully selected, up-to-date reviews of thousands of the Internet's most useful, entertaining, and functional Web sites. The searchable companion CD-ROM gives you direct, instant links to the sites in the book—a simple click of the mouse takes you wherever you want to go!

Developed jointly by Microsoft Press and the Microsoft Bookshelf product team, the OFFICIAL MICROSOFT BOOKSHELF INTERNET DIRECTORY, 1998 EDITION, is updated regularly on the World Wide Web to keep you informed of our most current list of recommended sites. The latest version of Microsoft Internet Explorer is also included on the CD-ROM.

U.S.A.	**$39.99**
U.K.	£37.49 [V.A.T. included]
Canada	$55.99
ISBN 1-57231-617-9	

Microsoft Press® products are available worldwide wherever quality computer books are sold. For more information, contact your book or computer retailer, software reseller, or local Microsoft sales office, or visit our Web site at mspress.microsoft.com. To locate your nearest source for Microsoft Press products, or to order directly, call 1-800-MSPRESS in the U.S. (in Canada, call 1-800-268-2222).

Prices and availability dates are subject to change.

Microsoft®*Press*

Use the ultimate computer reference!

MICROSOFT PRESS® COMPUTER DICTIONARY, THIRD EDITION, is the authoritative source of definitions for computer terms, concepts, and acronyms—from one of the world's leading computer software companies. With more than 7,600 entries and definitions—2,600 of which are new—this comprehensive standard has been completely updated and revised to cover the most recent trends in computing, including extensive coverage of Internet, Web, and intranet-related terms.

U.S.A.	$29.99
U.K.	£27.99 [V.A.T. included]
Canada	$39.99
ISBN 1-57231-446-X	

Microsoft Press® products are available worldwide wherever quality computer books are sold. For more information, contact your book or computer retailer, software reseller, or local Microsoft Sales Office, or visit our Web site at mspress.microsoft.com. To locate your nearest source for Microsoft Press products, or to order directly, call 1-800-MSPRESS in the U.S. (in Canada, call 1-800-268-2222).

Prices and availability dates are subject to change.

Microsoft® Press

Things are looking up!

Here's the remarkable, *visual* way to quickly find answers about Microsoft applications and operating systems. Microsoft Press® *At a Glance* books let you focus on particular tasks and show you with clear, numbered steps the easiest way to get them done right now.

Microsoft® Excel 97 At a Glance
Perspection, Inc.
U.S.A. **$16.95** ($22.95 Canada)
ISBN 1-57231-367-6

Microsoft® Word 97 At a Glance
Jerry Joyce and Marianne Moon
U.S.A. **$16.95** ($22.95 Canada)
ISBN 1-57231-366-8

Microsoft® PowerPoint® 97 At a Glance
Perspection, Inc.
U.S.A. **$16.95** ($22.95 Canada)
ISBN 1-57231-368-4

Microsoft® Access 97 At a Glance
Perspection, Inc.
U.S.A. **$16.95** ($22.95 Canada)
ISBN 1-57231-369-2

Microsoft® Office 97 At a Glance
Perspection, Inc.
U.S.A. **$16.95** ($22.95 Canada)
ISBN 1-57231-365-X

Microsoft® Windows® 95 At a Glance
Jerry Joyce and Marianne Moon
U.S.A. **$16.95** ($22.95 Canada)
ISBN 1-57231-370-6

Microsoft Press® products are available worldwide wherever quality computer books are sold. For more information, contact your book or computer retailer, software reseller, or local Microsoft Sales Office, or visit our Web site at mspress.microsoft.com. To locate your nearest source for Microsoft Press products, or to order directly, call 1-800-MSPRESS in the U.S. (in Canada, call 1-800-268-2222).

Prices and availability dates are subject to change.

Microsoft® Press

Register Today!

Return this
Introducing WebTV®
registration card for
a Microsoft Press® catalog

U.S. and Canada addresses only. Fill in information below and mail postage-free. Please mail only the bottom half of this page.

1-57231-715-9   **INTRODUCING WEBTV®**   *Owner Registration Card*

_____
NAME

_____
INSTITUTION OR COMPANY NAME

_____
ADDRESS

_____
CITY   STATE   ZIP

Microsoft Press
Quality Computer Books

For a free catalog of
Microsoft Press® products, call
1-800-MSPRESS

BUSINESS REPLY MAIL
FIRST-CLASS MAIL   PERMIT NO. 53   BOTHELL, WA

POSTAGE WILL BE PAID BY ADDRESSEE

NO POSTAGE
NECESSARY
IF MAILED
IN THE
UNITED STATES

MICROSOFT PRESS REGISTRATION
INTRODUCING WEBTV®
PO BOX 3019
BOTHELL WA   98041-9946